1

2

CASTANEDA FOR DUMMIES
A Simple Exploration of Power

A Francine Jesse Publication

Dedicated to my Loving Family, Friends and Readers

5

TABLE OF CONTENTS

6

INTRODUCTION

I moved to Hollywood to go to guitar school. It was the late eighties. Hard rock and heavy metal were the cultural mainstream of rock music at that time. There were thousands of rock musicians living in Hollywood, I had found happiness itself, gorgeous guys with guitars were everywhere. Southern California was a heady experience for someone from the East Coast. I couldn't possibly love NYC more, but this was new and exciting. A beautiful cool city in the midst of beautiful canyons, only miles from the beach. The climate was exotic to me, and the foliage intriguing. The people were very different. When I initially got there I really couldn't believe how outgoing and friendly everybody seemed. I liked the culture of a warm climate. The school environment was competitive and intense, designed to prepare you for the rigors of professional music. The music scene in town was prominent, it was a time when thousands of participants in the hair metal and hard rock blues scene converged on sunset strip almost every night. My concerns were playing guitar, not making it in the business. I got to see incredible talent all the time. Hard rock raged night and day in Hollywood. There was the excitement of the entertainment business, and the feeling that anything could happen at any time for people. Everyone was overboard in personality. Acting was an art form that seeped into the reality of who people were, who they thought they were. Life became more grand there somehow. It was nice in that, one felt more free to be their creative selves. Acting out was more accepted, encouraged and in many ways expected. Confidence was supposed to be displayed. Quiet, good manners received no accolades. I enjoyed the feeling of the right to be sexy. You could live in your sexy character without people thinking you were crazy. They wouldn't really take flirting, to be anything real. In fact, they didn't seem to take having intercourse as anything real either, but that's neither here nor there, only an observation. Being, acting, and feeling glamorous were expected. It felt good. It was relaxing. It felt good to lift the yoke of the maniacal work ethic and simply be natural and flirtatious. After school I decided to stay in Hollywood. I thought it was great to be there. I didn't find a record deal, but what I did find became more and more interesting...

1   THE LANDLORD

After school I looked for a studio apartment. I wanted to live alone. I had a roommate whom I enjoyed, but we talked too much. We spent usually two hours a day talking. It was great to have so much to communicate about with someone, but I thought my practicing was suffering because of it. I thought if I lived alone I could practice guitar ten hours a day and not have any interruptions. Oh and work, yeah work. I felt slightly spoiled wanting my own flat. I had seen these semi successful rock bands living with six guys in two rooms. All they had was their sleeping bags and their gear. I was far from that cool. I found it vaguely annoying even having one other person living in the room that I did music in, plus I had stuff. It wasn't expensive stuff, or something as concrete as furniture, but it was tons of books and music stuff. Lots of clothes too. Living alone sounded like paradise to me. I called an ad for a studio apartment across the street from where I currently lived. I had avoided that building in the past, because it had a sign on it that mentioned adult quiet living. That didn't seem to specifically invite electric guitar presence. The man who answered the phone had a rich masculine voice. He asked me if I had a lot of parties? I didn't. That was a good question

to ask. The sound of breaking bottles and the shriek of female

laughter never ceased to ring in the night from the outdoor

patios in the area. Another charming antidote was the gunfire.

Whether it was from, whatever group of people found it

entertaining to shoot their guns in the air, or bona fide

criminals, it was absolutely insane how often you would hear

gunfire. In my last apartment, there had been a loud banging

on the door at seven am. I opened the door to see two cops

with their guns out, pointing right at me. They yelled to step

out of the apartment with my hands up. My talkative

roommate was yelling from the other room about who the hell

is there at this hour! I'm freaked. I've never even seen a gun.

They said they had heard gunfire and it was said to be from

our apartment. I had heard that as well and thought it was from

up the hill. Someone had reported that we had been shooting

through the ceiling. I didn't say anything. Later in the day I

went to the guys upstairs to see what their take on these

accusations were. It hadn't come from them. They were three

guys from music school and the last thing they wanted visiting

were police. They had marijuana practically out in dishes. The

building manager asked me to come over to see a couple of

studio's he had open. He said to come by in ten minutes. I

went over and no one answered when I rang. I was mildly put

off, thinking it was far too close in time for the guy to have

forgotten. I went back home and rang him. He

unapologetically told me to come back over. The building

resembled an old Tudor house. It had within it twenty studio

apartments. The building gave you the sense of old

Hollywood. The atmosphere was casual and relaxed, and there

were paintings and plants in the hall. There was the aroma of

incense, and the sound of musical instruments filtering thru

closed doors. A cat meandered leisurely down the hallway.

The man who came to the door seemed too diminutive, to be

the man that I had spoken to on the phone. He led me upstairs

to the second and top floor. There was a nice skylight above

the stairs. "This is Jonah" he said. He knocked on the door and

then shuffled quickly away. Another man answered the door.

He was strapping and muscular, with handsome rugged

features and scant hair. He effected a modest ponytail, bearing

hint of his artistic nuance. He appeared to be in his forties, and

aggressive in a silent kind of way. He told me to wait outside

for a moment while he went inside to retrieve a large jangling

ring of keys. The first studio had no special charms, it didn't seem to be set off from the others in any way and was in the middle of the hall. The second one had two young striking blonde people. One was a perfect looking blonde woman with star power and much cheer, and the gentleman had perfect boyish looks and obvious gay pride. They were too much to look at to get much of a feel for the apartment. The apartment was also too much in the middle of the hall. I thought there would be more privacy and music privacy in some end corner unit. The third unit he showed had a feel that I liked. It did have an adjoining door inside to the next apartment, but I figured no one ever opened those things. He told me that a sophisticated drummer lived next door. What a sales person this guy was. He gave me the impression that the tenants were of a certain caliber to be here. He looked at me in an oddly piercing manner. I wondered why he gazed at me so intently. I expected him to try and sell me on the apartment instead of interrogating me. I asked him if I could play electric guitar here? His demeanor changed entirely. Instead of the bums rush I expected, he at once became graciously endearing. His knifelike gaze softened into gentleness as he said that he played guitar as well. As we talked about guitar players and music, I found myself becoming more and more absorbed by him. I was captivated by his subtle sense of strength and intelligence. For some odd reason I felt that he understood me. I told him that I wanted solitude to focus on music. He said that you could get a lot accomplished by concentrating in solitude. He told me that I could blast off anytime back there on guitar. That was my only criteria for a location, so I took it right away. I began to feel lightheaded while I spoke to him. I felt pulled towards him by some unseen current. I thanked him for his courtesy and quickly left. I left with the feeling that I had made a friend.

I thought of Jonah several times before moving in. I didn't want him to see me with school books. I told him I had graduated already and was employed. I had learned that the Hollywood landlords needed to know you were working. All very youthful and charming compared to the arm, leg and first born the NYC landlords demanded. One morning I spied Jonah on the roof in his white bathrobe. I felt somehow startled that he would present himself on a city street in his bedclothes, I thought he displayed a rare disposition of freedom. I tried to resolve that this was really not such a big city, and that the man simply felt at home on his block. Another time I was walking up the block and heard him playing guitar from his upstairs window. I stopped to listen

because it was very good. It rang mystically like chimes. It

created a mood that was already gathering in the evening dusk.

I felt almost embarrassed to be listening to someone without

their knowledge. I kept thinking about this new landlord, and I

didn't really know why. Our interaction was very professional,

and more of a cerebral nature than anything else. We certainly

had not displayed any personal affection, or even flirtation to

each other. In fact, our interaction had been purposely devoid

of any sensual overtone. He was straight as nails to me and I

responded accordingly. It was surprising that he stuck on my

mind so.

I moved in. It was disappointing that the place had not

been cleaned. There was obviously no memory of my

upcoming arrival, let alone preparation. The "sophisticated"

drummer next door, whose door adjoined to mine, turned out

to be the host of a perpetual rock and roll party. I adapted by

obtaining employment that started later in the day. Jonah did

come down at one point to see that I was not hysterical from

my neighbor's ebullient lifestyle. By that time, I was already

flushing phone numbers of cocaine dealers and amazed at

what was happening just outside my window. I saw men

running with machine guns through the underground parking garage next door, and hiding behind the concrete columns. Overhead were the ever present Los Angeles police helicopters flying around. I didn't know if this was real or filming. I didn't see anyone that had a camera or looked like crew. I stayed low and kept the shade down.

It was obvious to me that the fast friendship that I had imagined with Jonah was just that, my imagination. He didn't seek my company, and it was more or less clear that he was only to be contacted when it was about something specific. In one of our earlier conversations he had mentioned that he had gotten rid of all of the hardcore hangouts from his apartment. I took this to mean that plain social calls were not invited.

I saw Jonah now and again in the street and in the hall. His presence was felt in the building because he was often around talking to various tenants. The building had a communal feeling to it because everyone was loosely associated by their friendship to Jonah. The place seemed to have its own presence.

After a couple of weeks there, I began to observe that I had developed a few unusual habits. I began to notice that for no apparent reason, I was always thinking of Jonah. I thought of him so much that I actually began to feel that I could detect whether he was on the premises or not. It was like I could sense a sort of electrical presence from him, and that I could also sense the absence of this presence. The other odd thing was that I distinctly didn't think of him when I was away from the building. We spoke in passing whenever we met. He always had interesting things to say, even if we only spoke briefly. He never spoke rhetorically, he always asked about things specifically. He became like a pleasant backdrop in my life and in my mind. I started to see my life in a filter of .... oh what would Jonah make of this? or what would Jonah make of that? He was like a tenant living in the back of my mind somewhere. His presence on my mind became so strong, that when I actually saw him it was a little shocking. It was like the fantasy presence coming to life. All of this was for the most part unconscious. I wasn't really aware that I was obsessively thinking about him. I thought, that I thought of him because he was the landlord, and he was around, I did have a little bit of a life aside from my musings of Jonah.

One evening I decided to go up and pay the rent. I went into the bathroom and looked in the mirror, I said to myself... "You look good without makeup." I grabbed my keys and walked out the door. Jonah motioned for me to sit down. He got out his rent book and entered the transaction. Without looking up he said... "You look good without makeup." He said it in the exact tone of voice in which I had thought it to myself. I was very surprised to hear him say that. When I left, I thought... that's really odd, that he would just say what I had been thinking a few minutes before.

A neighbor had mentioned that he was slow on repairs, and didn't like to be disturbed with anything that wasn't urgent. Because I could play guitar there, I didn't care about anything like that. I had to call him about a clogged sink. He appeared at the door with something resembling 1920's farm equipment. It was a large rusty metal machine. For some reason, he was enraged by this device, I had never seen him this way. I had company over when he arrived. I got the feeling that he felt like I was treating him like the janitor, by not attentively monitoring what he was doing. My friend left because the feeling in the air was becoming charged with anger. Jonah let out a bloodcurdling curse that made the hair on my neck rise. By this time, I'm actually feeling guilty that my long messy hair could cause such a disturbance. I had just been thinking what a peaceful and sensitive guy he was before he let out that outlandish cry. I was shocked by his outburst, but it had made my blood run a little faster. Finally, he and his contraption exited my apartment. My girlfriend and I had been gossiping about the hotel where we worked, The Hollywood Roosevelt, a place with enough cold spots to imagine an audience of the dead. They were always holding extravagant séances there. I wondered if he could have found our conversation shallow and insipid and if that was what had set him off.

One morning I went over to pay rent. He was chattering away on a business call. I stood around for a few minutes waiting for him. I noticed that the room had an almost animated quality to it. It reminded me of a jungle. The windows were all open, and the Santa Ana winds were pouring thru the room. There were a lot of plants in the apartment and The trees outside looked like they were an extension to his room. The large windows looked as though the room was a tree house simply perched in the trees. Gentle sunlight brightened the room. I noticed how refreshing his apartment felt. My apartment, in contrast, had a cave like effect. There was little light, and the leak from the shower allowed a humid mist to permeate the air. I still loved having my own peace.

Jonah got off the phone and completed the rent transaction. He showed me the type of guitar stuff that he was working on. I noticed that he had a hard cover book on his music stand. I asked him what it was? He said it was called "The Eagle's Gift," and was by an author named Carlos Castaneda. I told him that I had borrowed that book from a friend the first week I had moved to Los Angeles. Ten years before in Germany, there had been a very interesting woman who had repeatedly recommended this author to me. Jonah said that for him the stories had rung particularly true. He recommended that I read the one focused particularly on women. It was called the "Second Ring of Power." I hadn't understood much in the "Eagle's Gift." I thought that perhaps if I had read the series in their proper order I would have had better comprehension. I thought it was nice of him to lend me a book. I liked him, so I felt happy when he extended such a gesture. I thanked him and left. The first book I had read was about an anthropology student who had met an Indian Sorcerer. He had had an apprenticeship with him in order to learn his knowledge. The book seemed very interesting, but a bit farfetched to me. The stories seemed very entertaining, but not particularly real. I read it as though it was a story, but not actual occurrences.

A few months went by with nothing much happening between Jonah and I. I became engrossed in an independent music, recording project. It was a great group of twenty- six studio musicians. It was the studio where Frank Zappa recorded his first record. My then boyfriend was quite gratuitous to throw me in with that mix. The people were in general far more experienced then me. I held my own, but it was definitely kind of him to put me in it fully, as he did.

I brought back the book to Jonah after reading it. He was playing guitar, but stopped. He started talking about life. He started talking about learning, art and creativity. He was very interesting. He lent me another one of the Castaneda books. I asked him if he was going to be around later? I felt nervous being around him. It seemed that when he would start talking, that time would sort of suspend itself. I felt he had subtly cued me to leave, so I asked him about later, and then left.

I went down to the hamburger stand on Hollywood Boulevard. A heavy metal drummer was thumping away on the table next to me. He had headphones on. I liked his hair. I asked him what he was listening to? He let me hear it and told me about the bands that he liked. I wished him well and then left. I rarely talked to anyone, let alone cute guys, so I was pleased with the pleasantries.

I knocked on Jonah's door around eight pm. He yelled that it was open and to come in. I was surprised that he left his door open when so many people might call on him and just walk in. I told him that I liked the Castaneda book, but that it hadn't completely made sense to me. He said that the books were true, and that he like Carlos, had had a benefactor. "You, in fact, have met a bona fide sorcerer." My body felt very heavy and my mind felt numb. I couldn't really believe he was saying something like this. Here I knew him for over a year, and he was a serious minded, business like person. It seemed entirely out of character for him to just say something, so strange. I'm not a sorcerer by choice, he said, "it just happened." I didn't know what a sorcerer was. When they talked about sorcerers in the Castaneda books, they seemed like larger than life types of characters, and more mythical then real people. I couldn't see how, if they were actually real, that I would have the unusual fate to run into one. He said that his benefactor was from the same line of seers as the warrior party in the books. I felt an inward hysteria and I didn't know what to say. One part of me was annoyed that Jonah would try and take me for a fool, and the other part was very curious.

Jonah went on... These conversations that we are having are not everyday conversations. You are having a gesture with power. Haven't you ever noticed that when you come over here, that I already know what you are going to talk about? I always seem to be on the wavelength of what is on your mind. I thought about it. I had always attributed that to him just being very smart. It had been somewhat flattering that he was so sensitive to my mind. The times when he had spit back my thoughts to me verbatim had taken me by surprise. "I'm psychic." he said.

I did not know what he meant by a gesture with power, I did notice this... As I would be talking to him, oftentimes I would almost fall into a light trancelike state. Everything around me seemed to be emphasized. Time would feel suspended, and I could only concentrate on what he was talking about, as he was saying it. Something said five minutes earlier, I could not think of. I couldn't really think at all when we would get into these conversations. I could understand implicitly what he was saying, but I couldn't think of anything else. Then, when he said this stuff about being a sorcerer, I suddenly felt weighted to the couch. Jonah lit up a cigarette and leaned back. I'm glad he was relaxed. I was beginning to feel a little wound up. You should be taking these conversations down on paper, he said. As I said, these are not idle conversations and you should be taking notes on all of this information. The stuff I am telling you is interesting to people. They don't all know these things. In fact, a lot of this stuff nobody knows. I got a little offended that I should be writing down everything that he was saying. I wondered again if he was trying to get me to act submissive to him for some reason. I had basically been under the impression that we were two individuals having a basic philosophical exchange together. It was almost a time honored activity of mine to shoot the breeze over coffee about all sorts of psychological and philosophical inquiries with people. I was dead wrong about that. This was an actual man of knowledge talking to me, but I didn't see that. I didn't know what he would have to say that I hadn't already thought of. Soon I could acknowledge that he did seem rather informed, much more than me. He was older, but he didn't seem older. He seemed to have far greater energy then I did. For that alone I should have noticed something was up. Here was a man, that even in his forties, had the energy, power and vitality of someone in their twenties. He was older in age, but that was it. I agreed to take some notes when these conversations would unravel. The air seemed to clear, or maybe it was my mind. Precisely at that moment Jonah said that he had something to do. I said good night and left.

I went to work at the hotel the next day. Everything stayed pretty interesting there. There was a lot of celebrities and other odd assortments of people. When I came home I sat down to think about what Jonah had said. I decided to call him up and see what he was doing that evening. He said to come up if I liked. I went upstairs around 7 pm.

The first thing he said to me was... "I feel you thinking about me." I thought he had some audacity to think that. I thought that he was probably thinking about me and just wanted to blame it on me. I said... "Surely you jest," and laughed it off. "I'm serious, my mind is usually quiet, and I can feel you thinking about me." Is nothing sacred? I thought. Now you can't even think of a man without them knowing about it. I remembered that I had been obsessively thinking about him, but it had had to do with paying the rent that week. We got off the subject of whom was thinking of whom.

I wanted to know what Jonah thought about sorcery now

that he had made this unusual proclamation. We live in a world of black magicians, he said. The white man has really screwed things up. The planet is in a state of desperate danger. Sorcery is just one level of things. Sorcery has to do with interactions between human beings. We call this the world of the black magicians. You have to become aware of what people are up to. Mostly what people are concerned with is having power over other people. There are masters and slaves, and the whole world is playing that game. We call everyday society the world of the black magician. I have been taken outside of this world. I am in this world, but I am no longer of it. I am outside the ring that presses upon people. You, on the other hand, are still part of that world. You let the doings of other people upset and disturb you. I choose not to focus and stay on sorcery. I think, there are more interesting things happening here then my concerns with people. Everyone is trying to get over on everyone else. You're a leader, or a follower, but to be bothered with being a leader, you have to be concerned with followers. I'm not going to get up on a pedestal and talk about my knowledge because I don't want to be bothered by geek followers. Being a sorcerer basically entails stopping people who want to control you, and you being the one to control yourself. Being in control of your life,

to the finest detail, is the substance of the value of sorcery.

People will respect you when you are honest with them. They

don't respect you going along with their phony behavior. It

wakes them up when you speak directly to them about the way

that you feel. They appreciate it. They would rather be their

real selves. So, if someone is giving you their phony mask,

and you cut through to the real person, they will like that.

People full of lying bullshit stay away from me. If they come

in my apartment, they will feel uncomfortable and just leave.

They might not even know that they are acting phony. People,

get so involved with being an act that they believe that that is

who they really are. Lots of people are sorcerers. If they exert

influence, they are being a sorcerer. Artists, musicians, they all

have the power to influence, and of course there is good and

bad influence. Anybody can be creative. It is a skill that can be

learned. Not everybody knows that. A lot of people think that

they are not creative, when they actually could be. Everybody

could be if they set about it in a proper manner. Basically, if

they did things slowly and did not rush ahead of themselves. I

just do things slowly., accurately, and one step at a time. You

can apply this to anything... music, writing, anything. You

don't write a book.... you write a sentence or a paragraph.

These are not idle conversations, he said. Some very heavy knowledge is being transmitted to you, if you would just pay attention. I am storing knowledge inside of you. As you live you will remember it. It will come back to you. I am storing it in your body. I didn't really know what he meant by this. I knew that again I was woozy while I was talking to him. He said that that was heightened awareness. Everything that was learned while I was in heightened awareness was being stored inside me. I only knew that when I got this feeling, which seemed like some sort of paralysis, I had a lot of trouble remembering what had been said. That was why Jonah had said that I should take notes.

Right off the bat Jonah had said that I should not look at him as any type of guru. He was belligerently against the guru/disciple type of relationship. I'm telling you these things because you came here and were interested. I'm a regular guy, and I don't want to be bothered with any of that guru bullshit. Got it? he said. Also, you should question what I tell you. I don't want someone just being a yes person to me. Think for yourself about what you think is true. Question everything. Even what I tell you. Too many people are herded around like cattle without ever questioning what people are doing or saying. Some people are naive. Everybody is happy keeping people naive so that they can be controlled. There is a lot of corruption going on, on the planet right now. These idiots are killing the one thing that could save them, and feed everybody. If everybody could just be themselves, do what they want and respect the earth, the earth would feed and shelter them. The fields of Kansas could feed half the world, but because of politics it could never happen. This is a wakeup call. The greedy people who are contaminating the planet and destroying the forests, are wreaking unimaginable havoc here. So much so, that they could be pushing toward human extinction. The time to stop destroying nature is now, and it's a top priority emergency. These people are asleep. They are sleepwalking through life and ignorantly baiting horrific destruction.

I stayed awhile longer before I noticed it was midnight. I thanked Jonah for his company and left. I felt all sorts of strange feelings when I walked downstairs to my room. I felt concerned about the warnings Jonah had talked about. Somewhere in the midst of his dialogue, he mentioned that he was an Indian. The way he said it did not imply that he was part Indian. I was confused. I had thought he was Welsh and French. Later that week when I was talking to him, he seemed to appear Indian to me. He said that I possibly could have seen his essence. An Indian is someone who loves the earth he said. I tried to figure out if he thought he had in a past life been an Indian, or something like that, but he didn't seem to corroborate that idea. Jonah had me hooked. I was frustratingly curious about him and his experiences. He did not give up his stories easily to me. He was very emphatic about his life being his business. He told me that he would tell me what he wanted, when he wanted, and that it would not be questioned. It was clear that if I were not extremely respectful of his privacy, that I could take my curiosity elsewhere.

One day when I was visiting, he mentioned that he knew that reincarnation was a truth. He said it was not a big deal. I'm probably the one person on earth with the amount of proof that I have. He said that a picture had once been taken of him, that a great painter had already painted. I wanted to see the picture. He said that maybe one day he would show it to me, but that maybe he wouldn't. He said that he was a great painter in the past. Overtime I guessed whom he meant. I looked at a lot of art books. I found an artist that painted things he had said that he liked. He admitted to me that that was the one. He said that he could have just let that become his claim to fame, because of the proof that he had. That's just another level. I don't want to get hooked on that. I don't want people becoming amazed by that. It just is and it doesn't matter. I noticed that he did have some large and interesting canvases around that he had done this lifetime.

Time went on. I joined a rock band reminiscent of Frank Zappa. One of his players was in it. I enjoyed Hollywood. One day I left work and walked to another part of town to an electronics store. I needed a needle for my stereo. I was well away from my neighborhood when I spotted Jonah. I was surprised to see him. We talked for a few minutes in front of a furniture store. A bum came up to us and asked him for a cigarette. Beat it pal, can't you see I'm in a conversation, he quipped at him. You have to watch who approaches you, he said. People don't always look like who they are. They might look one way and behave entirely unexpectedly. Keep the weirdo's and creeps out of your life. This path attracts strange people and situations toward you. I knew he meant to watch the seemingly safe as much as the obviously suspicious. I told him that I had heard that someone had been murdered in front of the health food restaurant across the street. He said that he had felt some type of violence when he had walked past there just now. Places can hold energy of events that had happened there, he said. I told him that I felt a sort of dismal and depressed feeling every time I walked into a certain local pub in our neighborhood. He said he had worked there and had probably personally left that feeling there. I still thought the place was really cool, but it had this sedating quality to it even before you had a drink. He then was on his way.

Later that night he told me that that had been a gesture with power and not a chance meeting. I didn't know what to make of a "gesture with power." I didn't feel fortunate enough to have something so elusive and mysterious happen, so I found the idea only vaguely possible. I did leave Jonah with a sense of his energy. It was always that way. There was something about him that felt like an actual magnetic force.

A few nights later I went out with a music school buddy I had known in a different city. We had seen each other on the street in Hollywood. He met Jonah and immediately liked him. We went out to a local bar. I sat next to an off duty clown still in his uniform. He sold balloons on the boulevard. He seemed either tired or just not needing to be putting on his clown ritz.

Around one a.m. I came home. My friend walked me to the door and then left. I was surprised to see Jonah emerge from the shadows as I walked down the hall. He came in to chat for a few minutes. He laid down on my bed, and I sat at my desk. I was mildly intoxicated from the JD and coke I had had. That nervousness I had, that accompanied that strange magnetic force I always felt from him, came over me. He started talking about sorcery again. I kept thinking that if my neighbors could hear this conversation they would think it really odd. The walls were excessively thin, but in retrospect these neighbors didn't seem like the type to be avidly discerning conversation through the walls. Jonah had made it very clear that I was not to be discussing these conversations with anybody. I thought it a little odd to have Jonah lying on my bed. We weren't that familiar. I wondered if he thought anything of it? Probably not. That was like when he would come to his door in his underwear. He would look at me like I was some alien square to notice such things. Another one of those California things I guess. He clearly was not in his underwear for my benefit, it was something I was just supposed to not notice. My ex from Europe had been that way too. On our first date, I came to his room and there he is in his briefs. And of course they're those euro briefs that are always seemingly more brief. To me it seemed a little odd to answer the door in one's underwear unless you know someone on some kind of personal basis. Obviously I didn't get the proper training in uninhibited coolness. We talked for a few minutes more and then Jonah left. I had the feeling that I was living in a strange dream of some sort. I felt excited by Jonah's conversation and presence. I liked him a lot. He seemed fair and honest, and always had great insight on things.

A few days later we got on the topic of altered states of awareness. There are a lot of deranged people walking around Hollywood. More than one would normally encounter in just about any community I had ever been in including NYC. We say that their assemblage point is in the left side of awareness., he said. He called that the junkyard of human consciousness. I told him I got anxiety sometimes. He said that that was ok to experience different states of mind, such as if you stayed up all night. We switched off that topic. Then Jonah said... I'm an Indian in spirit. My spirit loves the earth, which is God. This path of heart that I talk about is an Indian warrior path. We live in a world of sorcerers, and it's hunt or be hunted. The whole world has that game going on. Sorcery is the power to influence someone. It's the power to move their assemblage

point. The assemblage point is a point of attention. I told him

that I found it more virtuous to work on yourself instead of

trying to manipulate others. My only goal is to leave this place

better then when I got here, he said. In cleaning up your own

act, you will be able to heal others. You can't save the whole

world at once. You can be the best you can be and others will

change around you. A big part of developing yourself is to

shut off the internal dialogue. Slowing down the endless

chatter, that most people have going on inside their heads.

When your mind is talking, you think that it is you thinking.

How can you be sure that it is you producing these thoughts?

What if these thoughts are coming to you from someplace

else? It's better to be aware of the silence inside, then the

nonstop barrage that comes from you or from somewhere else.

To be present and not lost in thoughts was a better place to

operate from. It's like an athlete who must perform a function

without thought. To allow the natural function to flow, without

hindrance of thought or analysis, is the best. Like a child. If

there was no consciousness of self, then there wouldn't be any

fears of inadequacy. People's proficiency would soar.

Children ride this crest. They worry about nothing and they

just blow through things until inhibitions are taught. "Watch
the animals." They are in their intuitive states at all times.

2 BEING YOURSELF

One day in January I found myself again affixed to
Jonah's couch. This was the first time I conceded to take notes
on a conversation we were having. Prior to this I had felt a
little stupid about it. He mentioned that you should function in
your own element. I liked this idea. If you do what feels
natural, you will do it with ease and you will like doing it.
Find a work element that feels alright. Socialize with people
that feel natural to you. Basically, do what comes naturally.
"Listen with your body." Your body has good natural instincts
if you listen to it. I don't want to scare your body by doing any
kind, of what you would consider supernatural, type of
actions. You always want me to perform tricks for you. I told
him I was trying to not be gullible. Doing what came natural,
and putting yourself in with situations that flowed, came down
to being yourself. Jonah heard my opinion on how to treat a
work superior. He told me that to act in any special way was
ineffective because being yourself at all times was being the
best possible you. Being here is all it takes, he said. Being
present, to realize that each moment is unique in time, and that

you can change anything, at any time. Each moment is an opportunity to think more freely. Each moment is its own. The possibility to continually progress is available, when each minute is a possibility for entirely new realities. He continued... self- importance is an enemy to people on this path. You attract what you seek. Thoughts are like magnets. You attracted a sorcerer because that is what you sought. An artist is a sorcerer, positive or negative. Someone to tap and bottle the source, and to effect people positively or negatively. The hardest part about creativity is slowing it down. You don't write a book, a song or a screenplay, you write a sentence, a phrase or a theme. Learning had to be approached like this. Learn in chunks. Learn small bits of information well. Build on what you know. Jonah lit up a cigarette and paused, I suspected he wanted to change gears, so I thanked him and left. The only event I could recently remember where I had done anything that I could relate to seeking a sorcerer, had been with a drummer buddy of mine. I had known him from back east and he had come to LA to music school. We used to meditate together and take excursions into the woods to enjoy nature. We used to talk about sweat lodges and other native American customs. So maybe, in that way I was seeking to find a sorcerer, but I wasn't conscious that that, was what I was doing.

Around this time the riots in LA broke out. Jonah stopped by and said I could come upstairs if I wanted. Eventually I decided to go up there. He had his window open and was blasting away on guitar. I could not believe it. He was sitting there relaxed watching the news on television. Tonight is history in the making, he said. He said that he had been up on the roof watching before. I was more than mildly concerned. This neighborhood was stockpiled with young thugs with guns. Law enforcement had essentially quit. It was a unique feeling to have no active law enforcement on duty. Society as I knew it seemed to be gone in this time. All of a sudden it was a society without laws. It was a scary feeling. Where one always has to take care of oneself, this was a completely different experience. It made me see that what we take as absolute truth is a system that could just be gone. All of a sudden I felt confronted with how would people really behave if we didn't have the modern construct that we considered to be reality. It would be like caveman times. Women would need protection. The whole thing felt off kilter. Obviously there was an unusualness in the air for everybody.

There was a lot of miscellaneous violence erupting all around.
It was a sad and crazy time. In general, the thing I was most
prejudice against was prejudice. I just thought that in general
people should be judged individually, not by some creed that
they just were born into anyway. My favorite saying to myself
was that we were all born of a mother. I can see how stereo
typing and conditioning can seem real, but I never thought any
one culture was superior or inferior. Some seemed to have
more advantage which would make them seem better because
it was easier for them to be well. I asked Jonah if he wasn't
nervous? He said no. This is a protected place. Nothing will
happen here. It certainly sounded good. I wondered how he
could be so sure. I was losing it. I didn't want to be around
neighbors because it seemed a very real threat that buildings
were being set on fire. One would naturally have to exit the
building, and I kept thinking of bumbling around asking
people's opinions about which way to run, while getting shot
in the process. I really felt that to have your absolute wits
about you in a situation like this you had to concentrate on
your surroundings and not blunder by talking to another
human being. A shot rang outside my window while I was on
the phone with my parents. I stayed on the floor with the

shades down. They were a little disconcerted. This was not supposed to be happening. This is a power spot Jonah said. That is why nothing will happen here. I finally relaxed and went home. I slept with shoes on and my money and contact lenses in my back pocket. There was a very strange feeling in the air the next day. Gangs of delinquents sat on the four corners of the boarded up streets. Everything was completely boarded up. The most regrettable   burning in the area had been this huge Lingerie boutique on Hollywood Boulevard. It had been an amazing costume shop the likes I had never seen anywhere. The original Hollywood Lingerie.

I went down the boulevard to pick up a check from the hotel. I thought I heard Jonah's voice in my mind when I left the building. I thought I heard him say... "Where are you going?" The voice felt like it was in my mind so I didn't look around. Five minutes later as I walked down the boulevard I ran into him. He said... "Where are you going?" To pick up a check, I replied. He said O.K. I thought it was chivalrous of him to be concerned considering the mental climate that prevailed. When I saw him later, I told him how I thought I heard something said, five minutes earlier then it was actually said. He said that I had heard into the future. I didn't really question that much when he would tell me things that were seemingly outlandish. I figured that somehow, within his scheme of things, some things were possible that were just not ordinary. I accepted that I did not necessarily understand everything that he would say, but that it was open to possibility. He had told me not to become overly concerned with every piece of seemingly phenomenal experience, but to just observe it. He said not to interpret it. Just acknowledge it and let it pass. "Nothing means anything."

I had to go to the East Coast for a wedding. I went early and stayed near the city. I called Jonah to tell him things I thought he might find interesting. It was hard to judge what would happen when I called Jonah. Sometimes he could be immensely gracious and exciting, and other times he could come off cuttingly cruel. He was never kind with words. He cut to the core truth in any situation. A lot of times I didn't know what the core truth was. That was one of the things that was so amazing about him. He perceived truths about myself ten times faster than I did. I would never realize a lot of things till he said it. Then I would review or observe it and say, that is what I was thinking or feeling, but I couldn't get to it. He seemed to know ten times more about my psyche then would ever surface to my mind. In a way it was maddening because I didn't think I thought that way until he pointed it out. I was often on autopilot about being courteous and appropriate in my manner. He would rip that up until you said what you really thought about every damn little thing. He would say knock off the bullshit. I didn't think I was being phony, until he pointed out that I thought nothing like the docile veneer I was trying to pass off as what I thought. He sometimes misunderstood what I had said or meant, and would give me vicious interpretations of what he had thought I had said. Again, things were out of what I would consider acceptable in a normal friendship. This was not any sort of association like I had ever had before. He was so in genius, that I tried to put aside my horror at his meanness. I saw that he was beating my demons out of me, so to speak, and that beyond his scathing words were the intention that I transcend my conditioning that held me bondage to society's brainwash. He felt that although everyone got sort of chartered into it, a lot of misconception and brainwash was being perpetuated. The lost knowledge of our connection to the earth was a big part of it. The Indians had lived here for thousands of years, never disturbing nature's balance. In the last couple of hundred years, horrendous devastation was proliferated in the name of industry and progress. I just wouldn't have let someone speak so harshly to me normally. He seemed to career himself out of really bad moods into totally different states, so I tried to not dwell on misgivings but to stay focused on just how amazing his company was to me. I mean when he wasn't blasting me about something, we were laughing our asses off about all sorts of crazy things. His company gave me great joy.

I got the impression that even when he went on a verbal rampage, it was to illustrate a point. A point that would be useful, and that his intent was with affection despite its seething appearance. However, I did know that he was serious. He would periodically remind me that if he was wasting his breath, he would drop me in an instant. He told me that I was his last handout. He wasn't going to help people one on one anymore, because they became a burden. Certain people had taken advantage of his good nature. He had other, agenda's anyway. Having one person get involved in learning from him was one thing, but a whole bunch of people would take up his whole life. To outside ears, it would sound slightly bizarre his behavior at times, but to me it didn't matter. His information I found fascinating and I wanted to know it all.

Overtime we eventually wound up taking several road trips together. Just one occasion I wanted to mention here. We were in Colorado in a mountain region. We stopped in a beautiful souvenir shop. It was not standard fare, it had jewelry and crystals and rain sticks. The woman was older and very sophisticated and attractive looking to me. Jonah chatted with her for a bit. He made a point to talk to many people wherever we were. Sometimes it was mortifying. One time he said that the waitress was not on the ball at all. She definitely heard. Amazingly she then did seem to become attracted to him. After we left the shop we went to a luncheonette next store. We sat in a corner of the small establishment. It was a fairly rural area being up the mountain, so there was definitely a cozy otherworldly charm to the place. It was a location just isolated enough, as to make you feel that you were somewhere authentic. Out of nowhere I commented that I wanted to know what he knew. He seemed to take flight on this statement. I remember him becoming aroused over this, but I don't recall whether it was with annoyance at me wanting to be privy to his business, or just more of a deep foreboding like... now you are in for more than you might have bargained for. On one hand he seemed to take to the idea, but that the idea was preposterous unless I became far more then what I presently was. This came up time and time again, that he recounted that I had wanted to know what he knew. He said that I could not know what he knew, but that I could only experience what I knew. In other words, he was trying to say that I won't have his experiences, but that I will live my own knowledge. I didn't want to know anything he wouldn't want me to know, unless it directly affected my survival. I didn't want to be nosy, it was just that how does someone become as he was. What school did he go to? Said with incredulity, not common inquiry.

I was under the impression, that some intensely interesting event had taken place, and I was curious about that. He alluded to something that had affected him, but that it was something that may come up between us to discuss, or may not. Again, I wasn't looking to disrespect his privacy in any way. I just felt, that if he was interested in talking to me about whatever had happened, he would.

His nature seemed a complete paradox. He was undoubtedly the most interesting person I had ever met. The unique euphoria and energetic paralysis I experienced in his presence was extraordinary, and the other side of the coin was equally hideous. As great as he was, was as horrible as he was. I truly found his presence amazing. I bore that in mind when his terrifying side arose.

He told me that he had a benefactor. He said that his benefactor had given him all sorts of knowledge and experience. He talked about his benefactor with a lot of respect. He attributed all of the knowledge that he was giving me as being straight from his benefactor. I imagined his benefactor as being quite a person.

Later that night I was reflecting on a particularly hair raising row that had occurred between Jonah and I. I had been thinking about him and had wanted to see him. Sometimes it felt natural to go up and see him, and other times it seemed as though I should have some kind of legitimate reason. He probably sensed my reason as being some sort of decoy, because the sparks were flying almost immediately. I asked him if he could lower the action on my guitar. That meant adjusting the string height. After he did, he said .... "play this," and he played a lick. I was nervous about his demands and played it poorly. Then he said... "play this." I couldn't catch it. The next thing I knew he was insulting me inside and out. I left quickly before a less controlled side of me snuck out. I was hurt, but I was also furious. I played passionately the next day. I played in ways I had forgotten existed. I wanted to thank him for his interest in my musical wellbeing. That was the last time I used my guitar as a reason to say hi to him.

While I was in N.Y. I had my own room. It was comfortable. I called Jonah from Broadway. I wanted to tell him about all the wonderful things I had seen in Pennsylvania. I had visited some Indian Burial mounds, and had seen a lot of wildlife in the woods. I expected some wonderful meaning to the things that I had seen. He told me to knock off the bullshit. He had talked about something he called "seeing," that "the Indian" had talked about, all through the Castaneda books. I thought it had something to do with the earth communicating with you. I could never tell if the earth was just being the earth, or if I was "seeing" the earth in a different way. So, I was sort of looking at nature to see if anything would happen. He said to stop being an idiot. "It is what it is." If you see a table, it is a table. Stop looking for hidden mysteries and being such a bozo. Don't interpret stuff. When my friend and I had gone to the burial mounds, I had gone off by myself to listen to the silence. I felt an amazing silence in the woods. There was a beautiful feeling there. The farmland was lightly chilled and quiet. I was enamored by the feeling there. I felt I was stabbing in the dark about figuring out his ideas.

When I got back to LA I went to Jonah's to have dinner. He had mostly organic foods there. He had great taste in what he ate. We started talking and he said that the earth "communicates with you". The phone rang, he picked it up and no one was there. "That's my agreement" he said. The cosmos, or earth, does communicate with you, but you're not supposed to get freaked out by it. You're also not supposed to added meanings or interpretations to it. That's just the nature of things and it's not a big deal. The earth consists of everything. Since we are not just in nature, it is not just natural things that communicate with you. It is everything. You are not supposed to get jarred by these types of things. It has to do with the timing of a circumstance. "My benefactor eliminated coincidence." The earth is not how it appears. There's a lot more going on here then you can see. There is the known, the unknown, and the unknowable. You shouldn't try to know the unknowable. My benefactor never let me tell him about all the things I would "see." he didn't care. Just like I don't want to hear about every little thing you think and see. "Seeing is personal." That is what his benefactor's wife and apprentice had said. I tell you some of these things to point things out to you, but you can rarely be sure of these things, so we stay away from interpreting things. You might get an omen about something, but all you can do is witness it, because to add meaning to it is stupid. I don't want you to live in a haunted house, he said. The more that you get wrapped up in this, the weirder the stuff that starts to happen. Don't get nutty, he told me. Just acknowledge the earth, meaning everything, can communicate with you. It's good to listen, but there's nothing to fear.

"Be an observer." The point is that this is natural, and it is not supposed to draw you into thinking about this sort of stuff exclusively. What I'm telling you about are things that are meant to expand your awareness. However, the point of all this extraordinary stuff, is to put it to use in the service of your everyday life. There are interesting things here to explore, but the first order of business, is to get your life impeccable like a warrior, right here in your everyday existence. To live an impeccable clean life gives you the kind of energy for other explorations. It also gives you a tight orderly life that will make you successful. Money is time. Time to live life the way you want to live it. I'm not impressed, he said. I'm not impressed by anybody. I'm not impressed with people with money. All of the knowledge that you are getting is interwoven into ordinary language and concerns. I wasn't taken out of this world to go sit on a mountain. I'm right here in the city, and I work my magic in the fabric of everyday life. I think your concerns with supernatural phenomena are in part a wish to not be in this world. You are in this world and you must adapt to it. Money is survival in this world. Forget that starving artist trip that you were on. I told him that I always knew when it was time to move. My poster of the Antelope Valley poppies would mysteriously fall off the wall. The last three times of moving it had fallen on that day. It never fell any other time. He told me not to dwell on paranormal activities. It wasn't of particular use in business.

You are always coming to me with garbage that you think is so meaningful. That's left side awareness. No interpretations. Nothing means anything. The less garbage that you are trying to figure out, the closer you will be to perception. Perception is the point I'm trying to teach you. I'm trying to enhance your awareness. It's called cleaning off your island. I clean off all of the garbage on your island when you talk to me. Then you feel great. You go away and you are happy, and then you come back with garbage clogging up your brain.

The first thing to cleaning off your island, or, to clean off your life, is getting rid of the geeks. You, my dear, attract lots of geeks. You also seek them out. You go looking for these guru mystical types. If they say they are, they aren't. Listen to those who are quiet. Listen to those who aren't after you for anything. They might have something to offer. Keep intelligent, decent, goodhearted people as your company. "By their fruits you shall know them," he quoted the bible.

Your life is no longer an open book, he said. Do not go around spilling your life and your guts all over the place. When someone asks you about yourself say... "Why do you ask?" Your business is entirely your own, and you shouldn't feel the least bit uncomfortable about maintaining your privacy. This path attracts geeks. You must not invite them to invade your business. They become like vampires. They will suck out your life energy.

I felt annihilated by the long conversation. We finished dinner and I went home to sleep. Jonah invited me out to dinner later that week. We walked up the boulevard to an Italian restaurant. I noticed he maintained a formal and

commanding demeanor. We talked a little bit about our lives.
It was fairly relaxed. Once we were seated he seemed to lose
that perfect upright posture that he had walked there with. It
hadn't been, like he was just casually walking up the block.
He had walked there like a person with serious intent about
where he was going and what he was doing. It wasn't like a
leisurely stroll. It was different being in public with him,
because we chose not to talk about sorcery or any of that. I
told him that I had once known a great bassist named Jaco
Pastorius. He told me that I should play bass. I said "why?"
"Because from where I sit, I can tell you that and have it be
true," he said. Because you ran into Jaco, it was an omen to
play bass. I didn't see the logic behind that, but I knew that on
several occasions, I'd had that feeling about the bass anyway.
We walked home on the boulevard. He walked very slowly. I
almost felt it was annoying to be walking that slowly. I
thought he was doing it to illustrate a point about slowing
everything down. We stopped in front of a club that had music
pouring out of it. We listened for a few minutes, but were not
inspired to go in. We walked back to the apartments and went
upstairs to his place. He took a seat on the couch, and I sat in a
chair facing him from across the room.

Most people are not what they look like. Just because they have a certain exterior image, that is not really who they are. Some very untalented looking people could be very talented. The basis of our conversation thus far, was that it was possible to go from life to life, and retain your consciousness. That, if you could attain a certain wisdom, you could master going from life to life with your awareness intact. With the knowledge that I have been given from my benefactor, I have only one main desire. That is to leave the planet in better shape than when I got here.

To help the human race, you have to believe that the potential was possible. The planet will heal itself. People have to believe that if they do a turnaround, and take care of the planet, the planet will take care of them. Taking care of the planet would be the shortest distance to reach the potential of clearing the stage, for what could be man's natural inheritance of what could be heaven on earth. Where everyone was fed, clothed, and got by in a peaceful productive manner. If everyone could be themselves, doing what came naturally to them, the world would take care of itself. People could choose peace.

There is a magic in life that could be everyone's, if they

were able to tune into it within themselves. For everyone to be free, to feel the peace and freedom within, is the warrior's way. He got us some tea, then he kept talking. "Power is a feeling." Places have power. Watch what the animals do, because they go with their feelings. They are intuitive and always alert. They use their senses. Humans could do that if they made themselves aware to.

The inner silence, shutting off the inner dialogue, will bring you closer to your senses. What I am passing on to you is my benefactor's knowledge. A warrior's discipline is just like any other form of discipline. This is simply a body of knowledge being passed on from generation to generation. His benefactor told him, that to live long and to live well, it was important to relax. To even relax while you work, because to be in a meditative or relaxed way, was the way to peace and health.

Today's lifestyle was too stressful to the body. The chaos grew when the population grew. As the population grew, the lifespan dropped. "People used to live to eight hundred or so, when they used meditation daily." I noticed a change in my mental state. It was almost like I was going from a thick haze in my mind back to normal everyday awareness. I knew that he could feel that shift as well, and that that was

about it for tonight. I was subtly agitated about the lifespan

comment. I didn't know how to process that. I didn't want to

get confrontational at that moment, but I was just not

conditioned to consider a lifespan of eight hundred years to be

within a physical human capacity. We went back into some

brief regular conversation about work and music, and then I

said goodnight and left.

3 DREAMING

I have come to the conclusion, that one of the biggest
setbacks I have had, is that I did not know how to love myself
properly. Jonah had quoted Shakespeare in saying ... To Thy
own self be true. Jonah also said that you can't save the whole
world, but if you save yourself, the world will heal around
you. So really, by helping yourself, you would help other
people. I have spent years following those I was impressed
with. Which is great. I am in love with a lot of the talents I see
in other people. I inwardly thought it was somehow wrong to
celebrate my own worth. This leads to not believing in
yourself. This goes nowhere. When you don't believe in
yourself, you can't do anything for anybody else. Then you
become dependent on others for whatever you think you don't
have. Not honoring your own worth is messed up, because it's
like saying you don't believe in the gifts that you were given.
Jonah also said that there is a piece of spirit, or god, in all of
us. So, to hate yourself, is to not appreciate the god that is in
you. So, so self-deprecation in the guise of humility is
unnecessary. Although a little humor is ok. Whoever wanted

to taper my megalomania was off the mark. I choose to celebrate myself as a way of honoring life. If I can't love myself, whom can I love? Why not participate in healthy achievement? I feel empowered to discuss this. I have felt insecure a lot, and part of it was not giving myself permission to be who I am and to love myself. Why not honor all of the fantastic things that we have here. What can compare to the sublime beauty of the earth. The haunting whisper of the evening meadows. I say we should love ourselves by embracing our talents. When you love yourself it is so easy to love the next person. I was reading the bible today. Sometimes I feel that time is drifting and what am I doing? What is it that I am supposed to be doing? So, the bible said you should love people. I felt pretty good about that. I have never lacked in good will toward others. It came back to.... even the bible says to love yourself. I mean if you're going to have positive feeling toward everyone walking up and down the street, shouldn't you at least give yourself the same respect and love.

My ex-lover paid me a visit. A really good visit. Oh look, that's what it means to be alive. I remember that. I worshipped this guy from the moment I laid eyes on him. All the right everything. A person whose focus was square on himself. I loved focusing on him too. I felt better about me, just being in conjunction with him. We celebrated a lot of life and music together. He made me develop my talents all the while I was just admiring his. I hid behind his presence. He really seemed to love me, yet I saw him drink my blood like it was wine in the past. He was a self-preservation artist. He had to be and he was. I was conscious to not give up myself again. He'd had me really down before. The point I'm eluding to is that I think it's ok to put yourself first. When I put others before me, in the past, I was in bad shape. So when I ran across someone only capable of healthy self-interest, and I was able to keep mine intact, it felt like an honest deal. I still think he's really great, and he is supportive in that he thinks I'm great, but in this case we go home alone, or is it with ourselves? I wouldn't say all people should be that way. I would think there are people not undeserving of having one give themselves more fully. I would hope to share with people, but not lose myself. If I could love myself the way I needed him to love me. If I loved myself right, I wouldn't have that need. I'm glad I can feel that kind of energy with someone, even if I really have to control it. He brings out my wild animal nature. It's good to know it's there. The person

I'm saying is only capable of healthy self- interest, managed to put a whole lot of people in touch with themselves, because he was in touch with himself, so to speak. He was in touch with his own art. Bottom line, eventually you can only get paid for your own work. There it is.... Love thyself, because thyself needs to get paid. So, Jonah said it right. Heal yourself and the world around you will be healed. Jonah is a very kind person, but he was also the toughest, or second to toughest person I had ever met. His kindness was not weakness. He said to be careful that my good nature wasn't taken as an opening for people to misbehave toward me. Another time he accused me of having the humbleness of a beggar, as he called it. It was like a false modesty that I had, as well as low self -esteem. He said that my spirit was warped and that was why I had trouble with self- confidence. I had taken browbeating too much to heart. People had tried to beat me into strength and it had made me fearful. He wasn't exactly soft in getting this point across. He said something like why don't you go blow a bum behind a dumpster? I was totally offended and freaked out. I thought why on earth are you saying such disgusting things to me? I figured out that he was saying that I was treating myself in a poor manner, and that if I was going to be that rude to myself why not take it to the worst degree. He was pointing out, that I wasn't in some way defending myself from the insults of others. Not letting people get over on you and make you fall into their court was a big part of growing into being a warrior or a man of knowledge. Not being suckered into other people's lairs was big on the list of what he was trying to share with me.

I called Jonah to discuss cooking something. he commented on how undomesticated I was. Then he said... what I am introducing you to is stuff that is unknown to you now. I'm waking you up. "The whole story is how to wake you, in your dreams, and how to live in your dream state awake." It is also about staying conscious to life. Either choice sounded intriguing. Another thing important is to be yourself. Be your own best friend. Stop hassling and restricting yourself. You have to let yourself be free. I told him that I didn't want to be crazy. You go too far to be "normal," he said. It is important not to judge yourself how other people judge you. To be your own best friend, is the best.

I got back from going on job interviews, and was sweltering from the heat. Jonah had finally given me the go ahead to take one of the nicer apartments upstairs. I knocked on his door so that he could connect my phone to the door buzzer. He motioned for me to come sit on his bed, by the fan. he made a mock gesture of closing his robe more, but I knew he didn't have a modest bone in his body. I had come across him in his underwear before, and had always waited for him to cover himself. He seemed to admonish me for being so concerned whether a body was dressed or not.

I told him about some odd dreams I had had. He told me to look for my hands in my dreams. Each night tell yourself, before you go to sleep, to look for your hands. The Indians knew a lot of knowledge before people came in, took over, and killed them. The knowledge was about existence, not just them. I asked him about how that feeling of heightened awareness would happen whenever I talked to him. He said he didn't know how, but that it just happened. It had happened with him and his benefactor also. When we would get into these conversations, he said it was a "gesture with power." A feeling of suspended animation would come over me. My concentration would become intently focused on him. My body would feel heavy, yet good. It was a very profoundly unusual visceral feeling. You would be aware of feeling it but not able to do anything but stay intently focused on whatever you were talking about. You could not go back to previous thoughts.

I came over again later that week. He invited me in. He had been working on guitar chords. I sat down on the couch next to him. He said that he had a flash that I should become a court stenographer. The idea struck me with horror. The idea of discussing this now strikes me with even more horror. I felt alarmed that he would say such a thing. My mother and I had been quibbling about life as a guitarist, versus life as a secretary for years. The level of ability for such a feat as he mentioned, didn't seem a real possibility for me. I had come seeking the mysteries of creation and now he was suggesting the height of tedium. I felt resistant. I didn't see how a "flash" could come to him, that would cost me essentially thousands of hours of time. I felt the request to be somewhat of an imposition. He was serious. In fact, it looked like the continuation of our association seemed perched on this small insignificant request. He decided that this was going to be a sorcerer's task, as he put it. These were "tasks" that were supposed to be without question, because of the extreme exclusivity and unusualness of the entire situation. The time is going to pass anyway and you might as well do something with yourself. I decided that this was not the time to discuss the extraordinary amount of time that goes into being a real instrumentalist. I tried to tell Jonah that this didn't feel right. He said that I could greatly hasten my note taking and that he could accurately give me verbatim information. I have attained moderate facility of this, and he was bitterly right about the whole thing. I always fear he will depart and what would have been the use of this skill, but the other side of it is that it can be used for your own writing, to write at the speed of thought.

A cool breeze came in the room, as I had the thought, that all happiness came from the love of the spirit and not from the success in the popularity contest among people. I listened to some Jimi Hendrix music. I felt something in his music that electrified me in a certain way. I felt that whatever propelled him to such beautiful creations could also be something I felt satisfaction in. Jonah had said that the cosmos talks to us. It agrees and disagrees. Coincidence, he said, had been obliterated repeatedly to him by his benefactor. It is hard to know what is coincidence and what is not. I didn't like to make inferences. The times were countless that I had been helped by outside hints.

One time I was trying to get dressed for a recording session. A real one, with a release form from a record company and everything. I always like to wear comfortable clothes, but I wanted to be attractive to someone that was going to be there. I felt nervous about the session to begin with, and wanted to wear something that would make me feel confident. Dressing sometimes got me into fits of anxiety. As I opened the closet door and thought "be comfortable," the light bulb blew out. It was the timing that suggested to me to listen to that thought. I immediately felt strong and secure. I dressed quickly and did very well at the session. I played my parts perfectly the first time.

The heat raged on in a sweltering heat wave. I dropped in on Jonah to check his pulse, the pulse of his interesting existence. The topic of Art arose. He cut it to its simplest form. "Thievery." I loved it when he would talk dirty. He was serious. I always expected such clear honorable intention, when he would just see things out of the box of what I could see. Like the time in Vegas. We were down to little money. I think we had just enough to get back to Los Angeles. I was at the bar in the casino. I know I wasn't drinking so I'm not even sure why I went up to the bar. I found a wallet lying on the bar. I immediately thought the absolute and only solution was to hand this in. I was proud of my quick and proper thinking. I practically ran to him to show him my decent manners. I was astounded at his reaction. He was furious. He saw it as a blessing from the great spirit, (we'll never know how much of a blessing it could have been), to get us home easily and in comfort. He thought that if someone was so careless as to leave a wallet like that, that they deserved the consequences. He probably meant to toss back the id's etc... and just take the cash. I really think that, if he had opened it and found a lot of cash, he would have just taken practical money and somehow, without endangering his own security gotten the bulk back to the owner. I knew him to be a to the penny honest guy. After further discussing my staunch conformist conditioning, he relayed a story about how he once returned a wallet and didn't get so much as a thank you.

When he mentioned thievery as a preliminary in the creation of Art, I again was initially dismayed. Thievery was just a scary way of saying to learn from. To observe, to chop apart and to recreate. He told me that he took pictures of beautiful landscapes. Then he would blow them up on an opaque projector and paint the photograph. By the time he would finish the painting, it would be nearly impossible to trace the photograph. In the business world I think they use the word mentoring. It seemed like quite the sound and proper way to learn things quickly.

He changed the subject. "This Path of Heart," this is what a warrior follows. You've been on it for a long time in that you followed music for your pleasure. The path of heart is straight down the center. Warrior's don't believe or disbelieve. We are here to witness. We don't interpret we just witness. The path of heart is where the feeling is. The path with heart is pursuing the unknown. To interpret what you see, is to call yourself an expert, which makes us talk above our heads. People who give explanations are making it up. What you see is what it is. Seeing in a warrior's context is personal. That was what Kathy had told him. She was his teachers apprentice and wife. She was such a together warrior that it took them years to allow me to meet her. Jonah had always praised her sense of orderliness and attention to detail. Essentially her impeccability. When I did meet her, one thing that was very obvious was her unique radiance. Her skin seemed almost translucent. Her shine from within was remarkably strong. Her very appearance seemed magical. She had mentioned that she liked to make salads. She was the poster girl for extreme health. Besides being naturally attractive you could almost see her luminosity. She almost looked like she radiated light behind her skin. "Seeing is personal." Only you see what has been an observation for you. I asked him what "gazing," was? That was something he had mentioned before. Gazing was doing something meticulously. Staring at something and then recalling it in your dreams is gazing. This was a subject also covered extensively in the Carlos Castaneda books. Gazing is focusing, and then dreaming about it. Find a place to orient yourself in your sleep. This is about waking up in your life. Some people call it enlightened. On another occasion I had clearly recalled an event, where by gazing at something, it had shown up in a vividly awake dream state. I woke up staring at a large chocolate chip cookie. It was at the bakery in Penn Station where I bought soup every day. It was as though I avoided looking at it so hard that it actually showed up in dreaming.

The phone rang and Jonah went into a conversation concerning his business. I observed the wood carved shelving and the moose antlers that held up his bow and arrows. A feather hung from a nail. There was a fish tank carved into the wall going from his living room into his kitchen. All of his guitar stuff was strewn around the room. He said that his guitar was his spirit catcher. There were a couple of wicker items decorating the room. The most striking aspect of the room, other than the feeling in it, were the windows. The trees outside looked as though they were part of the apartment. Sun and wind were constantly streaming in, in an almost noticeable fashion. The branches were flowing in the wind and reflected a pattern on the floor in the sun.

He hung up the phone and resumed talking. "Nothing means anything, and seeing is personal." Get over the hump of being alone because everyone is really alone and they should feel comfortable about that. Be true to yourself. We sat a few more minutes and the most beautiful creature came to the window. Jonah had a birdfeeder on the ledge. It was a beautiful female dove. She had a tiny delicate face and big soulful sweet eyes. It looked different from any bird I had ever seen. Jonah said it was a dove.

A couple of days later I came over to tell Jonah about a strange dream I had had. I told him that in my sleep a wind had come and attacked me. I felt like it was trying to kill me. I mentally had screamed for Jonah. I felt like I was being drowned by a wind. I thought to calm down, and look for my hands, like he had told me to do in my sleep. I thought I had woken up, but I couldn't see anything but an amber wall of fog with a purple light in it. Moments later I was awake in my bed. I was scared to death. I had the feeling as though I had just fought something. I felt like I had just barely survived. I didn't move for a few minutes, then I kept the light on for a while. Jonah said that this was the most important thing I had told him since we had met.

A few nights later something else had happened. I felt as if I was awake in my dream. I saw a wall covered with green vines, and sunlight pouring onto the vines. Then someone dropped a utensil next door and I woke up in my bed. I had felt as though I had been vividly awake as I had looked closely at the vines. The whole texture of the awareness felt different then a dream. I had felt completely awake.

Some years later something happened that had completely bore out the truth of this for me. What happened clarified to me entirely the validity and reality of these types of experiences. Even though it was but a few minutes, it now showed me, beyond a shadow of a doubt, the reality of other levels of consciousness available to us. I had a doorman at my

New York apartment building who was a dreamer. He was an amazing, charming and delightful person. I could write a chapter on what an intelligent and good man he was. He was younger than me, but clearly versed in dream travel experience. My experience was that he and I were in a car driving. It was the early morning and it was a suburban street at the height of cherry blossom season. I recall being fully conscious, looking at houses, not seeing numbers clearly and remembering to not look too closely at details. Then I awoke in my bed. I saw this, I felt this, and now I knew that it was real. The doorman claimed that he had tried to wake me in a dream state, which he and his friends did together. If for nothing else, I now had proof for myself that the stories in the Castaneda books were not the creation of fanciful imagination. This was well within the possibilities of normal human capabilities. Clearly the supposed known world was a lot more, then people of this century were giving our capabilities credit for. Who knows how this knowledge got oppressed or submerged through time. Many cultures spoke of these things as normal. Why was this not forefront mainstream training. If this is a major part of what our rightful capabilities are, shouldn't the world be trying to develop these aspects of their natural human nature? Didn't societies in the past know and practice the normal abilities of dream travel. Why at this juncture in time when technology is so advanced would the simple developments of our own nature be considered an unimportant or subversive exploration. Jonah said that paradise is right under our noses. Right inside our own minds. Seek the kingdom of heaven within. When you meditate you are contacting a deeper part of yourself within you. He said that that was what the great masters were trying to show people. How to find peace and spiritual planes all within their own minds.

Later that night Jonah started to tell me more of his story then he had before. He said that he had been living close to a college campus, when he had run into his benefactor. One day he had gone into a restaurant to meet a friend. The friend had brought another guy with him. Then, for some odd reason, his friend started sputtering inanities and got up and left. He left him with this guy Dan. Dan started saying things and before he knew it his jaw started catching flies. He said that he was just amazed at how this stranger knew him. It wasn't long before he wanted to know what this guy was about. He was a man of strong presence. No woman could resist his energy, he said. How fortunate for him, I thought. He would visit Dan in his apartment, which was also in the off campus vicinity. A group of people would go over just to listen to this guy talk. That was really all that they could do. Shortly after he met Dan, really amazing things started happening in my life. He wound up buying a tavern with no money down. The scenario of his apprenticeship was in a large gorgeous Old English Tudor style tavern. They did great renovation there. At the beginning of an apprenticeship, everyone is drawn into the interestingness of it, but as it goes on it gets really hard and most people try to run away from it. It got so heavy for me at one point, that he just hitchhiked away to visit friends. My assemblage point had shifted, he said.

I went home to make dinner and play guitar. I thought about what Jonah had told me about him and his benefactor. He said that his apprenticeship had been fraught with danger. One of the things that really surprised him, was how little his benefactor really knew, of how he was being affected by the situation. That surprised me too, because he said his benefactor was a highly accurate mind reader. That had been one of the things that made Jonah acknowledge his benefactor. He would say things to Jonah, that Jonah had been thinking. It got his attention. The term he used to describe his benefactor and himself, was Nagual. That meant ... a container of knowledge. It was a type of knowledge that was passed down from generation to generation. He said that out of the people to associate with his benefactor, he was the one to receive the most. Even though he was a Nagual, his benefactor was the nominal leader of the warrior party. He again mentioned to me that my life was not an open book. In general, it was not good to talk out my whole life to people.

Later that week, Jonah knocked on my door. He wanted to see how the new apartment was shaping up. He said that being upstairs gave you a whole different feeling. One benefit to a future basement dwelling I had, was that you could stamp your feet, to keep time more when you were playing guitar. At least he was willing to visit me in this apartment. He had told me to take notes on our conversations. Now he told me to formulate them into a journal. Writing brings you into a state of perception, he said. Writing inadvertently expands awareness. It helps you work on seeing what's around you. That is what our training is. There's the world inside your head, and the world that is outside your head. Take for instance, music. When you saturate yourself with a certain style, you can hear similar stuff in your mind. Thinking is hearing. You think you are thinking music. I'm saying you are hearing it. Then, you can hum it. Hum it the way you are thinking, and hearing it. You can draw it out of the ethers. You can get proficient at listening to the music in your head and writing it down. That is how Mozart and those people operate. Stuff poured into their minds, and they had the skills to hear it and write it down. To be really creative you have to practice the art of listening. We are like receivers. There is an infinite amount, of things to listen to. It can be positive or negative. Don't identify with your thoughts. Observe your thoughts. Discipline stops negative thoughts. Food has a voice as well. It will go inside you and then talk through you. People don't immediately make that connection. If you put good healthy food inside you, then you will think peacefully and clearly. If you put garbage food inside you then it will come out in the form of negative feelings. The only redemption is to discipline yourself, have faith and have patience. You have to work for the earth. The raw truth rules. Mother nature presides. Wise men are learning men. Our place is to have dominion over the earth and to tend the garden.

Jonah was always saying to be honest. His version of

honest was unusually brutally honest. He never placated. He said what he thought, and he didn't give a damn what people would think of him. It wasn't a popularity contest for him. He said that that was what I liked about him. The fact that he was free enough and secure enough to be himself. He behaved in a professional manner when doing business. He acknowledged that he talked the talk and walked the walk, when he wanted to present or accomplish something. It was a little confusing because on one hand he said, "just be yourself," and say what you see. On the other hand, he said it was perfectly acceptable, even necessary at times, to act. I guess he meant that you should act to your advantage. In the situations that require acting, do it with preciseness. He referred to acting as controlled folly, or stalking. Stalking was another area of sorcery training discussed extensively in the Castaneda stories. A warrior party had members that were taught both the arts of Dreaming and Stalking, but some people had predilections stronger for either of the two.

　　After Jonah left, I had to hurry to work. Every time that Jonah would leave, I would feel better than before I had seen him. He did say a lot of interesting things. Every time that we would sit down to talk, he would pour out idea after idea. He was very thought provoking, I liked that though. It gave me a break from the Hollywood "I'm so sexy" competition. The LA lifestyle of competitive attractiveness had its benefits in that at least it kept you on your toes about fitness and nutrition. It made people do their best to take care of themselves.

I visited Yosemite Park over the weekend. The place was thoroughly enchanting. Gorgeous and inspiring fresh natural beauty. I brought back a huge pinecone for Jonah. I knocked on his door. I didn't think that he really wanted the pinecone, but he took it anyway. He invited me in. He was doing sight reading practice for guitar.

He started talking about a universal priority that we have. The leaders of the countries are small time compared to more immediate priorities. They can't do anything without the planet. The environment better be the top agenda they have, because without that there's nothing. As was common for Jonah, he would pause, and then change the topic. He would emphasize what he thought was important, and then go on to something else. He went on to discussing dreaming again. He said that in dreaming, you go from one level to another. He said that when I had awakened in the amber fog, that I had actually gone to another place. All along he kept lending me his Carlos Castaneda books. I read them one after another. I tried to understand some of what Jonah said through the Castaneda stories. He said not to get hooked on those stories because that was their lives and their "tales of power," and this was mine. He told me that Carlos was an excellent writer and organizer of this knowledge. He said that his reason for showing me the books was to give me a method of writing. He said that those books were a huge contribution to waking up society, and that they would last for generations. They were very successful in taking the Indian, Don Juan, and putting his knowledge out into the world. He referred to Don Juan as "the Indian." Don Juan was the teacher, the benefactor, in the Castaneda stories.

I was interested in the amber fog occurrence, because I had really had the sensation that I was awake. Jonah continued... "The spirit goes at the speed of light." Astral projection is the spirit. There were different pursuits, living forever not being the least of one. Healing the planet. The planet will prevail. He had said that living forever was not impossible. That was the number one goal of this. There was a way to achieve maintaining consciousness after death if you had developed yourself in your dreaming body while you were still alive. Saving your energy and becoming a warrior was to teach you how to train your awareness to function in your dream body to the degree that you could maintain consciousness on another plane of existence. The planet, he said, will collapse back to what it was. It will crack its bones, so to speak, and get rid of the parasites. A main pursuit is to take care of yourself. One could never achieve the mental durability to become a dream warrior if they poisoned their body. One way to take good care of yourself was to be aware, that it was important to take care of the thought process. "Try not thinking." This is the key to rejuvenate health. This is why people can last. This is why the swamis in the mountains can live to be so old. They stop thinking. Thinking and stress cause deterioration of the body. Meditate, or call it what you want, but stop thinking. Even for a few minutes a day. Keep your head clear and quiet. Slow down to speed up. Slow down to become focused, collected and accurate. Listen to the metronome of your life. Go at a good pace. More things get done if they are done in a peaceful coherent manner. For that you have to slow down. Rest when you want to rest, work when you're working, and play while you're playing. Be involved in what you are doing while you are doing it. Stop

the frenzy. Everything should be perfectly organized and

running smoothly instead of, never catching up with yourself

and living in a pressure cooker situation. I told Jonah that I

liked having things run fast. You can roll fast when you can

roll accurately, he said.

The most constant theme that Jonah began to emphasize

was getting organized. This was not a small situation for me. I

was organized in a basic kind of way, but I let a lot of details

slide. Jonah pounded into me the idea that everything should

have a place, and that things should be put back in their place.

It sounded like something you would tell a two- year old, but

the premise was sound. Being neat was a necessity, he said.

After getting organized, you could move on to become

disciplined. I asked him how this had an effect on doing things

like dreaming? You're always looking for magic to be

something like a man flying down from the heavens in a white

robe. The magic is in everyday life. At least at first. You have

to clean your room, your mind and your body before making

progress in those other areas. The will cannot be mastered by a

weak body. Besides the fact that you want to fly around in

your dreams, you have to learn organization to be an efficient businessman in the world. You can't master an instrument, run a business, or do anything else really well without having the backdrop of organization. "Get your ship tight, no loose ends." Do things properly. I can tell when you're not organized. It's better late than never. To get organized, don't look at the whole job. Look at parts of it, and get parts of it done. In cleaning up your area, do a corner at a time. Then when that is clean, keep it clean and go to the next area. When everything is organized you will literally feel more energy. There will be nothing weighing you down or cluttering your mind. Your surroundings are an extension of your state of mind. People don't realize that if they clean up their surroundings, they will literally feel better. Do it a piece at a time. When you look at the whole job, you get frustrated and don't do any of it. For projects, sketch a rough draft. Make an outline and then fill in the details. Almost like a grocery list. That's the way you can organize projects. At first, when Jonah would get on this topic, I thought it was pretty self- explanatory. I didn't see the point in him telling me over and over again to clean my room. Again he said, knowing something and doing it were two different things. Finally, when I did start cleaning more, I saw and felt the energy he was talking about. I did feel amazingly better. I actually got a real buzz of energy the more I did it. It was strange. I wouldn't have thought that it would be like an energy that you could feel. Later in time we got to visit his benefactor and his wife at their apartment. I was prepped on how they were very much regular business people. That aside, from being formidably ideal in intelligence, stature and energetic countenance. Most of the time youth are oblivious to their own inexperience. It was clear to me that I was not as mature or knowledgeable as these people. They were totally smooth about that. They didn't act like they knew that they were quite a bit more sophisticated than me. Later in time, I didn't further friendship or communication with them. That was because I wanted to only have concrete results to give them. It seemed like that was the kind of world that they lived in. There wasn't room for anything other than success and results. I mention them now, because I got to see two things by seeing their apartment, and another office space that she had. The apartment shone. It was a simple environment where nothing, not a speck of dust was out of place. Everything was on shelves in total neat order. Looking back, it's easy to recognize that there was serious energy in their place. Whether every clean room would have that level of subtle ebullience I don't think so. I think they added a measure of energy to their environment, but the fastidious cleanliness that they demonstrated undoubtedly aided them in being how they were. Growing up as the next generation to the sixties generation, I used to look at authority as being un hip. So, people with everything in perfect order seemed not as creative. That was a backwards viewpoint. It was like looking out of your feet to see the sky. These people were super cool, super intelligent and creative and had their things and lives wound tight and in order. And they weren't supercilious about it, it was just how they lived. It wasn't their whole point of focus, it was just the basis that they worked from.

One time Kathy took me to see an office she had just moved into. We were there for about five minutes. I remember a room in which almost everything was white. It was a pretty space in a semi wooded area. Years later I told Jonah about Kathy having took me there. He said I had missed something. That Kathy would not take you to her office, to exchange pleasantries. She was showing you something, and she was showing you something big. I agree with him on that now. The memory of that room, is that it also shone in perfect energy and cleanliness which is how a warrior should live. That is how to live to become a healthy warrior with natural healthy power. Those rooms had power. Their apartment had power just like a forest has power. I confess that still I have not mastered this and that a huge overhaul is needed. It's ok I guess that I have amassed an entire library, an incredible music collection and some other things, but they need to be placed better. Jonah was very positive about keeping just pragmatic things and really throwing unused stuff out. Useless sentimentalism was another pile of crap to go. Certainly limit it. Put memoirs in marked boxes if need be.

He changed the subject. People can make you feel good or bad, just being around them. You should clean people or situations off your island, that could anger or depress you. You have to deal with the bullshit or it kills you. To get organized means to make things simple. Jonah was hanging off his ceiling trapeze as he spoke. The Path of Heart is getting yourself together. Making things feel right to you. Becoming aware of something if it isn't right. "Warriors are outside the ring that presses upon people." They do not go up and down with it. They do not get sucked into other people's headaches. They observe the drama, but they stay in the middle of the road. They stay peaceful. They have handled everyday problems. They work, and do their work with enjoyment. People are asleep. They are asleep to doing something with their time. They are asleep to the emergency of the earth, to dreaming, to worlds outside the human band. They are living, but they are asleep to the spirit. Waking up is learning to expand your awareness. The way to wake up is to get quiet. To shut off the internal dialogue. First, everything in everyday awareness must be clean and completely organized. "A warrior realizes what an inept clod the self is and leaves it in the dust." This is one of the great challenges of becoming a warrior.

You start conforming to your surroundings. You start meeting your parent's expectations, and you start relating to the whole world like you would relate to your parents. You become messed up. You bend to everyone as if they were your parents. Do your thing. You are in control of your behavior at all times. People interact with you on your terms. I became saturated with his conversation. He could always tell when I was getting too tense to absorb any more of what he was saying. It was like a fuse would blow. Then I would get out of heightened awareness and go home and rest. A lot, but not all of the time, moods of heightened awareness would come over me as we would speak. My sense of attention would become more focused and intense. I invariably felt a super sense of wellbeing after speaking with him, unless I had incurred his wrath to a point where there was not a lot of ability to feel good about the situation. Most of the time if there was some sort of problem about something, enough other positive ammunition had been fired to put the whole thing in a good and productive perspective. Most of the problems that he would have with me is that I forgot a lot and had a really hard time getting things done. My level of confidence was not right. He said that my spirit was warped. That the browbeating that had occurred in my life, had undermined my confidence in myself. It was misdirected. People challenged me to make me better, but it just got me scared to do things. No one intentionally tried to make me unconfident, it was just the mixed up dynamic of them trying to help me and me getting too intimidated by their challenges.

I always felt pretty spectacular after seeing Jonah. I left with an elevated sense of exuberance. I started to see, at a certain point, that energy was something you could actually sense. I realized quite suddenly that the energy I projected would be returned. Words have power, he said. Watch your words, your thoughts and your food. All of these things work on you on an energetic medium. You could get a different sense of energy in different places.

I called up Jonah and asked him if I could list his ideas, so that I could organize what he was talking about. I could take the conversation down verbatim. The basic idea was to improve myself. We had mushroom soup with vegetables and some very good whole grain bread. When we were done eating, I relaxed back on the couch with my pen and paper. He started talking and I started writing and listening.

You are where you are at all times. Your mind dictates how you feel regardless of your actual location. How your mind is, defines your experience of any place or situation. When you're alone, shut off the self. The secret is in the silence. There is no meaning, no thinking, no talking. Find your hands in your dreams. Bring your hands up to eye level and follow your hands. There is the known, the unknown, and the unknowable. You can get to the unknown. Be quiet and shut your mind. Concentrate on not thinking. Stop talking to morons about life. Be organized. Follow only the path with heart. Follow your heart. "Listen to spirit." To stop disease, stop thinking. The disease is taken out of you when you stop thinking. Thought is disease. Thought ages you, not constructive thinking, but random obsessive thinking.

There are ways of keeping awareness alive, he said. Eternal life. Take gaps in the thinking process. Thoughts have an effect on the body. A state of no thought is the healthiest. I stand behind the peacemakers, but don't mess with me or you will be sorry. I am trying to drag up your awareness. That means putting you in touch with your higher self. That would allow you to connect with what gives higher creativity. Jonah turned on the T.V. There was a mildly sexy movie on cable. A naked woman kept walking around a room that had velvet couches and long elaborate drapery. She was engrossed in dialogue as she gracefully sauntered around the room. We watched for a while. Then the phone rang. One of the tenants was complaining that the building next door was making too much noise. Jonah had a reciprocal association with the landlord next door. They helped keep each other's buildings within social confines. I stayed awhile longer but then got exhausted. The next evening called Jonah to see if he wanted to go to the movies. He said no, but offered to finish the massage he had started to give me the other day. That sounded good. Jonah periodically tried out his chiropractic basics on me when my back hurt. We exchanged massage once in a while. On this occasion we never did get to the massage, because Jonah began talking. I got that dreamy feeling again while listening to him.

Turning off thought rejuvenates and wards off disease. Lie down for a sleep state for just five minutes. You could be totally stressed out, hit a sleeplike state for just fifteen minutes, and you would be totally recharged. Turn off the mouth inside your head. The internal dialogue is bullshit. Turn off the English language and just perceive.

Cross your eyes to the arch of your nose. See light refraction, with the eyes closed, and the eyes crossed looking towards the arch of the nose. Quiet the dialogue and focus on the third eye. Control your thought. Say shut up to random thought. Stop the English language. Shut off the head. Be gentle to yourself. Give silence to the head.

See light emanations, translucent light emanations. Keep the eyes shut and focus on the third eye. Translucent light becomes perception. It's interesting. Perceive with no thought. Lie with the feet and head propped up. Go into light sleep. Everything leaves the mind. The body now is not bothered by the ego. Internal dialogue, which is the self, leaves.

Save the body. When the self leaves the body, then the body is left alone. I kept writing as Jonah spoke... "A wise man does not grieve for the living or grieve for the dead." It is not wise if it accomplishes nothing. The hole when someone leaves will mend. They are part of the unknown then. Let yourself feel the pain, but don't overindulge. Jonah started talking about other stuff at that point. A few guys from down the hall wandered in to say hello. I went home after catching up with them. One of the things I thought about was how he had said you could feel everything if you shut your mind off. The mind fades in comparison to feeling. It's all based on feeling. Places can feel good or bad. Every place has a feeling, he had said. This is not about reason.

The next day I saw Jonah in the hall when I was taking in my laundry. He asked me what I was doing later? I didn't have any rehearsals, so I told him that I got home from work around eight thirty. He said that I should stop by. I felt a strange excitement every time I saw him. I had to admit that I found him strangely sexually appealing somehow. Our association was such, that I felt it would be entirely inappropriate to allow any nuance of that sentiment to escape.

I came upstairs around nine in the evening. I came in and

sat on the couch. He put down his guitar and had some juice. We started talking about health because I was feeling lousy. Relax the neck and tongue, he said. Tell the body you have no disease. Relax the tongue (throat) chakra. Stop the inner dialogue. In meditation, or when the inner dialogue is stopped, listen for other voices. The genius in you is quiet. You can plug into divine voices making music and write it down. That's called transcribing the music in your head.

Warriors have no weakness. They are disconnected. Keep growing. If you keep learning, you won't age. You learn to learn. When you learn to learn, the beauty is that you keep learning. Keep learning. People stop growing when they stop learning.

When you meditate, there is stuff in the air. Everyone's a radio. There is no peace and quiet. When you hear inner dialogue you are hearing something. It is a hearing process. Warriors don't pay attention to the self. Ignore the self. Find a quiet place where you can pay attention. You meditate by listening to the outside. Inside is the self. When you meditate you can listen to this faint buzz that you hear when you are listening to silence. It is outside yourself.

Your self is the hardest friend to make. To have peace

with oneself. Have the right food. What is in your body thinks your inner dialogue. Eat peaceful food and you will have peaceful thoughts.

My body and mind felt clean and clear just from talking to Jonah. It was nothing short of amazing. When I left Jonah's I went to the liquor store and bought a banana and a protein shake. One thought stuck out in particular. The difference between a man and a warrior is that a warrior observes his thoughts, and is detached from them. He does not claim his thoughts as his own.

Later that month a certain fondness became apparent between Jonah and I. One evening when we were relaxing, Jonah went to change his tee shirt. He put on a white tee shirt and came and sat down. I felt this intense magnetic feeling from him. It was not of a sensual nature. I stood in shock wondering how he was literally freezing me with his eyes. His face almost seemed to change, as if someone else inhabited his body. He looked very old, and yet brilliant and loving. I was shocked. He didn't look like himself. He looked like an old prophet. I stammered... "You look different." He said... "maybe I'll really change for you sometime." Shortly after he seemed like himself again. I felt an intense lightheadedness when anything strange would happen. I had felt an intense pull toward him when he had appeared as though he were a different person. When I would leave Jonah I was often a little bit dumbfounded. I didn't want to feel as though I was going crazy, and yet, the stuff going on here was simply not normal. What was really so unusual was the feeling I would experience in his presence. This would not always be the case. As he had said... sometimes I'm Jonah, a regular guy, and sometimes I'm a sorcerer. I would get different feelings around him. Sometimes he was just my buddy...an unusual landlord, and sometimes he was a completely prolific and intense individual. Most of the time I felt shockingly good after seeing him. I would feel extremely well physically, with an added degree of clarity and peacefulness in my mind and body. I actually felt euphoric ecstasy from his presence. Other times though, his words put me through the most intense hell. It was not always a smooth sailing amicable association. Jonah told me exactly what he thought, in detail about anything that came to his mind. He had no mind to placate me, and really this was one of his greatest values. His perception was so acute that I never would have figured out half of the things that he said about me. As astonishingly rude as something might have initially sounded, it was often deep revelations that I agreed with after having it pointed out. He was really gifted at seeing into things. He was always real, and of the mind to drag up my awareness. I was not mature in knowledge the way he was. He told me what he considered to be the right way about a number of things. He ventured to teach me, to improve me. He attacked my fragilities with unbending force. He was going to beat out the conditioning and maladies of life I had acquired. He tried to get me to forget about the self. To be conscious, aware, and to pay attention to what was outside my head. I felt strange electricity from him and constantly kept the buzz of thinking about him with me.

He was extremely funny. He put a humorous twist on things by his very nature. He was not a somber guru type of person. He was a fiery energetic regular kind of guy. Even though our association had taken on elements that could normally be construed in a number of ways, he shielded me from forming romantic attachments. This was actually very cleansing, because the whole thing was intense and crazy anyway, and to add complications of love would have constricted what was a phenomenal situation working on so many different levels. All ideas of traditional love were extinguished and that was cool. Besides, that was not was this was about anyway. That was not what was needed in a warrior party. Still and all it obviously helped us to be closer as people. Something about him struck me as very funny, his sardonic wit and genuine laughter seemed close to his core. We were always laughing and I mean really laughing. Hard laughing. Tears running down your face laughing. His sense of innuendo was superb. His energy created a wellspring of mirth.

A couple of nights later I went with a friend, to a fine cuisine health food restaurant in Topanga Canyon. It was a gorgeous setting up on a mountain by a brook. We noticed a coyote on the other side of the brook. People were throwing food to it. We watched it pick and choose what it wanted to eat. I noticed my friend was in a tense mood. I was also feeling stressful from the events of the day. While we were eating, two men came in and sat down. They sat partially hidden from my view by a vine covered partition. All of a sudden one of the men let out a piercing curse, then an awful sound. I lost my composure completely. It was as if his nervous sounds had gone directly into my nervous system. I could not keep from becoming hysterical. I tried to keep quiet

so as to not appear that I was laughing at the man. I was
extremely shaken by him. Tears were running down my face.
My laughter was an intense nervous reaction. Meanwhile, my
grumpy friend was becoming furious that I would be laughing
at a poor man with such a glaring affliction. I could not for the
life of me figure out how the waitress could be composed
enough to take the man's order. Every five or ten minutes, he
would let out another echoing shriek. I felt terrible that I was
the only one so unnerved. One man jokingly said...Hey
Buddy, how come I didn't get any of that in my soup? Finally,
I was able to subdue myself and concentrate on the meal.
There was pleasant classical music and a gorgeous summer
night. There was also a new age bookstore attached to the
restaurant. We were on the back patio.

That night I dreamed vividly about the coyote. I dreamed
that I went to his lair that set into the mountain. It was a
strange dream because it seemed so real. The lair had a blue
shag carpet in a little cave like dwelling. It was like a
doghouse built into the mountain.

The next day, I passed Jonah in the hall. He was
rummaging through a storage closet outside my door. I told
him that I had dinner with a coyote the night before. I was

referring to the one at the restaurant. He said... "oh really." I invited him in and told him about the coyote dream. We got to doing some massage and sitting around. Then out of nowhere Jonah asks me if there was someone strange at the restaurant? I remembered the man. I became shocked again. How did you know that? I asked. "That coyote was a sorcerer and he came to visit you." "I see it." I became deeply fascinated. I got a little scared too. I tried to understand what he said. It was not something I could easily take at face value. He said that a coyote had taken an affinity towards me. He said that he didn't particularly like coyote sorceresses. They were like scavengers. He had lost me. While it sounded sort of exotic, I didn't exactly fathom myself to be a sorceress, and I had no knowledge of an affinity towards a coyote other than the dream. I tried to ask him about the man and the coyote, but he got mad and made me drop it. He said not to fool around with this stuff. To observe it and go on. I kept trying to understand how a man, no matter how weird, could not be a man. He also said that there was no proof that anyone else perceived him in the same manner in which I did. It could all have been a show for me. How did I know what anyone else had heard or seen? Jonah left, and I was left to think about that for a while.

Sunday morning my parents called. They mentioned my father's illness. When I got off the phone a wave of terror hit me. I cried on and on and on. Ten minutes later Jonah knocked on the door. I told him my dad was sick. He said that death was a part of life. That wasn't exactly what I wanted to hear. He was very nonchalant about it. He said watch yourself before he left. I was glad he mentioned that because I was getting to that all out lying on the floor gagging stage. He would say that any extreme emotional states were indulging.

A couple of days later when I was at Jonah's he said... "Your father could die, you know." The idea was entirely shocking. My parents had spared me of knowing what was going on. He had been well for ten years. I had an exceptional father. Jonah continued on... "It's nice to be with someone while they're still well." I felt very torn at the moment.

I felt quite compelled to stay around Jonah. His whole presence and realm of experience, was the most interesting thing that had ever happened to me, plus I wanted to know the secret. Jonah had inferred to a phenomenal experience that he had had, that he would possibly share with me over time. I was so fascinated that I was willing to wait the time. At times I would try to be logical and say that maybe all this was crazy, but he would say and do things that were truly striking. One sunny day he shook his rain stick, and within forty-five minutes it was raining. That still had room for coincidence to me. He said that he had caused the floods that summer. He mentioned that he had caused the blackout in New York City, ten years ago. I didn't know how to probe these statements. I didn't want to flat out invite hostility from him, but again, I did not have the ability to comprehend him doing that. I found his statements almost plausible because of the feelings I had around him, although they still sounded extreme. He said... "Question things for yourself." I knew that I felt light and happy after every timeI spoke to him. Light and happy really wasn't enough to describe it. I felt a sense of ecstasy and vibrant health. I felt a current of positive electricity in my body, mind and spirit. I felt completely healed each time that I talked to him. There was no logic what so ever for that. He wasn't telling me anything that should make a physical difference in the way my body should feel, and yet it did. His presence gave me a sense of elation.

I decided to move to be with my father. One day I was obsessively thinking about Jonah all day. I couldn't shake this horrible feeling about leaving. I felt very morbid. The feeling would come in waves. Sometimes I would feel all right about the move and sometimes not. One day a friend of mine came over to play guitar. I called Jonah to borrow an amplifier. He said, sure, come pick it up. I came in and his business partner was there. He seemed very quiet. I tried to make it quick because I assumed that they were doing their work. We talked briefly about music. His partner asked me if I could read music? I told him that I did, but not very quickly. I could learn stuff by reading it. His partner was a very normal, healthy, and handsome looking guy who appeared to be in his forties. I took the amp and dragged it out the door. Jonah stopped by during the session. He called later to get the amp back and asked if I was still entertaining the troops? I thought that that was a very bizarre and out of character thing for him to say. I thought perhaps, that he was complimenting me for having a male over to my apartment. It would have been impossible to imagine jealousy.

On Sunday, Jonah stopped in around eleven. He was lounging around the building in his white robe. He always made jokes that I wanted to see him walking around in a white robe as if he was a holy man or something. There was something vaguely comical about him in his robe. Especially when he was in the yard or on the roof. Even though it was a city, there was a neighborhood feel there, albeit a slightly eccentric neighborhood. There was the chanting foreigner at dusk, the Indian rocker on the roof and a host of other Hollywood notables tucked into every corner. When I actually did see him in his robe, he looked funny. He looked funny to me no matter what he was wearing. It was not that he was funny looking. He was definitely masculine and handsome. His hair, in particular had a number of ways of appearing funny. It had a knack for becoming full of static, and flying in fantastic configurations. I had been thinking of Jonah so much on Saturday, that it was actually startling when he appeared at my door on Sunday. I was so accustomed to having him on my mind, that the reality of seeing him made me nervous.

He told me a story about what had happened one time when he was driving across the country on a motorcycle. He had stopped at a truck stop rest area after driving for about twelve hours. He would sleep in a sleeping bag on a picnic table by his bike. He observed that someone was observing him. He was alerted by a gut feeling. He had the feeling that this guy was a killer. He slipped away while the man was not looking. He walked around to a vantage point where he could watch the guy waiting for him. He watched the guy waiting

for him for hours. Finally the man left. He knew that this guy

was a killer. He said that there are a lot of killers around and

that not all of it makes it to the news. People disappear all the

time. You have to listen to your instincts and be aware at all

times. I asked him why he didn't just run immediately? Get on

the bike and go? He said that he was already exhausted. No

one can sneak up on a sorcerer, I can feel them coming. He

went on to say that people have no business making contact

with you unless you really want them to. "Why do you ask"?

was the best thing to say to any seemingly innocent,

busybody. His privacy was sacred, and nobody but those

whom he asked, were allowed into his space. Strangers asking

questions were to be put off immediately. His business was his

business, and he intimated that I should follow suit, at least for

safety. When I first saw you, you would have been lunch meat

for any crack sorcerer. Someone could have stolen your soul

without you being aware of it. I pressed him to clarify what he

meant. You are defenseless. Someone could just walk off with

your life and take all your time and energy. What if you

married a certain friend that we both know? Then a piece of

your life would have been given away. I thought it was too

hypothetical. Gradually I admitted that I let most people approach and talk to me, so that I wouldn't offend them. He said that offending them was their problem. They shouldn't have been annoying you in the first place, and they were rebuffed because they had put you out in some manner. People shouldn't, and don't have the right to push you around. It is your responsibility to stay true to yourself, and serve your best interest at all times. Even in such things that might seem small, such as going out to socialize when you are tired and would prefer to stay home. Instead of just going to be sociable, ask yourself if you really feel like going? Be yourself at all times. Never let someone talk condescendingly or make you feel uncomfortable. As soon as people start chit chatting and being their false selves you should cut them off and throw it in their faces. You can't choose everything in this world but you can choose who you associate with. If you withhold everything you think people will mash you into the ground. If someone brings you into an argument, it should never get into a screaming match because then they are bringing you down to their level.

People like to have their bullshit put in check. They also rather be themselves, if they can get to it. People expect that they have to act sometimes, and when you make them be themselves, they respect you for it and appreciate it. Again, not that you're looking for their approval. Don't be phony, and don't let others be phony. He said to be truthful, but that he also had a great respect for the art of acting. There were many cases where he felt acting was imperative and could be likened to an art form. He felt it was your choice to share what you wanted at any given time. So, in that respect, it is your right, to be whomever and whatever, whenever you choose. People act professional, and it's acceptable, agreeable and functional to do so. He alluded to my persistent adolescent attitudes. I did observe that as a rock musician, I did carry some semblance of youthful language. It slowly dawned on me, as to what he was referring to as getting my act together. My act was together as a freewheeling, high spirited musician, but as a business professional, there were always elements of my other life showing. It may be hard to accept this but people do play roles. Depending on what result you desire, you have to give them what they expect, and what they want to get the desired results. For your satisfaction, be whatever you want. It's all you, but if you want to sell a service, give them what they want. Years later, when the vicissitude of work honed my spirit down, I would relish how to hold onto the feeling of that freewheeling person. I finally stopped the struggle, and success and freedom from intense stress was granted. When I stopped fighting for money, it came to me. Not in huge rolling chunks, but it was just like Don Juan had said about the world being made up of energy. I realized that I did have the ability to have my work function in a way that would create sufficient income. This was really a phenomenal turning point, because as soon as I believed that that was the case, it actually manifested. All of the years, and I mean years that I struggled in pain and poverty actually could have been avoided by what I believed in. Once I saw to my satisfaction how my job could work, the work actually poured in the way I thought it would. When I thought that I couldn't make the money. I couldn't. It didn't come in. As soon as I stopped worrying, it would pour in. When my energy was not stressed out, people were happy to work with me and come support what I was doing. I was poor for as long as I thought I was poor. One day a more affluent and affluent minded girlfriend of mine, pointed out that the assistance I received from outside sources was entirely unnecessary because I had those ways and means by myself. The outside assistance had been heavily leaning on my self-esteem, and a person had almost made me their prisoner because I thought I needed them. I realized that their help was so minimal, that not only could I do it myself, that most of the problem had been my imagined dependence on them. As soon as I realized that I could do it on my own, I entirely could. Such unabashed joy and freedom. I'm still amazed that one conversation with this lady, actually freed me from a period of having put myself in a particular prison.

Later that night I went to Jonah's apartment and watched television. After about a half hour he turned down the sound. He mentioned that another woman that he knew, had met his benefactor several times. He said it as if his benefactor had appeared to her almost out of nowhere. I thought how lucky she was. I imagined some fantastic event of him showing up in some mysterious manner. Jonah said that he couldn't set it up for me to meet his benefactor. He said that if he wanted, he would just show up. I felt a little apprehensive about the idea of meeting Jonah's benefactor. I did think his other friend was lucky to have met the man Jonah was so interested in.

4   A GESTURE WITH POWER

I stopped working and took a week to pack. Jonah called and left a message on my answering machine. I had been out shopping and looking at art books. I was trying to see if I could find the artist Jonah had said he had been in a past life. I called Jonah back and he asked me to come over and attach his hair extension. One time I even gave him a ponytail that an ex had given me. I guess I wasn't totally in love. I wouldn't part with that if I loved the person more. The funniest part was when I told another friend that I had given away this guy's ponytail. He was horrifically upset by this. He had gone through ceremonies to become closer to an Indian culture, and somehow this didn't jive with that. I think he had found the ponytail lying around the room and found it macabre. If my most recent ex ever dispersed of his very long black ponytail I would give it a pillow. I might eventually move it out of my bed, but I wouldn't give it away. I went over and attached Jonah's latest fashion ornament and left. Later that day I needed to come back over and get boxes. I had this feeling that I wanted to dress very natural. I also had the feeling that I wanted to become peaceful. I wore a comfortable flannel shirt with a black camisole underneath it. I wasn't thinking about why I wanted to create a natural feeling in myself. I noticed afterwards that my mood had been one of peaceful anticipation although I wasn't aware that anything interesting would happen.

I knocked on Jonah's door to get the boxes. He always had them around for his business. I came in and noticed that he and his partner were doing business. I wasn't going to stay long because I figured that they were busy. I had no perspective on business at that time. Caught up in the throes of rock and roll Hollywood, I viewed any activity outside of creativity as a misfortunate use of time. In retrospect, my appraisal of "business" was oblivious to the creativity of business as well as the necessity. My immaturity of that assessment actually embarrasses me. Being spoiled caught up with me. Art was like a creed back then. I'm proud of the spirit of how I thought about it, but work is food, which is top. Nothing really rules above food. Every animal knows that.

I struck up some chit chat, regarding marketing and distribution. I was surprised when they began talking. In the past his partner had seemed pretty quiet. I stood around leaning a couple of flat boxes to my leg as we talked. I got the impression that it was ok to pull up a seat, that they were taking a break from their work. His partner started sounding like he was a guy from N.Y.C. He had a comfortable casual way of speaking that implied humor and familiarity. He was a good looking man, seemingly in his forties. He wore casual athletic types of clothing. He seemed limber and agile. His hair was thick and well styled. His face seemed brilliantly animated. He would go from dour to scintillating in a moment. he seemed like a regular upbeat healthy kind of guy.

We started out just talking about everyday sort of things, when I started to feel I was becoming lulled into a slightly varied physical state. Nothing unusual was being said, however I started to feel glued to my seat and all my nerves were jumping. Jonah mentioned to his partner that I was a writer, which I thought was kind of preposterous. I had never considered that I was a writer, but that I was just writing this story. Dan, his partner, started to talk about his writing experience. He said that he had a secret dream to travel, and that writing had proved to be his ticket to travel. He had been to the Masai Plains, Far East Asia and the Middle East amongst other places. He said that I should find a writing

agent. He said that he did technical writing. He said that he
had also been involved in acting. Never show yourself when
you are acting, he said. Have it, be real onstage. He had had to
work with a lot of people. A lot of actors had been on cocaine,
but they would piece it together and follow the best. He talked
about how people were so crazy, that they would take the
actor as his part. It scared him how people would react to him
as his part, if they could recognize him offstage. He was so
convincing while onstage that often no one would recognize
him offstage. I noticed then that Jonah had taken a less
authoritative posture in his demeanor. He had a sheepish look
on his face that was immediately startling to me. I had never
seen anything less than the stance of quiet dominance in his
persona. In business he seemed fair and serious. He always
had the manner of being in charge. The only time I had
observed unguarded behavior was in the presence of feminine
behavior. He seemed unarmed by their charm. He seemed to
be a softer person when approached in that manner.

Because I saw Jonah giving this guy the floor, so to
speak, it occurred to me, that maybe this was the man. Maybe
this was the benefactor. I didn't really think it was possible.
First of all, the guy really wasn't flashy enough. He had said,

and I quote... "My benefactor could get any woman in the world to sleep with him." Now that sounded like a pretty tall order even for Clark Gable. Taking into account the variety of taste in the world, I didn't see how any one man could have that capability. Granted, he was dashingly handsome and had an energetic sense about him, yet, he didn't seem to harboring any dramatically unusual qualities. A very well tempered magnetism. He just didn't necessarily look like the person Jonah had been talking about. And of course how could I really tell if this was the man with the great powers of seduction when that was certainly not the area of conversation we were addressing. He looked for the most part like a normal guy. A great guy, but a normal guy. I brushed off the idea that this was Jonah's benefactor. Dan, his partner then got into a very funny story about how he had driven the Jehovah witnesses away from his house screaming. He said.... Jesus isn't here today. If you're hearing voices in your head, you're schizophrenic. People should read his book, not listen to his interpreters. Dan started telling all sorts of stories. I noticed that I started to feel all different ways. First I would get tired, then all of a sudden I would have a lot of energy. I tried to be attentive to what he was saying. I noticed he started talking about things, as I would be thinking them. I recognized him saying a lot of things that Jonah always said. It slowly dawned on me that this was the benefactor. He seemed to immediately know that I had grasped that. It seemed to be like one of those occasions when the man shows up with your lottery ticket. I was a little surprised. I was already too mesmerized to be nervous. It occurred to me that the guy was really smart. I remembered Jonah telling me to act and look smart. It occurred to me that he had mentioned that for just such an occasion. I tried to look smart. It seemed as soon as I thought this, Dan smiled as if he had heard me. It occurred to me that this guy could hook you with his energy. He went on telling stories about how sometime he just knew things. He didn't know how he knew them, he just did. One day he knew that his wife was going to get into a car accident. He told her to please not use the car that day. She never listens to me, which is one of the reasons I love her, he said. She's her own person. But on this occasion I really wanted her to believe me because sure enough she had an accident. I felt terrible seeing her bruised.

Another time he knew some of his friends were going to get arrested for selling marijuana. He told them, don't do this now. You are going to get caught and go to jail. They got caught and went to jail.

He then picked up the pace in his stories. He went from one to another. His voice dynamics went from higher to lower, and from casual to angry to casual. He talked about Vietnam. He said you don't feel anything when you kill someone, only afterwards when you come home from war. When there's fear, I feel awareness, he said. Like an animal. I don't know how this intuition happens, but it does.

I started to notice that he looked very different from different angles as he spoke. He became theatrical in his emphasis. He walked over to his knapsack and turned it over. It looked almost like a part of the conversation. His body was fluid and agile and seemed to speak along with his words.

Marriage can kill creativity, he said. A partner has to understand how much time it takes to write or do anything creative. Material things own the owners. Houses will own you. Life is an adventure. Live it. Don't lock into "what you should do." Hear your body. If you get itchy, move. It's human nature to get bored doing the same things forever, so stay fluid and flexible. Never stop learning. He then told a story about an island he had visited, where the tourists and developers were discouraged from staying. It was because they couldn't understand that money wasn't everything, and they were obnoxious. He paused and continued... "Who is important enough to be phony for?" I thought that was really true. When it comes to sales he said... "Tell them about something, if they like it fine." He gets rid of clients by disagreeing with them. "People are always looking for approval." I mentioned something about appearances or looks. "I wouldn't cross the street to take a piss on good looks." "It's not how you look, it's how you feel."

He told me about the five children he supports in third world countries. The US is starting to look like a third world country. The body is a lazy piece of shit unless you make it do something, he said. I was becoming attuned to his continuous subject changing. It was understood that I could keep up with his train of thought.

He went back to discussing writing. Ask questions, he said. Learn by asking questions. Find out about people. Have people talk about themselves. When you are the best people will always hire you. Tell them that you can do it better, and that you can do it for less. I thought about how Jonah had said I had a learning problem. I attributed it to caffeine and lack of concentration. Dan said, as if to hear my thoughts... It's ok to be a slow learner, work harder. I'm a slow learner, I work harder. "Don't let anyone screw you over, even your friends." I knew something was going to happen today concerning boxes. I looked at the boxes I had beside me for the move.

I once went to an outdoor play of Shakespeare with Richard Dreyfus. I got up and shouted... "This is the worst Shakespeare I have ever seen." My wife wanted to roll under the picnic blanket. Dreyfus was doing himself. You couldn't find the character. Stars are weak because they do themselves. They do their acts and their personalities. Writers get paid the least. Everyone on a movie is replaceable except the executive producer. People believe what you tell them. That's what makes them stupid. They see even an actor and believe that he is the part. Bush and those guys are bad comedians, bad actors. They are some of my favorite characters. This was in the early nineties.

People rather be timid and conform then think and act for themselves. Parents become friends. They are no longer dictators. I again noticed the energy rising and falling during the conversation. Meanwhile Jonah had lain down on the floor and was gazing at the sunlight in the trees. Dan said that his wife did what she wants. Don't try and make a person what you are. Leave them as they are. Question everything. Don't just take the damn bullshit that people place in front of you. With the caste system those people should get up and say fuck you. "Nobody's law is any better then you're own. Think. Act freely. Challenge people on what they say." "People barricade themselves into their own views." Dan kept charging through story after story. I recognized that something was different about him by the amount of stuff he had to say. He talked for three hours. Jonah and I didn't really say much of anything. What he said, I thought was true. Everything he said, about how to think about certain things, I agreed with. A lot of things were ways I would have wished to act, but never gave myself permission. I would gauge my behavior on my surroundings, and no one ever invites you to be free and to be yourself. I began to notice that given the opportunity to control you, people impose their superiority and will, whenever they get the chance. I acknowledged that I didn't want to close myself off from learning from people, but I didn't want people trying to control me. I decided to make a conscious effort to shake off those people whom fed their egos by controlling me. I willingly let Jonah control me to a certain extent because I

learned from him in an undeniable way. He could talk as a
teacher to me, because I knew I was learning from him.

Dan said that it was after five and that he was going to
pick up his wife. I said that it was really nice to meet you. Dan
and Jonah walked out of the door. Jonah went downstairs with
him to the parking lot. I didn't know what to do. I didn't know
if I should leave and lock up the apartment, or wait for Jonah.
I felt extremely wired. Jonah came back and asked if I wanted
to go to dinner. I said yes, and that I would go take a shower
and come back in around thirty minutes. He said that he was
going to take a nap and that I should come back to wake him.
Before I left, Jonah gave me a big Riverside edition
Shakespeare book. It was a beautiful book, and I thought it
was a nice gesture of friendship for him to give it to me. He
signed it. When I walked down the hall my body felt as though
it had had some type of strange electrocution performed on it.
When I walked into my room everything looked brilliant and
shiny with the warm glow of the twilight. It seemed like my
room was illuminated in soft light. I thought it looked like my
room finally looked like Jonah's room. His room often seemed
to have an attractive effervescence. I felt like I was in some
kind of mild shock. I showered, dressed and went over to

Jonah's. We walked to a nearby restaurant. Jonah was in a

very somber serious mood. He acted strange, powerful and

silent. He seemed in some way intimidating. I wanted to ask

him a lot of things, but it seemed inappropriate to discuss

certain things in a restaurant. I couldn't very well make

chitchat either. He would have none of that. He refused to

discuss inanities. He told me that I had been very lucky today,

that my life had been changed. His benefactor, whom he

referred to as the Nagual, had done something to change me

but he wouldn't exactly say what. Pretty soon I tried to

investigate with questions, but he said to forget it. To dwell on

it would diffuse its power. He said that today I had had a real

gesture with power, with an awesome sorcerer. I did in a very

real way feel like my consciousness had been altered in some

way. He said that he had cleaned my awareness without my

knowledge and brightened my luminosity about nine time to

what it had been. I went home eager to clean up my untidy

life. The next day I came to Jonah's door to give him back

twenty dollars he had lent me. No one answered. I walked

downstairs to walk out the door. I ran into Dan and Jonah.

They had small grins on their faces and it crossed my mind

that they somehow knew I had been upstairs looking for them.

It seemed almost like they had popped out of nowhere. I still didn't know their capabilities, and I almost expected the impossible from them. I interpreted their grins to imply... Now you know what we are. I imagined them to be saying that in a childlike sing song manner. I felt a friendly wariness. They seemed like two clowning schoolboys. Jonah asked me to pick up some juice while I was out and to come back over. When I came back Dan and Jonah were in the kitchen. I handed Jonah the juice and told him to keep the change. Dan gave me a strong look and said... "No, be exact." I was sort of surprised, and I recognized him taking the role of a leader. Jonah had said that Dan, the Nagual, was the nominal leader of their warrior party. I was a little nervous. I still did not know what the protocol was for addressing a sorcerer. You know how to greet a doctor, or a postman, but I was still unsure how to mingle in this situation. As I thought that, Dan stated... "We're friends. Because you are a writer, we're friends." I tried to act normal. I didn't want to appear as though I had my head in the clouds and was looking for a mystical fairytale. I didn't want to look like an idiot looking for weirdness. Here were two normal healthy guys, and I wanted to act like a person with a normal healthy attitude. We went to another financial exchange, and by accident I did the same thing about keeping the change. I got embarrassed and hoped I didn't appear to be willfully disregarding Dan's comment on doing things impeccably. We moved to the living room and sat down.

Dan said that I could ask him anything. This opened a very large can of worms. There were a lot of things that I had questions about. Just being around the two of them was like an event. There was a palpable feeling of energy that they both had. I mentioned that I had read the Carlos Castaneda books, and that they were very interesting. He said that he had come across those books after he had had personal experiences. He mentioned something about not being gullible. I thought, well if I'm ever going to be gullible, wouldn't this be the extreme example of it. As Avant-garde as I would have liked to think of myself, I still found the idea of real sorcerers a bit on the exotic side. As cool as I liked to think of my life, it still didn't have real wizards and the such, running around. He then told me that he was an apprentice of Genaro. I couldn't imagine anyone being more fascinating. Genaro was a sorcerer in the Castaneda books. He seemed to have a lot of wit. He seemed to live by acting on things rather than thinking about them. I found it hard to imagine that he actually knew anyone from the books. I also was not sure if he had gotten to meet them face to face. He said that Don Juan and Genaro had come to his apartment in Ohio and had come inside his body. Even my imagination was at a loss this time. Before I could ask anymore stupid questions, Dan went on to say, that he had seen a cactus in the desert that was an old seer. Then he told us the story about when he had been a young boy he had gone to the movies with his brother. A man sitting next to him in the theatre had put something on his leg. When he turned around to see what the man was doing, he saw that the man had no face. No one else had seen it. Then he said that he had once been in a restaurant somewhere, where there was a mysterious looking man at the next table. The man appeared almost to be asleep. They found out that he was the tenant. The tenant is an old seer who takes energy from the Nagual, for continued life. He said that he was one of the new seers and that he was a dreamer. Then he said that he had seen the Great Spirit, and that it had somehow resembled hay. A cascade of bristling lights. It had happened at a rest stop on the turnpike in Florida. My mind was electric. I was peaking with curiosity and interest when all of a sudden there was a knock on the door. In walked Chin, the owner of the building. I was severely put off by his presence. It seemed the ultimate horror, that Dan, this paragon of fascination should be freely discussing his experiences, and then the conversation should be cut back to common daily events. I felt I was getting close to getting some answers to questions that I had had for about a year. I didn't expect Dan to just lay out his story. Jonah was always so maniacal about his privacy, that I assumed Dan would be that way as well. I would've appreciated anything that would help me sort out the confusion, of who Dan and Jonah actually were...And what was actually happening. All I knew was that I went into some level of a trance state just being in the presence of these people. They were extremely intelligent, and I felt extremely different by being around them, especially Dan. I had to continually eat, so as to not feel faint in his presence. I struggled with proper blood sugar levels normally, but this was even more erratic, though very good. Dan was unruffled by Chin's entrance. He started discussing world trade and other stuff as nonchalantly as he had been discussing the Great Spirit a moment earlier. I realized that that was a part of his talent in behavioral abilities. He could change gears in an instant. In looking back now, I don't think he was partial to either type of subject. Jonah continually stressed that higher consciousness activity was exactly equal to taking the garbage out and getting the rent paid. They were adamant to not get me tipped over into just obsessing over metaphysics. They felt it was a natural part of oneself that could be developed, but other than that a regular life was essential. The next day I came by to say something to Jonah and to say good-by to Dan. I noticed that he was not the mood of Nagual, and was just Dan. Jonah was like that too. Sometimes he was a sorcerer, and sometimes he was just Jonah the landlord, my friend. Dan wished me well, and I thanked him. I really appreciated all the good advice he had given me and the time and humor he had shared. I had thought I would have had the chance to meet his wife at one of their dinners, but it wasn't the right time. I imagined his wife to be a pretty interesting person too. It was alright that I didn't have the opportunity to meet with them over the weekend. I had the attitude that whatever was supposed to happen, would happen. I wanted to respect people's privacy. I didn't want to go barging in on someone just because I was curious.

5   LEAVING LA

I dismantled the apartment piece by piece. The day

finally came to leave. A friend came to pick me up with a van.

We were set to drive to Florida. I left Hollywood and what felt

like home. The building had really grown on me. The Eric

Clapton song "I can't stand it" played as we pulled away. My

good by with Jonah had been satisfying. It left a good

impression on me. It was a warm and comfortable good-by.

We decided to go to San Francisco first. I wanted to go

to Big Sur. The first night we stayed in a place called Half

Moon Bay. It was a gorgeous place. The rain was refreshing

after months of dryness in Los Angeles. At three A.M we went

out and bought shrimp and wine. We stayed in a friend's cabin

that was decorated as a nautical boathouse. The next morning,

we enjoyed a homemade hot tub in a greenhouse. We drove to

the ocean that was below huge verdant cliffs. A huge thick

mist hung languidly above the clouds. The air was moist and

clean. I walked up a path leading to a small hilltop

overlooking the water. It was a glorious place. The mountain behind us was a deep bright evergreen. We drove to San Francisco for lunch. We walked into a fabulous art gallery by Fisherman's Wharf. There was a huge brass eagle, and a 60,000$ silkscreen. It amused me that the salesperson thought that we might be collectors. We decided that it must have been the expensive leather jackets. We walked into a restaurant. There was a table with three Indian men and a woman with Blonde hair. From the restroom I could hear their speech and laughter. One of the men had long white braids. I noticed him staring at me when I came in. I wanted to observe them over lunch, but our table was in the next room. The man had been striking and radiant. I found their energy almost visible. We then went and looked at the Golden Gate Bridge. It was a cool beautiful day. On the way to the car, we stopped in a few shops. I was shocked when I turned around and saw a friend of mine from music school in Hollywood. I hadn't seen him in two years. He was one of the more interesting people from school. I had recently told a story that had had him in it. There were a lot of people around and it would have been very easy to have missed him. He said that he had been camping in Alaska, and was going to England.

We took off towards Monterey to see the northern

coastline. We saw pelicans. I was momentarily able to get

Jonah off my mind. Leaving him had been crushing. We drove

through the Artichoke capital of the world. We stopped in Big

Sur for dinner. We went to a gorgeous restaurant set high on

the cliffs overlooking the sea. At sunset a group of people

gathered on the back terrace to watch. I noticed that the

ketchup holders were the same wicker baskets as one Jonah

had given me. It seemed that there were reminders of him

everywhere. I was still in a strange state of mind from the

recent occurrences with Dan and Jonah. I was far from feeling

in my normal state of awareness. Something they had done,

had left me with feelings of strange mental and bodily

sensations. I felt euphoric, but a little dazed. I still feel an

incredulous feeling towards them and what they may be about.

I still didn't in some ways know what to make of them. They

were far more intelligent than anything my experience had

been exposed to. I didn't know what their capabilities might

be. I had vague ideas and fantasies, that when I saw a pair of

crows I imagined it could be them, watching me. I felt silly

having these imaginings, but a part of me was searching for

answers. Answers about what "seeing" was. I kept having the

feeling as though I was in some strange kind of dream. It

sounds cliche but it was true. All of a sudden the earth seemed alive in a slightly different kind of way. I watched nature intently as we rolled across the country. I knew that there was some sort of answer in nature, but I didn't know what it was. I watched nature, just to see what, if anything, would happen. One could jokingly say I was being suspicious of nature, but it was nothing malevolent. I also felt strangely connected to Dan and Jonah. I felt as if they were a presence in my mind. I knew that that didn't seem rational, but it felt as if they were right there with me at all times.

We left the cliff side restaurant. We then took a perilous ride around the mountain ledge road. A white sliver moon shone over the black rolling sea. The distance down from the cliffs looked about five thousand feet. My stomach was lurching as he swung around the curves. My friend whom was arrogant in many ways, was particularly so, about being told to slow down his driving. I finally demanded that we stay over somewhere, because I was actually terrified of going over the ledge. It was dark, and even though we hadn't been drinking, it was still too easy to make a mistake. The guardrails were minimal for that type of road. As it turned out, we stayed in the most beautiful place I have ever stayed. It was a cottage, high in the cliffs overlooking the sea. It was in a town named

Gorda. That also reminded me of the Castaneda stories

because one of the sorceresses was named La Gorda. We

could see otters playing in the water. The radio station was

called the Otter, and there were pictures of otters in the

cottage. It was a gorgeous cabin, made of fine woods, filled

with art, and had a half wall window that overlooked the

ocean. There was a picture of a pretty Indian child on the wall.

They shut off the power generator at eleven p.m. The only

light was from the moon. My friend and I weren't exactly

lovers, and weren't exactly friends. We were getting along

peaceably which was a lot of fun.

The next morning, we had breakfast in the coffee shop in

the main building. The waitress was like someone out of a

psychedelic time warp. She had an extreme Californian lisp,

and a manner of expressing herself that reminded me of

someone running through a field with flowers in her hair. She

was very nice, it just seemed a little crazy. Big Sur was

gorgeous. It was a lot more appealing to drive there in the

daytime. We made it down to Bakersfield that day. Outside

Bakersfield, we stopped in a lonely tavern, to use the

restroom. It was a biker bar. I did not feel like I was in a public place. This was clearly their place, and they looked at me like they wanted to know what the hell I was doing there? I sat on the toilet wondering if there was going to be a problem. I wasn't really used to small towns. This strongly had the feeling of a small town. We left and everything was fine. I kept thinking about how Jonah had said listen with your instincts, and your body. I observed that my body had definitely taken on a feeling of wariness in there.

It was turning into a really great trip. Jonah had said that since my meeting with Dan, my life was going to be like a journey. He told me to clean out my body. He said that if I ever did anything like cocaine, he would have nothing to do with me. I wasn't interested in that anyway. The trip had all the elements of an exciting exploration. We stayed in nice hotels, ate in great restaurants, observed different cultures, and saw the nightlife on occasion. We drank wine, watched cable, enjoyed hot tubs and relaxed. Each state had its own collection of experiences. We took our time. You can make it across country in three days. We took two weeks. After California, we finally got to Arizona. The last element of fascination in California had been miles and miles of yellow fields and mountains. It was absolutely gorgeous. We came across a group of buffalo behind a wire fence. I got out to look at them more closely. Then there were the wild horses. They were spectacular.

I had a strong feeling of peace in Arizona. We stayed overnight in Williams, one of the last towns before the Grand Canyon. We went into a large tavern and saw a country band. We peeked in a minute to see the people. A group of Indians caught my eye. The next morning at breakfast, the same Indians were in the coffee shop. I thought... this is a small place.

We took off for the Grand Canyon. The pastel coloring of the mesa walls was breathtaking. We decided to find out about the Havasupai village, because we had heard that there were waterfalls there. We went back to Williams to sleep. I felt a little frustrated because it seemed like we were losing time. The next day my friend decided to take a shortcut road to the village. I should have reminded myself that there are few shortcuts in life. The road appeared to be on the map. After twenty-five miles of being on the road alone, we passed a red bronco with a large group of Indians. We waved to each other. When we passed a group of wild mustangs off to the right. It was beginning to have a surreal look to the environment. The desert was gorgeous. We came to a sign that read... "State road ends here." Under that it said... "Continue at your own risk." Flocks of swallows swarmed over the desert foliage. We had gone this far, so we figured that it was about forty miles to the Havasupai Village.

My friend was a good driver, although arrogant. The road was treacherous. It had two feet drops an either sides of the tires. Had we become lodged on any protruding rock or land formation, we might not have made it out alive. A forty mile walk in the desert might have been out of my natural capabilities. We didn't even have extra water on us. This crazy road went on for an hour. Every move counted, to avoid an accident. No one was anywhere for miles, and it seemed unlikely that anyone would pass by again. We stopped at one point to admire the silence and the land. It was truly like a different world. We finally reached a real highway. There were yellow budding cacti all along the road. Large brown tumbleweeds passed us on occasion. The earth was many colors in the desert. There was red clay and white rock. There was yellow straw grass and white grass in front of a grey mountain range. I felt I could stay in Arizona forever. We reached the rim of the Grand Canyon that had a group of

Indians that would take you down into the canyon on donkeys. They were very nice. They seemed almost to have been numbed by the sun. They spoke in a slow deliberate manner. I was surprised that people lived in such a remote area. It felt very peaceful in this area of Arizona. We decided to pass on going down into the canyon. We would have had to leave the van unprotected all night. The thing I worried about losing was all my guitar institute schoolbooks. In retrospect, even that would have been replaceable.

We headed east toward New Mexico on Route 66. We spent two days in Gallup New Mexico. I liked being in an Indian town. I loved looking at the jewelry and crafts in their trading post stores. My friend bought me a beautiful bracelet. It reminded me of what I might have seen on the rock singer Robert Plant.

The next day we visited the Zuni Reservation. We visited an incredible place called the Zuni mission. It was an old style church just off the road, by some houses. I didn't know if we should be driving around there by people's houses. We went into the church. Amazing murals were adorning the walls. The most gorgeous painting work I had ever seen. A man named Alex, told us about the paintings, which were of

Kachina dolls, and other religious symbols of his people. I got a really good feeling being there. He was very generous and elaborate in his explanations. We then had pizza at the reservation.

On our way out of New Mexico we visited an ice cave. A man was taking money at the entrance where there was a small store. It looked as though his house was attached to the store. I asked him questions about how he liked living in a place so remote from any city. I felt very dependent on the stimulation that N.Y.C and L.A provided. I liked talking to the man, and getting another perspective. He was a handsome Indian man. The kind you would see in a movie or have a wild fantasy about.

We eventually rolled into Texas. The next stop was a place called Carlsbad Cavern. This was a truly incredible place. We stayed in a very artistic motel cottage. It had gorgeous Indian rugs and ornate wood carved chests. That night before sundown we went to sit outside the bat caves. There was a huge audience sitting on the bleachers outside the cave, waiting to watch the evening bat flight. They would come out to do their nightly feeding. We had to wait awhile before they came out. The ranger said that it was possible that they had taken off for Mexico, for the winter. Finally, they flew out. It was quite a show. Something like 300,000 bats spiraled out of the cave in a line, out into the twilight sky. Meanwhile swallows were trying to nosedive through them to get back into the cave. The bats made a high pitched little cry and let off a musk type of scent. They flew too fast to really see their features. Everyone was excited to see this. It was such a timeless, natural, phenomena. As if seeing this wasn't enough, the next step was to go through the ice caves the next day. It was an astounding place like nothing I could have ever imagined. Crystallized mineral formations that formed rooms of splendor. It was an entire underground world. It took hours to walk through it. It was a very special place. The next day we went to the Sonora Caverns. They were more of a wet nature. They had walls of shimmering crystals. Next we passed through San Antonio, Houston and Beaumont. I felt a strange feeling in Beaumont. The people stared a good bit. San Antonio was a wonderfully vibrant place.

We finally got to New Orleans. I had waited years to come here. I felt a thrill thinking of all the Jazz that had been played here. I felt an energy in the French Quarter, that I really liked. I could feel the passion for art and music in the air. I felt an undercurrent of adventure on Bourbon Street. I was so impressed I thought I wanted to move there. An extraordinary guitarist I knew from Mississippi had told me that really great musicians lived there. The next day we visited a very fine restaurant. The service was a talented presentation. One could also feel the horror of how slave trading had occurred here.

Soon after we were in Florida. We stayed in a huge pink hotel in St. Petersberg. We saw an incredible sunset from the room. I was getting used to living on the road. Of course it wasn't that difficult living in high style. I was really enjoying it. I didn't necessarily want to get anywhere. This was a satisfying, if not realistic life. I liked new stimulus every day. We visited the Salvador Dali museum in St. Petersburg. That was great.

6 FLORIDA

My adjustment here was slow. The culture shock made
me crazy. The sudden stillness where there had been
movement was terrifying. It was a smaller town life. I hadn't
had a car for years in Hollywood, and as appalling as that
could sound to anyone from LA, it was far more frightening in
a retirement village in what felt like a scalding zone.
Hollywood and Florida were just extremely different. I now
see South Florida as an exciting and upbeat destination.
However, at the time I was pining for my rock and roll
Hollywood. There were not thousands of musicians living on
my street. There was kind of one hip gardener, who was still
much older but bore a vague resemblance to Jonah. I
absorbed the fabulous beauty of the nature despite my
discomfort with the tropical sun. Jonah had excellent timing in
calling me. The very first day I got home he left a message
while I was out. I called him back from a supermarket
payphone. He said it sounded like a rocket station. I told him

how exciting the trip was. He said I sounded hysterical. I was just trying to be positive. I was getting such a horrible feeling being there. I mentioned something about how desperate I was starting to feel. He got really mad and said that I was setting it up to be horrible by not giving it a chance. You're creating this lousy experience, he said. When I got off the phone I felt much better. I felt he was right. I could create this to be any way that I wanted. I was happy that Jonah said that I could call him on his 800 number anytime. He said that by going home I got a chance to see how life could be. He said that my anxiety was from feeling out of control with money, and letting people step on me. He said that I was really good at letting people step in and take over my life. He said that I was an experiment to him. He also said that I had left weirdness. Florida, which felt strange to me now, was not weird. He said that I had been ready to go to sleep for life in Hollywood, in some treadmill job.

I called Jonah to tell him I was thinking of him. I told him I was feeling less chaotic, which was what I was used to. I asked him if he didn't find the term warrior, a tad strange? He said, corny? Yes, that's it I said. There weren't really too many fitting titles. If you could become a warrior that could see, then you could become a man of knowledge. He said that the term Yogi or Swami could be used on some occasions, but warrior was just the phrase being used. The maturity of the average man never even got to the mid- twenties. If your maturity got to the mid- twenties, then you were doing well among the race of man. He said that it was no illusion that you would see adolescent people in old bodies. They reach a plateau, and then they kick off their learning process and go into a sleep state, hence you get people completely closed in a pattern of some sort, and they have little interaction with the world outside them. They're almost not alive in some respects.

Why don't you forget about yourself? He said. A warrior is free from the circle that presses upon people. Stop concentrating on yourself. I called Jonah on occasion and I would actually go into a state of heightened awareness over the phone. He said that he was doing something called "cleaning off my island." He was in some way cleaning out my awareness. This act that he called "cleaning off my island," was a definite physical occurrence. When I would get off the phone with him there was a very physically tangible difference in my mind and body. In the course of our conversation, at certain times, something would happen to me.

I would feel as though a mild stupor would come over me. When I asked him about it, he said that I was going into heightened awareness. It would just happen as I would talk to him. It was very pronounced, and yet it wasn't entirely like some of the descriptions that Carlos had made about heightened awareness. For instance, I didn't leave the premises so to speak. It wasn't like dreaming where I was visiting another location. I was pretty conscious of sitting in the same place wherever I was. Mentally shifts occurred. On one spectacular occasion I did mentally go somewhere with him that was not only far away in location but bore the reality of being in another time. So things did happen. Carlos would even describe heightened awareness as having him participate with people that he wouldn't even recall out of heightened awareness. That sort of totally different plane of consciousness I could relate to as, closer to dreaming. As I would talk to him I would fall deeper and deeper into another state of mind. I could still function, if someone, were to run into the room and yell fire, but I was intensely absorbed into an energy that would numb me. I would always start to feel very good when I spoke to him. I felt very happy and positive. I would feel that everything was entirely right just to be on the phone with him.

I got an injection of energy just to be talking to him.
Sometimes he would repeat things that he had said before, to
emphasize them or because they were pertinent to a current
situation. Also, I would forget a lot of what was said in
heightened awareness, and so a lot would be repeated because
of that. That seemed to be a normal effect of that experience.
That was why I would try to write down what he said shortly
afterwards.

"Turning off thought rejuvenates and wards off disease.
Lay down for a resting state for five minutes. If you are totally
stressed out and lay down for a fifteen- minute nap, you can be
totally recharged. Turn off the mouth inside your head.
Internal dialogue is bullshit. Turn off the English language and
just perceive. Cross your eyes to the arch of your nose. See
light refraction. Quiet the dialogue. Control your thought. Tell
your mind to shut up. Take the challenge to shut off the
random bullshit. Focus on the third eye. Shut off the head. Be
gentle to yourself. Give silence to the head. Ward off disease
and feel better. See light emanations. Translucent light
becomes perception. It's interesting. Perceive with no
thought."

At later times when I would visit Jonah after I had

moved from the building, I got to see some of his daily routines that I hadn't seen when I lived down the hall. While I would prefer to raise my blood sugar a small degree upon arising, he seemed perfectly stable to begin his meditation as soon as he got up. He would sit up in either a cross legged or lotus position on his bed. I'm not exactly sure how long he would stay meditating, but he was consistent and in the groove of doing it. I just knew not to talk to him then. He wasn't playing at it, it was a part of his life. He had said that even if you just do it for fifteen minute periods of time here and there it's going to rejuvenate and relax you. To what extent were his experiences, I don't know. I just know that the game plan, was to shut off the inner dialogue specifically while you are meditating and as much as possible in your daily life, to bring about greater health and expanded awareness. He believed in napping as well, which I appreciated him having made clear and positive mention of. I'm glad he said that, because otherwise I probably would have considered it being lazy or a sign of weakness to nap. He believed it would save and better your health to take naps whenever needed. When you gave yourself that benefit, you probably wouldn't over nap because you would just do it as needed. He said .... lie down when you're tired and get up when you not. You would typically have more energy if you gave yourself permission for rest periods.

Lie with your feet and head propped up. Go into light sleep. Everything leaves the mind. The body is not bothered by the ego. The internal dialogue stops, and the self leaves. Save the body. When the self leaves the body, your body is left alone. I told Jonah that my father kept going into the hospital, and that it was very upsetting. He said.... A wise man doesn't grieve for the living or grieve for the dead. It accomplishes nothing. The hole mends. When you lose someone there is a hole in your life. It mends. He continued... Relax the neck and tongue. Tell your body it does not have any cancer or disease etc... Relax the heart chakra, which is the inner dialogue. Listen for other voices. The genius is very quiet. It's like reading music. Plug into the divine voices. Transcribe the music you hear in your head. Warriors have no weakness. Warriors are disconnected. I was taken out of this world. The first person in two thousand years. The planet is heaven. We're on our own. The religious stuff is right here. Jesus shifted people to a different world, so that we could use our potential, be in peace with nature and the planet.

Everything is happening now. There is going to be a chemical accident. Stay away from it. We were born into it, so we don't see the disintegration around us. We are too close to it. It's serious now. Don't mess around with the world. Save yourself. Save the world after yourself. Save yourself through meditation. Every day is unique. Be on to better days. I do not have religious ideas. When you have wealth, don't misuse it. Be an ordinary guy. Be conscious of who is affecting your thoughts. They're witches and sorcerers. Not the ones who say they are. If you can gather the totality of yourself, there is no going back to the egg pile of humanity of birth and rebirth. You can gather your totality and leave. Be the best of yourself. Do what you are doing when you are doing it. In other words, concentrate and be present as you do each thing. Don't be thinking about everything else to do when you are doing one thing. Cut out the inside talking. Be in meditation and be peaceful. When you want to, lie down and take a nap. It rejuvenates you. Things can be chaotic. Be at peace. My goal is to leave the world better then when I found it. You have accepted the greatest task, when you leave the place better then when you found it. Everyone's story is different. Everyone looks at a moment and sees something different.

Everyone who reads Carlos's books sees something different.

Mozart and Bach tuned into another level of existence, that dictated their music to them. They were master transcribers. He paused and went on.... We're on our own. There's nothing but earth for light years. The cosmos is here.

My mind and body felt very light as he talked to me. I again had a vague feeling of shock as we spoke. It was a very physical feeling. It wasn't because I was feeling shock at what he was saying. I couldn't move or think as I would normally. Everything felt more concentrated. It was as though I could only process his immediate words. Everything else was knocked out of mind. I always felt lightheaded but good after conversations like these. Other times when we were talking he would just be Jonah the guitar buddy or just another friend. He talked in a couple of different manners. Generally, after talking about something serious, he would get grounded and talk about regular stuff before I left. If his conversation became more pedestrian, I took it as an indication that he was going to be getting off the phone or leaving soon. You could feel it in the air, the shift of mood and feeling. On the phone he would end his dialogue abruptly. It seemed to be his style. It seemed also to be an indication that I had better start using the knowledge he was giving me, and apply it to cleaning up my life. He was emphatic that these were not chit chat conversations, and that he was not going to waste his time teaching someone, who would then go back to their old lazy habits. You keep wanting to be the old person that you were. Quit being a fuck up. You can quit that and change right now. At any moment you can just change your behavior.

While I would be talking to him I would be in a state of heightened awareness. Afterwards I would return to my normal self. My normal self, did not remember all that was said. That was why I took notes. I called Jonah from Key West on New Year's Eve. It was an exotic place. I called him later that month. I told him that I was shy to go to clubs by myself, but that if I didn't do that I would wind up doing nothing. He said that going out alone depends on what you're going out for. I never felt shy about going out alone again. I realized that I went out for the music, and then perhaps for the good cheer and company of others.

I told Jonah about going to the beach with an old roommate from music school, and wanting to kiss him, but all I could think of was death.

"Like what, like a bus trying to bite the tires." I was

astounded. I was once in the Bronx when a very odd
occurrence had happened. We were driving through a
seemingly violent neighborhood. All of a sudden I saw a crazy
looking white guy running after a truck growling, making dog
like gestures as if he had wanted to bite the tires.

I started stammering and Jonah said.... "See I told you
I'm an awesome sorcerer." That's how this stuff works. The
experience was so long ago. It had had such an unusual quality
to it when it happened. Right after I saw the crazy guy, then I
saw another guy across the street running at top speed with
what looked like a spear raised over his head. He was thin,
black and wearing only shorts. I'm not making this up. I
couldn't imagine what the hell I was watching. I couldn't
fathom how Jonah could pick this faint remote memory from
my mind. We said good night.

7 MODERN STORIES

I called Jonah about a week later. After we caught up
about current events in our lives he said... The white man got
off track. Places have feeling. People are weird. They may be
suffering in a place, but it doesn't occur to them to leave. They

should go someplace else if things are not working out for them continuously. Their mental and spiritual health has to do with places. Teach yourself to do something. Don't mess with anybody. The Christians took it to the other extreme trying to convert everyone. Being selfish is really closer to being a seer. We get out of the human band. We leave other people alone. Don't be responsible for other people. Being aware is enough. Sorcery is just a level. There are other levels above sorcery. Anything that has to do with influence is sorcery. A real man of knowledge is the jumping point. A man of knowledge knows that, that knowledge is where it is at. A warrior is independent. An independent person. They are not impressed with anyone that uses celebrity status or possessions to flash their wad. We live in the world of the black magicians. They're all running their master and slave game. To me it's all boring bullshit. I'm not inside the circle that presses upon people. Being happy is not having to worry. I like to be an artist. There are invisible people here. They're doing their own thing and have no public image.

Cosmically and biologically raise awareness to what's possible. The earth is something to take care of everybody. Instead of killing nature take care of the earth. Everyone can be rich. The rich are afraid of everyone being rich. If the rich were also taking care of the planet, then we would be harvesting greatness. Religious stories stood the test of time. Now there are more modern ways to say these things. Modern stories are aimed at saving the planet. We could become extinct like the dinosaurs, by a freak accident or a meteor. Man created God in his own image. There is a God. A positive creative force here. I pay attention to the earth and my allies, because I picked up interesting things. The Indian, Don Juan takes coincidence away. It's not a big deal if the earth wants to communicate with you. If there wasn't a force, it wouldn't have sprung us up. You can get through to people, through art.

I'm telling a story, he went on. I have an opinion on how things are. People have to realize their own stupidity. The bible is real. I found Jesus in a way that is unquestionable. I'm not a religious person. It's about the planet. People make billions and then they stop. When you make millions without helping the planet then it's misuse. Don't waste moves. I want this planet put together.

Keep the boogie man stuff off your island. Keep your island (life), clean and the spirit will talk to you. Make progress every day. Don't worry about the overall picture.

Take your time, but don't let up. What's creative and is genius, is being successful. Chip away at it. Every day I learn a little guitar. The odds are against us. Having my back up against the wall is the only way. Let's see what I know. There's a nightmare on the way. Learn how to get tough and survive the elements. Money can help. Learning to survive is a great art form.

I thought about how Jonah had told me to keep myself calm, and not allow other people's bad vibes to influence me. I had a situation with a teacher where she began to make me nervous. I was in the ladie's room at school, straightening up when I began to think of this teacher. I felt nervous just at the thought of her. At that moment I tapped my glasses by accident with the hairbrush. What felt like a light tap actually sent them smashing to the floor. What was so ridiculous was that I only felt the brush lightly hit the glasses. The force with which the glasses flew had the distinct sensation, of being of their own volition. At that moment it seemed like it happened in direct response to my losing control of my nervousness inside. It happened at that exact moment that I became inwardly hysterical about the teacher.

I told Jonah about the glasses and he said it sounded like

an agreement from the earth. The earth is everything around us. The Indians were in nature, so they got communications with the earth, but even with technologies, everything around us is considered the earth. The glasses shattering could have been to say shut up to your inner dialogue. You are where your mind is at. You can be in a different world out here. That's why you stay in total concentration while you are driving. I expand your awareness. I won the cosmic lottery ticket. The Nagual knew of me before I knew of him. We are radios. Most people are on automatic pilot and are on their instincts. They can smell power. They can smell another person's essence on you. I told Jonah that I felt like hell physically. I told him that coffee made me feel sick, but that I felt immobile without it. He told me to cut back on the coffee and drink eight glasses of water a day with vitamin C. He told me that this was a sorcerer's task, and not to call back if I wasn't going to take care of business. Just now as I typed this the desk cupboard door closed by itself. This is still a current pertinent issue to me. It took a long time to have it be real or ok that the earth can talk to you. It seemed like a pretty unconventional topic to take at face value. I still have this very specific way that I have been trained to acknowledge as the only way, things are possible. What continually happens is that little by little I'm being exposed to things that would have conventionally seemed impossible. One striking example of this happened in Florida. I had a short period of time where I was under the impression that I may have become pregnant. Not something planned, invited or even a vaguely acceptable notion. Had that been the case I have no idea what I would have done. I was completely hysterical contemplating this. Not once in my life had I been able to at least think about whether I wanted children. I couldn't even rationally try and think about it. I didn't dislike children, it just didn't seem like I was supposed to do that, and I don't know why. I was in the bathroom and out of nowhere I shouted either out loud or to myself, I'm not pregnant. At that precise moment my bookcase crashed to the floor entirely of its own volition. I was instantly sure that it was true that I was not pregnant. I just couldn't believe that that happen. Soon after I realized that I was fine. That was one time that it seemed like a hell of an agreement from the earth. There again it wasn't anything to be too freaked out about. Just observe it and move on. Later in time another incident happen that looked like it was the result of mental electricity. I couldn't definitely say if I caused this, it only seemed that way. I was at a nightclub performing with my boyfriend. We had a very heated and passionate relationship for years. We still have it but it is no longer our relationship. It is like lovers reuniting in a controlled but safe environment. There was always high emotional drama at these gigs. It was the best and worst of every rock and roll relationship that ever was. The fury was helpful to the development of my musical aggressiveness and ability. So one evening something happen. I don't even recall specifically what it was. It could only have been where I was jealous, or I was told not to play. Either of these things on occasion had me well over the edge. Perhaps it was the combination of the two. My guy was gorgeous and insane. Our battles were not something I'm proud of, but one has to mention this to illustrate just how high pitched these aggressions became. He was also a love God. This only enforced how temperamental I allowed myself to become. So one evening I storm out of the bar and walk away down to the water. It was by water. My rage was at an extraordinary peak. All of a sudden the overhead electrical wire catches on fire. This one I can't say was me, but again the timing of how hysterical I was and how this fire erupted out of nowhere seemed as though my mental energy could have done it. I don't dwell on it, and again I'm not even saying it was me. I will say it was odd and surprising. It reminded me of the movie Carrie.

8 BEING PROFESSIONAL

The next time I spoke to Jonah he turned to something I expected him to speak about. You are always trying to get me to do tricks for you. To prove to you that magic exists. I'm telling you the magic is in everyday life. Everything you do should be done professionally. By professionally I mean organized. Cleaning out all of your stuff until everything has a purpose, and there's no excess baggage. Only when everything is in impeccable order, will there be room for creativity. You are weighted down by the bullshit in your life. Your weighted down by unresolved relationships, and undefined clarity in your interactions. You should be professional in the way you walk, talk, order in a restaurant and clean your room. You're always looking for other worlds, other experiences because you don't want to deal with this one. You have to deal with everyday business before you can reap the rewards of going beyond that. Learning is doing. Moving is creativity. Forget about thinking. You can think forever about something. "Normal is relative to yourself." You set your standards. Fair and honest is impeccable. Who is worth lying to? His benefactor had said. That had impressed me. Be perceptive. You are not your art. Never let idiots run their bullshit on you. Call them on their phoniness and particularly on their manipulation. Clean up your life. Wake up and become professional. Jonah said that professional was not just the common meaning for the word. It encompassed every facet of your action. He abruptly ended the conversation and we hung up. I felt pumped up and ready for action. I cleaned everything of my belongings, and I noticed a definite shift in the amount of energy that I had. I actually had much more.

I went to Manhattan for a week. It was great. I loved the place. I stayed at the Chelsea Hotel. While not the most luxurious, it had a longstanding history of artistic nuance. It was known for a lot of things, but in my narrow world I knew it as where Grace Jones, possibly Patti Smith, and other 70's rock and roll and fashion cult hero's had their groovy apartments. The place had an antique feel to it. The lobby seemed an endless parade of characters. Years later one would not seek the elusive glamour of sitting there, but for the first time it was cool. The second time I stayed there, I cursed the fact that I hadn't gone to the Hilton for the same price. Another time there I went to a party. Me and two girlfriends decided to see the roof that was accessible through a skylight door. Once up there a wind almost promptly threw me off the building. It was incredible. I was terrified. One of my friends that brought me up there was a scary lady herself. The kind that you could imagine would not have been overly distressed had that occurred. Once inside it got weirder yet. A Japanese actor/artist was doing a performance art act of his. I don't know what it was, but he got on a very sensitive nerve of mine. It was a group of artsy well to do sophisticates, so I did everything in my power to not allow myself to express any inappropriate behavior. He made me feel purely hysterical. Had I emitted any sound it would have been akin to insane gurgling. I was aghast and trying to remain calm. Whatever that was finally subsided and we finally left. My other girlfriend there had another issue. It seemed that she had made a drawing of some sort of a particular thing. It had been somewhere, and now this artist guy was drawing this picture and putting it all over the place. When I told my boyfriend, the musician about this party, he had a million assurances that

that hotel was completely evil and that spirits would take down whatever they could there. True to form on my initial stay, there were lots of unexplainable footsteps, but like I said, they were unexplainable.

On the plane back to Florida, a very unusual man asked if he could sit next to me. I had seen him from ten rows back as I had glanced up from my book. His features, from a distance, reminded me of Sid Vicious from the band the Sex Pistols. He, by the way killed his girlfriend at the Chelsea Hotel and later died there himself. I had thought of him that day because of staying at the Chelsea and because of a book I had seen. I was surprised to see someone who would resemble him. When I looked up again he was asking to sit down. I said sure, and continued to read. As it turned out, up close he didn't really look too much like Sid Vicious. He did look rather distinctive though. He had a very large bone structure and a very deep voice. When we talked I found him to be quite intelligent. Still, there was something alarming about his appearance. Also, there was something unusual about the way he was making me feel. I felt locked into his presence. I felt obliged to be generally honest because it seemed like he could tell if I wasn't. When there was a short stopover, I stayed in my seat, because I couldn't get myself to get up and leave. He was a seemingly nice person, but strikingly unusual looking. He was an athlete. I gave him my number. We said that maybe we would play music together. He said that he played four of five instruments and spoke five or six languages. I wanted to get to know him because I could tell that he was highly intelligent. Those types of people I found very interesting. He was handsome, but intimidating due to his overall large nature. He was super fit with dark hair and dark eyes.

When I got home I called Jonah and told him how strange this guy was. He got very stern and said...You invited an Indian sorcerer into your life. That man is a sorcerer. He's not even a real man. He could have stolen your soul, without you even being aware of it. I can "see" this guy. You better watch out and you better be more careful. You are carrying around awareness that isn't yours, and it will attract weirdness.

He then changed gears. Your parents at a certain point become friends, and past a certain age they don't have any almighty power over you. They could drag you to their graves if you let them. He told me that I was awesomely lucky to have met his benefactor, and that it was especially unusual to know that he was his benefactor. He said that I had had the privilege to meet two of the most important people in all of

history, and that I should be thankful for every word. He said

this in reference to the fact that I was not doing all that I

should be doing. It wasn't so much as tooting his own horn as

it was to alerting me to pay better attention and to not be so

scattered that I couldn't appreciate what was going on. How

do I know you're not swindling my mind I asked him? There

are no guarantee's in life, he said. I reflected that most of the

stuff he said was pretty logical. I told him how I thought the

spirit or something had spoken to me. It seemed like my mind

spoke to me while I was passively listening. It was like it

wasn't me thinking, but as if something spoke to me. I had

been watching the Solid Gold dancers on television. They

were marvelously healthy and fit besides being talented. The

thing that came to mind was that they didn't do extreme things

to achieve their health, as much as they didn't do things to

abuse it. I remembered Don Juan telling Carlos that it was not

what he did to his body to keep his youthful vigor, but what he

didn't do.

I tried to get Jonah to tell me more about his experiences

and life. He alluded to some magnificent occurrences that I

felt could be enlightening. He said that if he told me his stuff, my assemblage point would just roll away. Your mind would leave your body. I didn't fully understand the concept of the assemblage point other than to be your state of consciousness, and that if it shifted, your consciousness would shift. Perhaps point of consciousness might be a more accurate analogy. He said that in your sleep it would shift naturally hence regular dreams and the state of dreaming, which he said were two different states. My understanding was that when I would go into heightened awareness, which was similar to a sober like trance, my assemblage point would have shifted slightly. He said that if he knocked my assemblage point too far, that if might never come back. I said o.k. I rather be safe and staid, then have my mind blown apart by some wild force of nature. I had been seeking to know what he knew for years. I could tell that he wasn't kidding about me not being able to digest too much energy, because I would feel the wired feeling intensifying. Once he had started quoting some scripture, and the feeling of energy and power kept rising and rising. My head felt like it was going to explode. My mind just started to shut off and I backed down. I said... oh my god, and he knew that I had had enough. It was as though he was feeding me an electrical flow of spiritual or energetic power right into my body.

He said that to shut off the mind was the key to other experiences. To stop the chatter in the mind, and to not own that the chatter in the mind was actually mine. The monks long ago decided that they didn't know where their thoughts were coming from. Because of this, they thought it was a mistake to be listening to all of these thoughts, that they didn't know where they were coming from. They began to practice shutting off the inner dialogue. Supposedly, this started them off in the ability to receive other information into themselves, other than the normal chatter of the everyday mind.

I called Jonah two days later. We again got into a relaxed conversation where I fell into a feeling of heightened awareness. Music is in the ethers. Quiet the mind and listen. Absorb culture and let it flow out of you in a quiet moment. Save the earth. It could have the species become extinct in our lifetime. Clean up your own spiritual environment. Pollution and overpopulation, which is pollution, are the bomb. Environment is the disease. If you clean up your environment, you clean up your disease. Develop dreaming like you would guitar playing or anything else. Program yourself before you go to sleep, to look for your hands in your dreams. The dream body can live in the world. Yogi's stay alive for hundreds of years because their body sits in a cave not enduring wear and tear, while their dream body is out and living. There is no life and death. The dream body and the physical body coexist. Don't grieve for your parents or your friends, they're to their dream body. They'll get another chance. The scene with Koresh, was a perfect example of tonals acting crazy. Some of the language Jonah used had a basis of understanding between us, because of the reading of the Castaneda stories. They were principles we had previously discussed. The Tonal was the part of the person that represented their conscious everyday thought. Their Nagual, was that other side, the dream body, the side with unfathomable capacity. It was also the name of one more energetically equipped, to be the leader of a warrior party. I wholeheartedly would recommend reading the Carlos Castaneda stories for their wisdom, talent and fascination. Jonah said that they were a manual of life and blueprint left for society on how to live life and expand the knowledge of your human capabilities. Other members of his warrior party have also put out books. They are Florinda Donner and Taisha Abelar. Incredible books. Another student of Don Juan was Ken Eagle Feather. His books seem to diffuse the knowledge into available methods of practice. All of their books are unique and valuable. Jonah continued... If you are not in the totality of your awareness, you will be eaten by awareness, or the eagle. People will try to put you in their world. Everyone's in their own little world. When you're thinking about someone else, you're not thinking about anyone else, so you're in their world. I know human character. We are perceivers. If you dream or think about someone they can perceive it. I told Jonah that I had a mildly sensual dream about a classmate at school. They came to school the next day and came up behind me and started caressing my neck in a sensual way. I was extremely surprised because that was the first time this individual had ever made any gesture of this sort, even though it was not any kind of invitation really.

A couple of weeks later I called an ad in a paper for a guitarist. I found out it was for a top professional rock musician. One of the most famous. Michael Schenker. I had the opportunity to talk for a couple of hours with someone I had admired for a long time. He was a very expressive and fascinating individual. I told Jonah about it and admitted to having considerable anxiety about the audition. He said I was acting like I was trying to get a part in the circus. Music, is a lifetime event. One job shouldn't overly influence your life. We talked about seeing each other sometime and hung up the phone.

A lot of conversations we would have would repeat topics over and over. Because of the nature of forgetting a lot in heightened awareness, he would repeat things until they became something I did and not just something I conceptualized about. He was extremely fastidious about the idea of organization. When things were in order, the stage was set for things to happen. There would be energy and contentment when things were in order. A Nagual opens the door for us. It lets us know of other realms to pursue. A lot of people's mentality gets stuck at 10 to 20 years old. You really have old people with adolescent minds. That's where they got off, they stopped learning. To stay young is to continue learning. The path to open the door to new realms, is silence. If you shut off the mind, the self leaves. A warrior realizes what an inept clod the self is and leaves it in the dust. That was said by Don Juan. Intuitive wisdom is not through the mental process.

To become quiet is one of the great challenges of becoming a warrior. To expand your awareness, you must get quiet and become totally organized. If you can become a warrior that can see, you can become a man of knowledge. "Seeing is personal." Jonah recalled Kathy having said that. Shut off the self and you will see. The secret is in being silent. Don't attach meaning to things. Just look for your hands in your dreams and call me when you find them. There is the known, the unknown and the unknowable. You can get to the unknown by being quiet and shutting off your mind. Concentrate on not thinking, he said. For me, the only path is the path with heart. Follow your heart.

Another continuous thread that ran through our conversations was his relentless insistence to be myself. Be yourself at all times. Cut the phony crap and be yourself. People will respect you for it. Never take any guff from anyone ever. As soon as people start chitchatting and being their phony selves, you should cut them off and throw it back in their faces. If you withhold what you think and let everyone ride, they will mash you into the ground. It's not that you go around looking for a fight. You let it be very clear what your boundaries are, and either people operate outside of them or they can take their leave. Also, when someone tries to get you into an argument, it should not get into a screaming level. That would be bringing you down to their level.

9   OBSERVING THOUGHT....THE INNER DIALOGUE

I looked forward to calling Jonah. I found him endlessly interesting. I was continuously curious as to how I could feel such an intense feeling from just talking to him. We led entirely separate lives, but every now and then he would speak to me and it was unique in some way. It wasn't always pleasant. He felt I needed great change in order for him to bother to talk to me. What he made me understand, was that... oftentimes in our conversations, he would go away. He would be talking, but he felt as though someone else had stepped in. He didn't know where the information was coming from. This could occur for two hours sometimes. That's why you should write this down, he would say. This is interesting because we don't know how or why this is happening. He said that it would take a lot of his personal power to do this. You are being loaded up with knowledge. You are a container of awareness. I didn't fully get what he meant by it, but I was fascinated about the whole thing going on. I had a great deal of speculation about what he would say because it just sounded so fantastic. I didn't really feel skeptical, I just felt inquisitive. He said I was like a doubting Thomas. I didn't feel the negativity of a skeptic, I was just trying to feel out the checks and balances of what I had been conditioned to believe. I just knew that I felt inexplicable joy after I spoke with Jonah. Not just a little good. Seriously high energy, excited, empowered and ready for takeoff. I felt deeply happy and refreshed. I felt robust, healthy and strong. I felt this tangible energy usually for several hours. He would say that I was a plugged up fool, "you have the light of god burning straight into your eyes and you can't see". It was true. I was so unconfident, so full of fear, insecurity, doubt about my abilities. I had a very "contrary mary" association with my mother and it was a case where she believed in nothing until the cash was on the table. I have learned to relentless admire her astute professionalism and brilliance in that area. My stupidity was that time and time I would try and make her happy or positive about whatever it was. I should say.... here are the results. Don't drag her through the game plan. I have to own getting my own security about myself at some point. I mention this because like I said, I could objectively say that all the power of god was given to me and I can still be shy and unconfident. It's messed up. I don't think it's beyond repair. I think one of my strongest points has always been looking on the bright side. I appreciate nature and people in an extraordinary way. On one of our journeys across America we were observing cloud formations. I could write chapters about what those cloud pictures would look like. Funny crazy stuff. You would think you would need acid to see stuff like this, but such was not the case. But one time I felt really sad by what I saw. Jonah said something to the effect of ...... it asks you why you are sad? There was a sad face in the sky. I didn't know I looked or felt sad. I certainly would not want the spirit, or God or whatever is out there to feel that I dishonored the amazing blessings of just seeing the beautiful earth, and was sad. How the hell could I be sad? I could be sad for the horrors in the world, but I should be damn grateful for my personal blessings. So I felt really embarrassed. I didn't want anything out there to think I was sad. If I was, I wasn't particularly aware of it. I think the long term result of this lack of confidence or sadness is not allowing the force of power to illuminate my way. I should be holding the vision of great energy and power that I have significantly felt, as my guidepost and not some nagging detractor in my inner recesses that needs to be extinguished. Here brings us to the topic of the flyer. There was a topic brought up in the last book Castaneda wrote before his definitive journey. I say definitive journey, because his life's training was supposed to be in the service that perhaps he could evade the dissipation of consciousness when the material body passed and fulfill the sorcerers quest of retaining conscious awareness in their dream body. It is believed by my benefactor, Jonah, that Carlos's teacher Don Juan Matus and his apprentices succeeded in taking their physical bodies with them consciously into another conscious realm. In his last book, called The Active Side of Infinity, he wrote about the experience and concept of an awareness that was called the flyer.

Suffice to say momentarily, that some of our thinking is something other than our own, and some of the "devils" inside us are really of a different type of awareness that is not really us. Thereby explaining, that some of our inner traits are something other than ourselves. I will go back to the idea of the foreign installation and what was said about that. It explains some of our weaknesses that we go back to over and over again.

Jonah called at about four thirty this morning. I had taken a product that was supposed to rebuild your internal organs and muscles in your sleep as well as burn fat and tone you. It had liquid protein and collagen in it. It had the effect of giving you a really deep sleep which was quite the relief. So even though it was difficult waking up, I was still fairly relaxed and could speak with him once I grabbed a bite of tempeh and a smidgen of coffee. There were few preliminaries before he played me a recording he had just made. It was a synthesizer piece that reminded me of a Latin and Brian Eno kind of groove. I wanted to write this conversation as soon as I could because by tomorrow it would be just another interrupted dream. We talked about a lot of things. He was saying that people could tell something was going on and they were waiting for something to happen. He said that the world was being run by people that did not have the information to address the most serious issues. The most serious issues being the entire ruination of our natural resources. It not being the romantic ideals of an enlightened few, that had recognized nature as their supreme ruler, but the imperative that people are made aware of the heinous catastrophe that is being beckoned by the inconceivable destruction of nature. The state of emergency that is at hand because of the ecological imbalance that our species at this point in history, is creating. He felt the whole situation was at a crossroads where, either the rulers could recognize the severe danger and change the outcome, or the planet and all of the living and breathing organisms will perish. What is more important then breathing? Is there something more important then air in your lungs and pure water to sustain your life? Why is the scientific community screaming disaster and not enough can be done? No one wants to lose any piece of whatever lifestyle they can have, but without the natural resources such as clean air, and water, there is nothing. Whatever is tipping the ecological balance must be stopped. It's not just for the hippies, or the naturalists, or the American Indians or any of the other cultures that respected the sanctity of nature. This is the most serious wake-up call that has been stated in the history of mankind. Because now the technology has advanced to the level where destruction has become easier, and therefore must be attended to and dealt with. It's not like one person washing baby diapers in the river. I have never been one to question other people's actions or lifestyles. As a culture that I have participated in and enjoyed I am not here to point fingers. The leaders must recognize the seriousness of stopping ecological destruction. If we kill the planet, the planet will kill us. It's really that simple. We can't expect one person to wield the power to save the planet or the world. This is not about pointing fingers at specific leaders and expecting them to be able to do everything. This is about waking up the whole community to the fact that this is the only priority. Complete environmentalism is the only religion anyone should be adhering to. What I mean by that, since anyone's religion is their business, is that it should be like a religious adherence that one does not disturb the ecological balance of the planet. It should be second nature that another solution other then any type of natural destruction is the only acceptable recourse. It must be known that if we destroy our own resources we will have nothing to live on. If we destroy our air and water, we will die. We will die as individuals before our time and we will become extinct as a species. Until I was told these things, I didn't recognize it. I didn't know what to do about it, because hey I'm one person. I thought it was terrible that the oceans and rivers and rainforests and oil were being sapped, but I really didn't know a whole lot about it. I still don't know a whole lot about it. I do know that I personally have every reason to believe that it is my responsibility to get the message out. The message being loud and clear that the world must prioritize not destroying nature, and that nature will save and feed all of them or it will kill us as easily as we have killed it. This type of industrialization is baiting horrific destruction that must be reversed. Our science and technology must be used to resurrect our natural planet. The health of our planet must be brought to our leader's attentions as the key to universal survival and abundance for all.

10   THE FOREIGN INSTALLATION

I mentioned before that there was something preventing me from getting over basic character flaws and feelings of general insecurity. There was a chapter written about the foreign installation in the book ...The Active Side of Infinity, by Castaneda. It's difficult to describe because its sounds so completely impossible. It sounds that way to me, and it sounded that way to Carlos, only the problem is that it makes so much sense as to why we are the way we are. Don Juan said that the foreign installation is an entity of inorganic awareness. That is like a form of life that shares our world, but is unseen to us generally. What they said of this awareness was even more insidious then some outside life force. They said that this type of being invaded our consciousness and made us think that their mind was our own. One of the first ideals that Jonah had told me about was that a sorcerer doesn't claim their thoughts as their own. He used to say, how do you know where your thoughts are coming from? How do you point out

to someone that their mind could almost be likened to a radio

receiver picking up a frequency. Over the years in the few

times that I went into a very conscious meditation I can say

that I heard a whole barrage of things that were clearly coming

from somewhere else. I sat there listening to musical passages.

I believe this was somewhere between a regular dream and a

lucid dreaming state. The point was that I was listening to

something outside myself. They say in meditation to listen to

the white noise humming in your head. People would always

describe visions and things happening in meditation. I was

always sure I wasn't doing it right because if I didn't fall

asleep, I wasn't hearing anything too unusual. But here was

the example that I was clearly listening to something else as

clearly as a radio. This was not an example of the Foreign

Installation. Don Juan said that the foreign installation was

something that moved into our awareness and stayed there.

It's reason for being there was that our emotional fluctuations

caused a certain type of energy that was actually this beings

food. The way to dispel this entity out of your mind was to

continually practice stilling the inner dialogue. To keep the

mind quiet as much as possible would eventually dissuade this predator from taking a person's energy. The more one meditated and kept the random thought and the compulsive mental rambling to a minimum the quicker one could alleviate themselves of this other awareness that systematically hindered the true potential of human beings. Don Juan said that if the flyer, or foreign installation did leave, the person would initially be very intimidated by their own lack of personal experience. It was said that those were the hardest days of a warrior's life when the flyer left, because a person's natural abilities had been stifled for such a long time under influence of this other entity. He said a person's luminous cocoon could grow back if the flyer ceased to eat the coat of awareness. Then a person's ability and perception would be closer to the actual potential of a human being. Discipline made the coat of awareness no longer palatable to the flyer. By adulthood the person's awareness had been compromised by this energetic entity feeding off its awareness, however by disciplining the mind and lessening the hold of this force, one could regain their original vision and potential as a magical human being. The abilities of humanity are strikingly beyond what is taken for granted as the current norm. Ridding the mind of this predator could bring a person back into their natural birthright of operating as a more magical and illuminated being.

The next time he called, we again spoke about a lot of things. He would change topics rapidly, but I understood how he spoke and followed along. If you're going to know people, have meaningful relationships. People effect the way you think. Disassociate yourself from people you don't want to think about. We are a fragile system. Be careful who you are running into. Warriors don't buy the bullshit. We look at the world and nature, what god created, and see a perfect world that was damaged. The potential is extraordinary, but the ingrates who hate life, are destroying the planet. The Christians think they are going to heaven, as if this can absolve the damage done here, as well as misleading the life of millions who need to attend to the heaven on earth here, and not waiting for an afterlife. There might be no recourse but for the planet to strike back. The planet will retaliate. The Bubonic plague took eighty- five percent of the population in Europe. Parents have kids so they don't grow old alone. The seers I come from are the top of the line, the best. Knowledge is dreaming. He went on and on talking, pausing between sentences where he would change topics.

Make sure you do business with accuracy. We're about business. Stop thinking. This is a major problem for you. You can be a morbid person. I cheer you up. I cheer you up more than anyone. A good sorcerer will walk away with your soul. They'll do it tactfully, so that you think that it's you that has made up your mind. I'm a sorcerer, but I'm a regular guy because I enjoy a regular life. You can do all of your mantra's etc.... but basically it means shutting off the internal dialogue. Don't think! Do! You have been a hippie with false dreams. You've lived well on nothing. That is knowledge, but not a way of life. Be professional. Be a business person. Being a professional is a whole lot better than being a rag in the wind, controlled by whatever force blows by. You're the only thing that matters. Keep your shield up. Get busy with life. Once everything is sorted out and you have organization down, then begin learning. Learning whatever. Learning music. Then enjoyment of learning is about a lifetime. Writing music, it's about a lifetime. You were a borderline transient, switch gears. Don't let the past hang on you. We deny. We deny that we do nothing. Get busy with life. Get a shield so that nothing in life bothers you. It's called impeccability. Focus on money, learning and creativity.

He continued... the planet needs help. Problems need confrontation. The planet will erase the species. The Bible stories made it. The Bible stories were word of mouth. There should be no time wasting. You're up to doing art, music and writing. Art is accessible to the public. Jesus was a warrior. He changed their world. You effect your own life. Write books to better their lives. To leave the place better. Wake up to doing with your time. People are living, but asleep to the spirit. To wake up, everything in daily life must be spit clean organized. The body, and outside of the body, your environment. Follow your heart, and listen to spirit. He continued.... there is the known, the unknown, and the unknowable. You can get to the unknown when you shut the mind.

Jesus shifted people to a different world so that they, and we can use our potential to be at peace with nature and the planet. We are born now at the time of the end. A time of great emergency and catastrophe. There will be a chemical accident of some sort. We are too close to it to see the tremendous destruction taking place as never before. Ignorance has gotten out of control. Forget saving the world. Save yourself through meditation.

I felt very heavy as he spoke to me. My head started to

feel as though it would explode. A great pressure started building on a sensory level in my mind. He sensed this and relaxed the conversation. We slipped into a less intensive conversation, then said good night.

Later in the week he was home and available to speak to me again. He started by telling me that if I am bothered by somebody, they're getting over on me. I'm expanding your awareness, he said. I won the cosmic lottery ticket. The Nagual knew of me before I knew of him. We are radios. Most people are on automatic pilot, and are on instincts. They can smell power. They can smell another persons essence on you.

Sometimes Jonah would repeat things over and over to me. It seemed that when I would come out of heightened awareness, I would forget many things that he had said. He started again after getting a cup of tea. The earth is everything around us. The Indians were in nature, so they got communication with nature, but even with technologies, everything that is around us is considered the earth. This reminded me of the other night when I was playing at this artsy cool theatre and the amp and guitar starting doing these completely non volitional sounds. I felt very lucky because although I suspected a mysterious glitch it seemed of the highest quality and quite exciting to ride along with.

Forget you.... your personality. Tune in to what is around you. Calming the mind takes the garbage out of you. Reverse the disease process. Heal the body and strengthen it against disease. He told me to drink eight glasses of water a day with vitamin c. Being a warrior was entirely about being super healthy. He always said to go to gym, do aerobics, weights, whatever it is.

You can get into a creative state by going to a deeper level of meditation, where you shut off the mind... and the stuff comes to you. You catch it.... write it.... play it...diagram it.... invent it... Art is a rip off business. Rip off and recreate, or model after, so to speak. The Path of heart is down the center of the road. It is where the feeling is. The path of heart is pursuing the unknown. To interpret is a pitfall. To interpret is to be an expert, which is false. People who explain phenomena are lying. It is what it is. Don't interpret it.

Gazing is focusing on something and then dreaming about it. Find a place to orient yourself in your sleep. Wake up inside your life. Some people call it enlightenment. Organization is the key to success. Seeing is personal. Nothing means anything. Don't add meaning to what you see. Observe without interpretation. Be true to yourself. Keep learning and you won't age. You learn to learn. The beauty is that you keep learning. People get locked in. They stop growing.

I tried to write as fast as I could. He was jumping topics so I just wrote down thoughts as he said them. Stay organized. If you're not using something put it away. Have only useful things. Toss out excess baggage. Think about nothing. When you meditate there are things in the air. Everyone is a radio. There is no peace and quiet. Warriors don't pay attention to the self. Ignore yourself. Go to a quiet place and you can pay attention. You meditate by listening to the outside. Inside is the self. The self is the hardest friend to make. Make peace with oneself. Have the right food. What is in your body is what thinks your inner dialogue. If you have peaceful food, you will have peaceful thoughts. Let go. When you die, you do not have to return to the cycle that is birth and death.

Do the job in piece's, the left foot follows the right. Creativity is a piece at a time. Take corners. This applies to everything. There should be no sliding backwards.

Your own natural self is the best possible you. Stay on the funny side of serious. Divine comedy. Comedy cannot be underestimated here. Amongst the much of the seriousness of the conversations we were having, Jonah was extraordinarily

humorous. Jonah sensed that I was getting overloaded with

energy again. We went back to talking about guitar playing

again, and called it a night. I was full of vibrant energy for

hours after the call.

Jonah continued doing what he called ... cleaning my

island. This was endless. The island was a reference for

everything that pertained to your daily life. Everything, that

pertained to your mind and body. He referred to cleaning my

island as... clearing off the accumulations of perceptions and

things in my head from the outside world. An example would

be.... if someone told you, you were ugly, and you went

around trying to deal with your feelings of ugliness. Their

interpretation of you, had gotten on your island. When I talked

to him, I went into a state of heightened awareness. No matter

how awful I felt, I would feel this subtle trance come over me

and pretty soon I felt light, happy, free and actually in a state

of peace and ecstasy. In mentioning the activity that he

performed called cleaning off my island, it brings us to the

subject that eventually we are meant to clean off our own

islands. This is done by a sorcery exercise that is supposed to

energetically remove the debris and hindrances that you have psychologically and psychically picked up in the course of your life. This was a main theme in the Castaneda books as well as clearly delineated in Taisha Abelar's book, called The Sorcerer's Crossing. The goal of removing mental energetic debris is that you will be free, clear, and better able to attain conscious dreaming awareness. This exercise is called the Recapitulation. In Taisha's book, Clara was the sorceress that was her instructor. She said that the recapitulation is the most important technique of self-renewal. Clara said that recapitulation is the act of calling back the energy we have already spent in past actions. "To recapitulate entails recalling all of the people we have met, all the places we have seen, and all of the feelings we have had in our entire lives." From now going back to the beginning of our lives. It is sweeping clean all of these experiences one by one with the sweeping breath. Jonah made it easy. He said .... read her book and do it. We cross referenced the books all the time because it was the same subject and the same party of warriors. Jonah said to follow what she had written about the recapitulation. He said to make a list of everyone you knew and everyone you could think of and to do the breathing exercise to release them from your consciousness. The breathing exercise was described by

Clara, in The Sorcerer's Crossing, in this way…Inhale through the nose as you turn your head to the left. Exhale as you turn your head to the right. Next, turn your head to the left and right in a single movement without breathing. She said that inhaling allows us to pull back energy that we lost, and exhaling permits us to expel foreign undesirable energy that has accumulated in us through interacting with our fellow men. After I wrote this I was looking at some of Taisha's lecture articles on the net. I was relieved to hear how at a later date she described the recapitulation. She said that it didn't matter which way you breathed as much as doing it with regularity and intent. That was a big load off for me because I had limited myself by just thinking of the technique. It will be easier for me now to simply do it and not get overly concerned with technique. Not to say that the technique is without importance, it's just that I had a stumbling block that is erased if I'm not concerned about exact technique. It is an activity well within my means of concentration. I have done it in a mini form in doing the recapitulation of daily events. That is a good quick clean method for at least the aggravations of each given day. There's people that you meet that you can't wait five minutes to recapitulate them out of your brain and spirit.

Dan used to do it all the time in front of me, Jonah said. I thought he had a twitch in his neck or something. He didn't care. He would do it on a bus if he felt like it. Dan being Jonah's benefactor.

My association with Jonah was not a lighthearted matter. Sometimes his treatment of me became outrageously difficult. Had this been a normal male and female interaction I would have considered his manner intolerable. He harassed me to the point of fearing a nervous breakdown. This was undoubtedly a "quest" situation, and his methods were to cure or kill me. It concerned me that I was obsessed with appeasing a person who was less then affectionate towards me. There were times on the road where it was just mortifying. One time I remember distinctly was in a mountain town in Colorado. It's a miracle he didn't pull me through a supermarket by my hair like a caveman. I was scarlet embarrassed to have things look like this in public. I knew that we weren't any kind of couple in a normal way and that he was usually more than right even though his behavior to my mind was real antisocial. An enormous aspect of what he was trying do was break my self-importance. To kill whatever part of me tried to uphold my ego. I was raised, to not exactly be a prima donna, but make sure it's not too far off the mark. A man was supposed to

make you his queen. Likewise, you were supposed to make

him your king. Certainly in public never to mistreat each

other. So like I said, these were some embarrassing moments.

I was also raised to have the man wait on you in social

situations. Now granted, this was not exactly a courtship, but I

was illiterate as to how to be a faithful servant. Had I fully

understood at that time that intense depth of this man's power,

although I kind of sensed it, maybe I would have caught on

quicker. I was trying. I'm reflecting on certain road trip times

where things were immensely beautiful, but supremely trying.

I had no confidence in myself to even do things properly and a

lot of the time I was scared piss less. In some ways it was like

being on the road to hell with a madman. His anger was

terrifying. I was not familiar with angry men. My father had

been the epitome of gentle, and immense in spirit. He got mad

but never in a threatening way. None of my dates or

boyfriends at that point had ever raised their voice to me. In

short, his behavior was shocking. I still can't point my finger

at him as wrong in any way about how he acted about certain

things. The fact is that his intelligence bordered on

omnipotent, and even though the delivery seemed insane, what he said was so true it was sickening. I was a weak spoiled person and had no survival skills. I took note that through all the coddling and protective behavior from men in my life, it had never made me feel good about myself. I never felt more independent in those situations. It didn't make me feel strong. I invariably became weaker and less self- reliant. Like the house pet that lacks the strength of what its counterpart has, to live in the wild. I must reiterate that my father's care and upbringing was flawless. I might have gotten to tough love from outside sources, but my father's wisdom was nevertheless bordering on Holy.

I concluded that what Jonah's function was, was to enable me to become a warrior, and that it wasn't insane or inappropriate for him to play hardball, for the purpose of developing within me, the striving for impeccability.

He said that I could occasionally open one of the Castaneda books, and power would point out an answer to me. I didn't want to be hokey about it, but sometimes some solace could be achieved this way.

I found a very clear and satisfying comment that made his tough behavior reasonable to me. Jonah had shared his personal power with me. I was now up to obtaining my own personal power. The comment in the book, was that... personal power is all that matters in a warrior's world. The way to round up personal power is through impeccability. One does not achieve impeccability by being spoiled and indulged. He was trying to get me "up to snuff," meaning, impeccable. To treat everything that one does as being important, and to do it right. A great example of this was in a rest stop on the road. It was the early morning and there was a lady in the bathroom cleaning the toilets. She was happy and she was meticulous, and she felt obvious pride and good will toward her job. Doing everything with impeccability. Especially with food, exercise and work. There should be no wasted moves, no wasted energy. Live on strategy, instead of flopping around never directing energy toward goals. Focus your energy on doing things instead of wasting energy on unconscious activity. Doing things consciously. To be conscious of what you are doing. It is important to not roll around in life on automatic pilot. It is important not to fall asleep in life. People can fall asleep in routines to the point where they are on a treadmill they got on at some point. This is not uncommon. You have to stay awake. I felt thankful that someone demanded perfection, and didn't stand for complacent mediocrity.

Our conversations were serious, and yet we were comfortable and casual most of the time, if he wasn't haranguing over something. When he initially read what I wrote, he thought I was not in the least bit picking up on how funny we actually were together and that a lot of what he conveyed to me was in the context of a very relaxed and enjoyable type of conversation. At this point in time, he said I was taking so much for granted, that if Shakespeare showed up in blue suede shoes, I wouldn't turn a glance.

Taking care of your self is the first step. Taking care of the thought process is a number one priority. Try not thinking. Slow things down. Don't rush through things. Do things calmly and accurately. To speed things up, slow things down. Doing things thoroughly creates progress. Do things in pieces instead of looking at the whole job at one time. I became exhausted and we said good night.

Life went on in Florida. I had friends, work, it was a pretty regular life. What I tried to absorb from Florida was the vast beauty of the nature. The atmosphere there was completely different from the climates I had lived in. The sky was an array of ever changing vivid hues. The colors were brighter and significantly outstanding. The scent in the air was awesome, raw and natural. The scent of flowers often permeated the atmosphere. The thunderstorms were a marked display of passion. The sun was strong. The sound of insects and frogs at night were a cacophony of evening song. The earth was a part of life there. My life was isolated in many ways. I didn't walk outside and see hundreds of people to grab my attention. I walked out and saw nature. I thanked the Great Spirit continuously for the beautiful sunsets, ocean, and life. One of the things that Jonah told me, that I found hard to fathom, was that people don't see nature. Many people apparently walk on by. Neil Peart, of the rock band Rush, put it succinctly.... "Once I loved the flowers, now I ask the price of the land." People actually don't see that our greatest gift and inheritance is literally showered all around us. It takes nothing to be happy for the good earth around you. People feel disheartened that they can't find the joy in life. It is as simple as the song of a sparrow in the early light of day. If we pay attention, the indescribable beauty of the day will attract and nurture us. It was imperative to be conscious, of the feeling of grass beneath our feet. To be more consistently aware of the earth. He considered the earth, being nature, to be intrinsic to the concept of god. He said that the earth had energy, and that if you were feeling drained, all you would have to do to heal is sit on the ground and relax for a while. To be more consistently aware of the earth around you is to invite a sublime pleasure that is here for all of us. The most fabulous of all beauty gives us energy and well-being. In return we must respect, cherish and love the earth. If everyone had an awareness of the power and sanctity of nature, the polluting and mass destruction would need to find other alternatives. People act as though we are on endless resources here. It is not ok for our rivers, oceans, air, trees and ecological systems to be destroyed by us. It is not our prerogative, to decimate the earth. Everyone is just part of a system. The system has to reroute itself. The human race, with its "dominion over the earth," has been given the god given honor, and position, to "tend natures garden." The earth is a living thing. To strengthen yourself go out into nature. The earth will give you a boost of energy. Jonah and I marveled at the simple beauty of nature, and how it can heal you just by paying attention to your natural surroundings.

I didn't call Jonah for about a week. I never called him unless a certain mood told me to do so. When I did call him he was finishing his dinner. He was interested in talking, so we got into a relaxed conversation. His thoughts started to run together. I jotted them down because I could never remember all that he said. Oftentimes I wouldn't be able to concentrate on anything other then what he was saying at the moment. It was very much like that when I would slip into heightened awareness. I could only retain each actual moment as it was occurring. He began by discussing the guitar, but this applied to learning anything. Don't play anything faster than you can play it accurately. Learning takes place at a slow pace. Play with the metronome. Don't skim over stuff. You'll know what you're supposed to know when you know it. That he mentioned more in accordance to me seeking his knowledge. Inner dialogue is called thinking. We think in words, pictures, and the English language. The difference between a warrior and a man is that a warrior observes his thoughts, and is detached from his thoughts. He does not claim his thoughts as his own. He observes what he is thinking about. To be a warrior is to never come back. I believe he was referring to dying with the totality of your awareness, so that your awareness can stay intact elsewhere. Leaving the physical body, but having the dreaming body so intact, as to have

mastery over going somewhere else in your dreaming body.
Waking up in your dreams was the cornerstone activity of
becoming enlightened, aware, and a man of knowledge. To be
an observer and to not lose your cool. Observe the world, but
don't get caught up in it. He would often say... "I'm outside
the ring that presses upon people." He meant that he observed
the world, but that he didn't go up and down with it. He kept
himself detached from becoming internally affected by what
was going on with people. That's why he said to watch out
who is affecting you. Who is affecting you is being a sorcerer.
Good or bad. He wasn't perfect at it. There were people he
knew that had tried to take advantage and he was pissed. Some
people are good at getting over on people. They are talented,
smart, beautiful, needy, whatever their hook that allows you to
get weak in a situation. It's that way today. I let people hang
me up because I don't want to offend them. He says, the hell
with offending them. You wouldn't be in the position of
offending them if they weren't the ones offending you. How
much of my life is going to be squandered not trying to offend
someone when actually I'm offending my-self. I'm offending
myself by pushing my spirit down to accommodate some other
person. And for the little bargains we make that we think we

need, get over it. Get so self- reliant that you are free of allowing people that injure your spirit to invade your space. If they belonged there you would be comfortable with them being there. I recognize this in myself. Why do I offend myself to be kind to someone.else? Why not be equally as kind to myself. If I was totally happy myself, what I would have to offer to people would just flow naturally instead of some contrived effort on my part. Jonah said that he didn't let his mood get hooked by the activities of men and situations. He observed that world without letting it unduly influence and add stress on him. He said that the Castaneda books describe situations. Your apartment is a reflection of your mind. Be impeccable. Catch things now. Do it now. Clean up your life. No backsliding. Stay in charge and be professional. Clean off your island and be what you are, whatever that is. Logic runs interference on creativity. Be yourself, it's my art. You can hear into the future, as well as see. The body is the spirit. Don't let people get beyond your first base. Don't let people run their games on you, whether they realize they are games or whether they are on auto pilot. Watch the animals. Human beings are animals. The body knows. The body tells you. When you're in the wrong place with the wrong people, the body reacts to tell you everything. Listen with your body. Instincts tell all, like the animals that we are. Jobs kill. Do things on your own terms. There should be less pressure. You will live longer. When you feel something tugging on your stomach, something is making you tense. You can feel thoughts. Your body feels thoughts.

Periodically little unusual occurrences would happen. Jonah told me that a Mexican man from across the street had asked about me. I woke up from a dream and remembered Jonah passing on the greeting. At that moment, the compassionate sensual voice of a Mexican man said hello inside my head. I became alarmed because I had been awake. The voice was closer to a thought. It was spoken into the room, but I heard it in my mind. I also thought it was odd because I had been thinking about what Dan had said, about Don Juan and Genaro, coming into his body. Don Juan and Genaro were sorcerers written about in the Castaneda books. Don Juan was the old Indian that was Carlos's teacher and benefactor, and Genaro was a member of Don Juan's warrior party. He was extremely fluid and talented in his dream body abilities. He demonstrated his abilities for Carlos on numerous occasions. I was fascinated that Dan had said that Genaro was his benefactor. I had wondered what that actually meant, when Dan had said that, Don Juan and Genaro, had come into his body. I couldn't jump to any wild insane conclusions except that a very warm clear voice had resounded in my mind when I was seemingly awake. I told Jonah about it. I told him that out of nowhere, on the level of thought, a voice with a Mexican accent spoke to me. He said that it could have been the voice of the emissary, the voice that Carlos had talked about having heard. He told me not to make more of it then it was. He told me that I didn't have to report back to him like a girl scout. He told me that if I got communications, it was ok to tell him about it, but not to become jarred by anything you see or hear. We are observers. I observe a lot of crazy things here. Things are not as what you have grown up to believe. Now you're getting a taste that things are different. Like that things about aliens. They're trying to get known slowly. I didn't stop him to question that. Just don't interpret, he said. Don't become an expert. You're demonstrating a higher level of expertise by acknowledging that you don't know where this stuff comes from. People get bits and pieces of this stuff, and then they're convinced that they're talking to god and that they know everything. At least Don Juan and the warriors say this is in the unknowable. He seemed concerned that I would become excessively frightened by the experience. I told him that I was not disoriented by the experience but that I had thought it worth mentioning. I actually felt nervous when it happened. I realized that this stuff was bigger than my expectations, and that perhaps I did not have the guts for this path. When I heard the voice, after my alarm, I thought of Don Juan and Gennaro communicating with Dan. I did not have the pompousness to imagine that Don Juan or Gennaro would have any reason to greet me. I thought about the possibility because they were supposed to be on some other level, and this was not a call on the Bell telephone system. Again, Don Juan and Genaro were two of the accomplished sorcerers in the Carlos Castaneda stories. Jonah laughed when I told him that when I heard the voice, I had immediately turned on the light.

Jonah was available later that night. He said... Everything is equal. What you seek is within you. Try to perceive outside you. I took a walk in my benefactor's dreams. You make this professional, or you lose it. This is not a love affair. There are two ballparks to play in. The everyday world, and the dreaming world. That was why I hardly had a mind to even inquire as to what could be possible on other planets. Recapitulate bad feelings and they will fall off your body. Don't be a bottom feeder. Stay away from slime. If I tell you my tales of power, you better learn how to write. Stay out of office gossip. Be professional. Be organized and impeccable. The tenant had the only game worth pursuing. Eternity is one minute after the next, forever. I have a strange knowledge, and I have a normal life. Life was supposed to be very wide open. Over the centuries things that were common knowledge became unknown again. It became too radical to discuss other natural aspects of life. The con artists constructing today's society didn't want to be found out. It threatened them to have the real information lain down that would expose their lack of perception. Seek and you will find. Seek the real stuff, not the fake stuff that appears to everyone in their travels of life. Don't be afraid to be your real self. Trust your real self. Trust your instincts. Talk only as your real self. Be quiet and watch. Don't engage in stupid conversations. You were dead before because you had no job or career. You, messed up, but now you can get on track. I sniffed at his lack of regard for my music. I remembered something I had forgotten to ask Jonah. He had said that dreaming and the emissary were natural parts of the human experience. So why was it, that anytime something of this nature occurred, I would become very frightened? He responded... The world of heaven is within. Seek within the kingdom of heaven. Stop looking outside. You have to go inside yourself to get out of yourself. I thought of a Frank Zappa song. Stalk that guitar, I thought, and the door closed loudly by itself. Dreaming and Stalking. The dream world with its mysteries and stalking your everyday life into a state of impeccability. I'm keeping all of your stuff together. I don't even know if it's good to be laying all of this stuff on you. He said he had to go and we hung up.

He told me that it was extremely important for me to get into my body. I called him a few nights later. He started talking about what the prerequisites for a warrior were. He said that you had to be intelligent, responsible, financially stable, physically fit and eating clean like a warrior. You had to be involved in learning something. It doesn't matter what you look like. It's what is inside you. It's who you are. You are a warehouse of knowledge. I have stored things inside you. Millions of people would be interested to know these things. I don't think you realize that. I know what's going on here, you don't. People feel comfortable with me because I'm in control.

You want me to play in your ballpark because men have always played in your court. I wouldn't put myself in the hands of someone whose life is out of control. I'm in control. That is why you feel safe around me. You received unspeakable gifts that you didn't earn. Now work. You can fake your way through college, but not with me. Learn the writing machine and earn the gifts you've been given. You're a secretary to me.

I'm messing with you on purpose, because you are an egomaniac. You're like a little kid that comes to my door muddy. I have to dust you off at the door. Love is not being taken care of. Your parents love you. They took care of you. When you grow up you don't need a man to take care of you. You don't need to be sick to get love. You don't need to be a damsel in distress. When you are an adult you can clean yourself off. You are an obsessive person, he said to me. Realize it's your thoughts. Your thoughts are messing with you. When I met you, you were worshipping rock stars. Worship yourself. Work harder. Let's see what you're made of? I felt positive and we got off the phone.

I felt I did Dreaming today, but I'm not one hundred percent sure. Towards the end I was very aware of bodily sensations and I was telling myself to gently glide back into my body. I thought I was at the edge of some sierra's standing right at the edge of a desert. I looked onto it and it was very sunny. I saw desert plants and a small fox or coyote. Then I felt myself flying through a tunnel. I felt the breeze over my body. That's when I told myself that I was doing dreaming and that I should go back to my body. I felt an itching ticklish sensation in my head, as I thought that, I thought that I must be reentering my body. I opened my eyes and was in my room again. My body had an almost painfully weak feeling to it.

11   NOT ABSORBING NEGATIVITY AND BEING

      YOUR OWN BEST FRIEND

My life changed all the time, but I maintained

association with Jonah. Every conversation had me glued to

my seat with interest. Jonah told me to read and chant the

Desiderata. Get it into your mind. It was a writing found many

years ago by an unknown author. He felt this one writing

covered a lot of bases. Just understanding this could help one

immensely. It read...Go Placidly amid the noise and the haste,

and remember what peace there may be in silence. As far as

possible without surrender, be on good terms with all persons.

Speak your truth quietly and clearly, and listen to others even

the dull and ignorant, they too have their story. Avoid loud

and aggressive persons, they are vexatious to the spirit. If you

compare yourself to others you may become vain and bitter,

for always there will be greater and lesser persons then

yourself. Enjoy your achievements as well as your plans. Keep interested in your own career, however humble, it is a real possession in the changing fortunes of time. Exercise caution in your business affairs, for the world is full of trickery. But let this not blind you to what virtue there is, many persons strive for high ideals, and everywhere life is full of heroism. Be your- self, especially do not feign affection, neither be cynical about love, for in the face of all aridity and disenchantment it is as perennial as the grass. Take kindly the counsel of years, gracefully surrendering the things of youth. Nurture strength of spirit to shield you in sudden misfortune, but do not stress yourself with imaginings. Many fears are born of fatigue and loneliness. Beyond a wholesome discipline, be gentle with yourself. You are a child of the universe, no less than the trees and the stars, you have a right to be here. And whether or not it is clear to you, no doubt the universe is unfolding as it should. Therefore, be at peace with God, whatever you conceive him to be. And whatever your labors and aspirations, in the noisy confusion of life keep peace with your soul. With all its sham, drudgery and broken dreams, it is still a beautiful world. Be cheerful. Strive to be happy." Jonah had me put the Desiderata on a large paper and laminate it. Chant it and get it into your mind. When you are

alone, shut off the self. The secret is in the silence. There is no

meaning in what comes up in the mind. Look for your hands

in your dreams. There is the known, the unknown, and the

unknowable. You can get to the unknown. Be quiet. Shut the

mind. Concentrate on not thinking. Stop talking to idiots about

nonsense. Be organized. Follow only a path with heart. Follow

your heart. We got off the phone. I went to the beach with my

mother and had dinner. I came back and called Jonah around

ten o'clock. He lit up a cigarette, put down his guitar and got

on a roll. Religion is all the same wearing different uniforms.

The Tonal's get together and agree. They worship a God they

created. The Tonal was a term that describes the everyday

normal state of awareness. They referred to the Nagual as the

dream body consciousness side of man, while his Tonal side

was his waking everyday awareness. It's limerick sorcery,

language sorcery. He referred to a book about women

sorceresses. They said that women generally have too many

worms in them. That meant to have too much, or too many

people's semen in you, which is the essence of someone on

you. Too many people getting their essence on you, they felt

would cause a draining effect on your energy. You are picking

up pieces of their karmic essence when you sleep with them.
Life is a series of picking up experiences and also the habits of
others. Try to stay around people you find admirable, or at
least worthy of picking up habits from. Birds of a feather flock
together. Whomever you spend a lot of time with is going to
have some sort of influence. You are going to hear them in
your head if you are around them long enough. Go with your
instincts. Develop instincts. A wanting and desperate person
gets sucked into things. They want things and company, and
they allow negative and possibly dangerous people to
influence them. It's like having a devil and an angel on your
shoulder at all times. Listen to the spirit. There's the big voice
and the little voice. The big voice is the outside persuasion.
The little voice is the spirit inside you. It only talks once so
listen for it. You pity people, you empathize with them. You
put yourself in their shoes. That's why you are always so nice.
Well, the hell with that. That's not the way the world is. They
don't respect nice. They don't want business or anything from
the nice guy. Their bullshit runs them, their mental games.
Don't let them run their act on you. I don't let you run your
lies and falseness on me. Your garbage runs you too. You
have to stay on it to keep your mental garbage from you too.

Stop being locked into your own mental garbage. Speak up for yourself! Don't take garbage from people. Be fair and professional, but if you don't want to be licking boots, then cut out that lousy low self-esteem behavior. This needed to be pointed out to you, that you go around like Mr. Nice guy. People don't respect overly nice or bootlicking people. You keep putting yourself in other people's places. Don't do this, it's not real. If they look weird, they are weird. Stay away from weirdo's. You have no business talking to creeps. Protect yourself. You have no obligation to start talking to someone just because they run up to you somewhere and start talking. Tell me if you think your right about something. It sickens me to have you kissing my ass. Don't allow browbeating. You don't have to take garbage if you choose not to. It's in how you run your life. People will do that if you let them. Stop this knee jerk niceness. Niceness sucks. It means you have a sign on you that is saying... I'm easy, take advantage of me. They see you coming.

I am a mirror. When I reflect your garbage and your real self, back to you, you catch a glimpse of yourself. That's why you can't get enough of me. I tell you the truth with no shields, and you can't get enough of seeing the real you in the

mirror. You understand these things as concepts. That is not
enough. You have to reprogram the old habits and put the new
ones to use. No accepting licking boots and browbeating. Put
this to use. Your mother mentally browbeat you too much and
your father spoiled you. You came out a babbling idiot. You
act as if they'll reject you, but if you're nice enough, you'll
win out. Your mother rejected whatever you said, but being
nice was understood and accepted by your dad. Take no
garbage, take no prisoners, and kick ass. "Be your own best
friend." Be powerful to yourself. When idiots run their
garbage on you, for example when men try to intimidate, treat
them like the poopy butt little children they are. These are
little kids acting smart. Acting up running their game. Do not
take their garbage. You are in control. I felt empowered. We
said good night. I was exhausted, but exhilarated by his energy
and conversation.

A week or so later I called Jonah again. He got onto a
similar track as the week before. Be yourself he said. Speak up
for yourself. Don't act polite, be yourself. Be true to your
spirit, not by being miss nice. Listen to your spirit. You better
be on par with me, or it's over. There should be no more
disciple behavior. Be a warrior now. If you can't act like a

warrior, you are gone, he threatened. Don't be the garbage inside you. You're on warrior time now. Don't pay attention or claim your thoughts. When you're annoyed at someone they're thinking about you. Act up. Act up in the business world. You know it's acting, but act business. You shouldn't be giving things away. It's better to be firm and correct with people. When the Nagual thinks you are messing up, he'll sic the environment on you. He went on in sentences that didn't necessarily connect, but I was used to his chain of thoughts changing rapidly.

This is the last conversation of this kind. I'm sick of cleaning off your island. Defend yourself. Don't let people come at you with their garbage. See through the human race in their costumes. No hand-outs. Save yourself. The earth is going to shake its bones. Keep out of its way. Don't get sucked into other people's schemes. If you still worry what other people think of you, you're an idiot. Beauty comes from the soul, not from the flesh. You carry around a mirror of what you see yourself as. You've had some of the best conversations of all times. Speak up for yourself. Recapitulate. Stand up and be counted or get out of here. No more being meek and timid. Speak your mind. Be your own best friend.

Be straight forward. No more being needy. Be your own best friend, let the stuff fly. Be open-mouthed.

I called up Jonah later that night. I realized the main problem I had was self -hatred. He said... be aware of hating yourself, so that you can kill that feeling. That feeling that drives you to showing pain all the time. Your body knows that this is the real deal when I talk to you. I'm inside rewiring your brain. Your study habits must be put into gear. Nothing is more important than anything else. Work and art and hygiene are all important. You choose to be a warrior or it's over. You clean up your act or it is over. Get busy. The gig is to do all of the knowledge, not just to know it. Clean everything.

People are in a sleep state, because they are unaware that they are listening to the internal dialogue. We are looking to master the art form of being detached with ease. Detached from the inner dialogue. Not thinking. Thinking is tiring. It stresses the body. Not being pulled by the inner dialogue is being awake. Awake to the fact that there is an inner dialogue pulling us around. People are asleep in their inner dialogue. Moods are just the inner dialogue getting free rein and going off. Bad moods could be unused energy building inside you, yourself wanting to be independent. You are an artist. You should have learned from the beginning. People are unaware, asleep to the forces that are working on them. Food, earth and people all influence you. These things contribute to the inner dialogue. We live in a state of self-realization. No one knows what is. Humans, or animals. Humans create. Does that seem like we're smart? We should learn from the animals. They survived. We're self-realized. We live with the awareness of being and end. Taking care of the planet is the humans lifework. Taking care of the living planet. The Indians were right. They lived here for thousands of years without effecting it in the least bit. This here is not successful. You make slaves, and you have a problem with Black society. Karma connects. Slaughter Indians, and things will go wrong. There is deep karmic trouble. They need a savior. Ignorance is societies biggest enemy. They need a catalyst, to reach their minds and shake them up. Shake them up to the priority of saving the land and waters. This is an emergency. Ignorance cannot prevail. Wise men are learning that our place is to have dominion over the earth. Tend this garden. Jonah changed his conversational posture and I could tell that he had to go soon. He was going out to the driving range. He was devout in his meditation and athletics. My mind was extremely numb from the intensity of his conversation. I relaxed and said good night.

12   ROAD TRIP #1

It had been two years since I had seen Jonah. He was coming back east to visit family. He was driving from Los Angeles. He asked me if I wanted to travel back with him from the Ohio area to LA. He made it sound really intriguing to go into the wilderness with an Indian sorcerer. By this time, though I couldn't say for sure what was happening, I would have to admit, there was tangibly something happening. To feel the kind of feelings, I would get just talking on the phone to him, was clearly not normal. And to say that I was just being gullible, would not have sufficiently described these mood alterations either.

I left West Palm Beach at four p.m. I slept all the way to Atlanta. I had four hours to wait for my next flight. I was exhausted from working the night before. The flight from

Atlanta to Louisville was short and uneventful. I got off the plane and didn't see Jonah. I went to freshen up in the restroom. When I came out I was starting to head toward baggage, when I heard my name called. I turned around and there was Jonah. I walked toward him feeling fascinated to actually see his face. He looked tired but good. He seemed shorter then I had remembered. But he looked really good. He said that I looked alright. I had felt insecure that my appearance would not have indicated a dedication toward his information about healthy food. My lifestyle in Florida was distinctly slower and softer then in Hollywood. I had begun to long for New York to pick up the pace and put the energy back in my body.

We got into the car in Kentucky and got on the road. I was very excited to be with him. He gave me an orange. My innate anxiety about seeing him quickly filtered down into a strange sublime peace. We were soon driving in Indiana. The air was clean and cool. It was a marvelous contrast to the summer in Florida. We got involved in talking and forgot to go to a motel. We drove another hour and a half. We stopped at a rest stop somewhere deep in the country. We bought some water and crackers. The area had a very remote feeling to it.

We found a motel nearby. It had a long bench outside and reminded me of a ranch. I again was exhausted, nervous and uptight about being there with him. I hadn't slept at all the night before. I felt ashamed of my body and out of sorts from living away from a city for so long. I hadn't been around the public for so long. I felt alienated and out of touch with the world. My stomach on this occasion was feeling extremely painful from stress. He massaged my stomach until the pain left. I couldn't believe how much better I felt. Before we had gone to the motel we had found an open all night Walmart. This was a fiasco. Walking around with Jonah felt like the funniest thing in the world. Just the sight of him alone, and the feeling of being with him, put me into a twilight zone of hysterics. I can't recall what could have been so funny in Walmart, but we were just hysterical in there. He bought me some white clothes for the desert. I was feeling feminine toward him, so I liked the idea of him buying me a personal item.

The next day at breakfast he said loudly.... this chick doesn't have anything on the ball, referring to the waitress. I felt embarrassed that she had heard that. I thought that he was pointing out that people often didn't pay attention or care about what they're doing. Somehow after that the waitress seemed to really like him. It was as if he had woken her up to the fact that she was asleep. She seemed enamored by him.

The first night in Kansas we stopped at a deserted rest area along the highway. The Sun was brilliant red. The sunset was amazing. Jonah was getting me to relinquish my black city clothes to be more dressed for summer. He went to the water pump and started pumping. He told me to get white shorts and a tee shirt out of my suitcase. I held the pump while he bathed himself. I felt like he was somehow putting me in a strange type of trance. The dusk was calm and angelic. His movements were steady and slow. Everything had to be done to perfection. He made it clear that he was in control and that I had better subdue my adroit arrogance that I had used with him, when he first started bossing me around. I was not in the habit of letting men talk to me in a domineering fashion. However, one would have to admit, that even though we shared passionate intimacy, this did not remotely resemble any kind of normal male/female association. Around the bathing pump I relaxed my indignation at having been talked to so condescendingly. While we were at the car, dealing with the clothes, I saw a woman pass by. I thought that very odd

because there were no cars. It was impossible for someone to
be there without a car. I mentioned it to Jonah. Then a group
of young party types of people showed up. Jonah led me up a
path through the woods. It led up a hill. There was a picnic
table under a gazebo. There was a circular walkway diagonal
to the gazebo. He told me to take off all my clothes and wash.
I initially felt shy being naked outside. There was a certain
thrill that cops could come any moment and catch me in the
wild. I wanted to dance around the walkway, but the feeling
was not strong enough for me to actually start doing it. A
magical feeling fell around me. It was a serene twilight on a
deserted highway somewhere in Middle America, and it was
beautiful. I put on Jonah's white shorts, a white tee shirt, white
high top sneakers and socks. It was the first time I had worn
summer clothes in a while. The change of clothes and the bath,
had put me in a more feminine state of mind. However, things
were still far from amorous between Jonah and I. Despite the
buoyancy of our phone calls throughout the year, we had come
close to a nail scratching brawl in subsequent days. I had
greeted him in the same spirit I would treat any of the men that
I knew. Basically that I was a total equal, and that I had better
be treated as an equal, or preferably as better. I was extremely

unaccustomed to being shoved around in a subservient manner. I was trying to hold myself in check and not go off on Jonah. He completely pulled out the stops. He dragged me around in public as if I was his cave woman. I was mortified. After the bath I started to mellow out. I kind of understood that to be a warrior, this was some odd charade of psychological boot camp. After a time, I realized he was attempting to get me to be more attentive to detail, and structured behavior. I was very sloppy and inattentive in my general actions. I was a cross between a person with attention deficit disorder, caffeine addiction and out of control hypoglycemia. Following instructions became an exercise in exercising perfection. He was really insistent about doing things right. No half stepping, gliding over, or skimming. Later that night we pulled over to a rest stop. It was the first night that we were going to sleep in the car. I was aghast that we weren't going to a motel. He had promised me on the phone that we would have beds and showers. I couldn't believe that he wanted to start sleeping in the car so soon. I made a few inferences to the Hilton thinking he would somehow get the hint. He forebodingly set up what I considered an appalling arrangement to spend the night. Every now and then he barked out an order. I couldn't believe I was going to spend the night locked in a Mazda with such an ill spirited, cantankerous man. He was the most difficult man to get along with. Feminine wiles were definitely out of the question. He settled himself down on the better piece of foam and was soon asleep. Meanwhile on a skimpy piece of foam I tried to lie down. A metal bar went right under my back. It distinctly affected the part of my back that tended to go out. After an hour of this I started to go crazy. I twitched about trying to go to sleep. I held my bladder for about an hour before I got the nerve to creep out of the car. It was freezing and it seemed like a slightly rough crowd at the rest stop. When I got back he had locked me out and stolen the hat that I was sleeping with. I had had, the Madison Ave sombrero over my face so that I wouldn't wake up baked into a reptile. When I got back into the car I refused to go back to the metal bar that had been breaking my back. I crawled into the front seat behind the steering wheel. My back was ok, but my legs were like a pretzel. I hovered in this state of semi solace for two hours. When I woke up Jonah was willing to relinquish his golden mattress for about an hour. Meanwhile they repaired the car next to us. They banged and clanked for upwards of an hour, then their kid raged for whatever was left of my morning nap. He finally drove out of there with me stone cold out under my black sleep mask. We crossed the Missouri line before stopping for breakfast. There was a huge overhang under which we parked. I felt happy solace at this. I was feeling unusually uncomfortable with the sun. I have since devised ways for me to be content with a few barrier accessories, but I hadn't become that creative yet. My hair had transformed into a viciously intense frizz knot. I discovered that by soaking it down in the rest stop bathroom I could get it to appear somewhat normal. It was long and wildly unmanageable. I mention this because it was just one more thing contributing to my already out of proportion sense of anxiety. I tried to relax and settle into breakfast. Jonah began to speak in a tone that was comforting and informative. It was a tone of voice that he would take up when he was going to share information. It was a relief because he would stop being the cruel disciplining man that would come out on so many other occasions. One thing that I just was not aware of at the time was that he was trying to break my sense of self-importance. I could understand the value in doing that, but I didn't realize that that was what he was doing. I was unbalanced anyway, teetering between arrogant self- assertion and fearful self- hatred. And then here's this guy, whom is actually a lover, just shredding whatever self -esteem I was trying to find. And yet I knew he was far too intelligent to be doing this arbitrarily. I knew that no matter how furious and terrifying he was, that it was one hundred percent because he cared. In some ways, although he did care, he was doing it just to be an impeccable warrior. If making me intelligent or without self- importance, was what he was doing, he wasn't going to tip toe around it. Niceness elicited abuse from me. I wasn't a quick learner from coddling. I understood being brought up to only allow a certain standard of behavior from others. That was like you get what you accept in life. Maybe that's why I have trouble eliciting respect sometimes because I have this knee jerk niceness as Jonah called it, that has nothing to do with the whirlwind of opinions I have swimming in my head. He says let it hang out. Be who the hell you are. Live as yourself, not a robot of what societies expectations are. New York seemed a little more adhering to that idea. Say it like it is.

If there's stuff on your island, you can't get off onto the next island. You get off your island to go into the next world.

There is a next world here. I know that. Those Indians came

back here to get their bodies from this earth. I assumed he was

talking about Don Juan and Genaro from the Castaneda books.

"I'll see you in the next world and don't be late." He made an

inference to a Jimi Hendrix song. Get busy. The hardest part

of work is sitting down. Once you sit down, it's automatic. I

give you my energy. I can't afford to do that anymore. I will

instinctively know when you are not working. You have three

friends in this world. Three good friends. You have earned

that. They are the types of friends that you would never go to,

unless it was something entirely out of the question, for you to

figure out. The Nagual said that he was genuinely sorry that he

didn't have an opportunity to talk to you. He wanted me to

pass that along. It's time for you to figure out what you want

to do with your life. You're not an average person. You have a

strong connective link to the spirit or else these conversations

would not be happening. You recognize the earth, and the

earth recognizes you. I saw when you were sitting on the

couch once that you could be a good guitar player. You never

had a good teacher and you had this learning disability. I told

him I was frustrated with my body. He freaked out and said

that I was one of those neurotic people looking for something to stress about. Forget about the self. You are obsessed with the self. Being invisible is being at the other end of the spectrum of being a look at me. Writing is your best therapy. Writing is magic. It truly is magic. If it's who you know, you're in the know. The only way you are going to figure out any of this is by doing it. If you do things to enhance awareness, and the earth, good things will come to you. If you exercise, everything will fall into place. He got the check for breakfast. I was lucky enough to catch something in a magazine that really surprised me. It was that for abdominal work, it was best to do cardio. I was doing at one time a thousand crunches a day. Jonah said I was starting to look like a foot ball player. It was not what I was aiming at. This was exciting, because as soon as I did the eliptical machine my stomach started toning properly. All of those sit ups were for naught compared to a little cardio.

We got back on the road and enjoyed the serenity and beauty of the land as we drove, for hours. We cruised for hours down the long gorgeous highway. It was a constant array of subtle and more dramatic scenery. Once the sun tapered its intensity, I was happier and more at peace then I had ever been. Jonah lit a cigarette and began to speak. People are like an insect on the earths back, annoying it. The earth

will have the last word. It will dispose of the problem, the

people, in some way. Maybe the ebola virus, or maybe some

loose bacteria. The earth is a living intelligent being. If we are

having this conversation and all the technology around us is

here, we are the caretakers of the earth's intelligence.

Religious groups like to make religion out of seers. Seers were

talking about human awareness potential, not religion. All the

"tonals" agree on everything. When you should die, when you

should do this, do that. The earth favors creativity. I'm trying

to toughen you up. Ruthlessness is impeccability. Keep the

assholes off your island. See the Shining. They're all con

artists in one way, until they prove themselves honest.

Friendship takes a long time to cultivate.

"Your one of the best friends that I have ever had."

Thank you, I said. I'm telling you this because I saw a person

with a little potential that might not have been able to use it. I

cleaned you out, to use your potential better. Dan cleaned me

out too. It looks like I manipulate you, but it's really the other

end of the spectrum. I'm telling you to wipe your own ass. I'm

not your guru. A Finnish guy once took English lyrics and

made songs and sung them without knowing English. Music is

the same way. Copy and listen, listen and copy.

Mankind has one priority. Cleaning up the earth. We all have our personal tribulations to go through. I should be a man with means, but it's my lot to work through poverty even with the vast knowledge I contain. Reactionaries will stalk literature that disagrees with their viewpoint. Don't challenge their religion. Don't upset their minds. You're being shown lots of geeks. Get a life. Get something to do. You're judged by the company you keep. Life offers you a choice. Your bait. You're a minnow if your friends choose you. You choose whom to associate with. Even if someone likes you. You have things to do. If you're any bodies friend, you're no bodies friend, and everybody knows that. Even the nobodies. Tell people to back off. Marie was an omen for you. She never cleaned up and got her head free because of her surrounding garbage. Marie was a woman in our building in Hollywood.

The first thing that you do when you write something is put a date on it. There are two forms of life. The mundane and the artist. The warrior path is the path of heart. The warrior life is the life of an artist. The path of heart is the path of creativity. The mundane hate the artists because they are free. Each culture has music. That is the universal language that speaks to the soul of all people. Music is the first art form. The mundane people blow off artists, but they listen to them. The life of a starving artist sucks, so you have to be a self-sufficient artist. Writing is the last of the art forms to evolve. Music, then painting, then writing. Writing only started five hundred years ago or so. The education systems are designed for the autocrat. People on automatic. Time goes by, but they never become what their heart desires. They could spend their whole life trying to win their mothers approval. It's subtle, but it's real. You could spend your whole life doing something that you want to. People are asleep.

We were crossing the Great Plains. Where we were, millions of buffalo used to roam, he said. Like seeks like. Display success and attract success. Always leave them hanging when writing. You can write any kind of book that you want. You could write a book as a diary. Your mortal gap is open. People can disturb your tentacles. If you let them you're a chump. The mortal gap was something he referred to as being in the umbilical region. It was the base of your will and intent. He described the will as the tentacles that came out of the stomach area and could attach themselves to something. These ideas were only things I could conceptualize at this point. I will say that he once said that if someone was upsetting you, you would feel it as a pain in your stomach. That happened yesterday when someone was arguing with me, and I had to take an Advil before I could go out. My stomach was screaming.

Put people in their place. If you feel a tugging at your stomach when you're talking to someone, you're letting them get over on you. I'm not intimidated by anybody and I'm not afraid of anyone. I know what power is. You let assholes intimidate you. Your mortal gap is open. It's been open for years. Recapitulate. Do the head rolls. Get everything off your island. You take everything at the drop of a hat. You're afraid to hurt someone. You're judged by the company you keep.

We rolled into a truck stop. He began giving me directions. It was understood that taking directions impeccably was in order for an apprentice. As much as my ego hated being ordered around, I tried to remain alert and adaptable to his requests. I wholeheartedly felt his insights to be extremely valuable and therefore felt more compliant to his demeanor. I did cringe inside when he bossed me in public. I felt very embarrassed. He loved to raise raucous scenes whenever he felt like it. Again the magnitude of the magnificent experiences, warranted allowing his bizarre displays of public machismo.

Several hours later we stopped in a quaint country restaurant. That particular air of magic at sunset descended around us in a cloud of exhilarating exhaustion. A feeling of peace fell over us. The land looked calm and beautiful. The restaurant was pleasantly not overcrowded. We ate in a relaxed silence. He rarely allowed conversation while we ate. He liked to pay full attention to eating, and doing so in a meditative manner. He lit a cigarette and relaxed his back. He began talking about acting. Everything is acting, he said. You can be any character that you like. You can play anything. Writing should be in a simple clear manner. You are either in a groove or in a rut. Your whole day should be scheduled for maximum production. Wasting time is laziness and stupidity. Jonah reminded me of some of the things that Dan had been saying, the last time we had all met. He had said that he knew what the tenant knew. "I am the tenant." I believe I even heard him say. This was pervasively shocking when he had made such a comment. The tenant was a character that I initially read about in the Carlos Castaneda stories. It was said that he or she had retained consciousness for two thousand years.

They had retained life by somehow borrowing energy from each Nagual of the line. When Dan was commenting on this, my body was in extreme heightened awareness. It was a sensation that seemed similar to a form of shock. He had said.... Death is a big black thing. When I die I will walk into the gateway to eternity. The gateway to eternity opens at various times. This thing goes on forever. Opinions of things don't matter, because they are not your experience. Make things clear and simple when you write. It should not sound preachy. Thinking is not as good as direct experience. When you are acting, never play yourself. He continued on randomly. Liars have to keep moving. Watch people who flatter you. No free hand-outs. I'm not into power over women. Once men look at women as people the mystery is over. People become people. Love sucks. Look at housewives. They look overworked. They appreciate their men going to strip clubs so they'll come home and have sex with them. That was some of what I remembered Dan talking about the last time I had seen him. Every conversation with him had been riveting if he was in the mood to talk.

We finished dinner and drove a few more hours before going to a rest stop. We set up our car for the night and went to sleep. I was more adjusted to the car being a camper by this time.

We rode out in the morning. It was a beautiful temperate day. We were heading towards Colorado, one of the high points in the trip. After breakfast we got into a discussion about some things to do to creates a warrior's body. Jonah said, that to meditate you had to relax. Relax the throat, then the base of the tongue. Relax also the third eye, the top of the head, the solar plexus and the groin. When you shut the inner dialogue, you open to awareness. He jumped from subject to subject as was his usual form. Jealousy, is a form of ownership. Trying to possess another's body. What's love? It's a four letter word. Love without attachment means there's room for real love. The first priority for anybody is their body. You should have aerobic activity daily. You must drink eight glasses of water a day. In meditation, relax throat, listen for outside sounds, and focus on the third eye. Wear cool colors to stay healthy and cool in the warm weather. Eat fruit. Don't chase food with water. Limit coffee to three diluted cups daily. Baggy clothes will give you energy. No wearing tight jeans all the time. For meditation, concentrate on the throat, which is the inner dialogue. Lie in dreaming position (feet propped up), or in a half lotus. Prop small of back up and fold hands in lap. Light incense and candles. You can pray. You can pray to the holy spirit. Pray for peace for yourself, for things. When you are a doer you will be able to realize and actualize things. No being overboard in anything. Not in writing or in work. When you're tired, lie down. Get in tune with the body.

You're employer is not your boss. I am my boss. You... are my employer. I am always my boss. Business is business. There's a line. People will always be encroaching on you. Be yourself. Clean up meticulously. Be neat like a surgeon. Nurture strength, spirit and body. I have met seers from two thousand years ago. Stay out of the hokey stuff. Stay out of left side awareness. Get busy with life. Loose clothing will give you energy.

The road stretched out before us. The land on each side of the highway became more expansive and fascinating. Jonah continued talking... Let go. Let go with the writing, with everything. Stay outside the circle that presses upon people. If you haven't noticed, this is a comedy. I'm glad he reminded me to let go with the writing. I was having a problem with this. I kept having the urge to try and make this very nice and logical. And the truth was that much of this did not fall into the mindset of what I had been previously conditioned to accept as rational. So... I kept trying to write things in a simple and coherent way so that people would understand that everything was nice and normal and that I wasn't a gullible or maniacal person. This went on for a while. So long as to say that I am now in a different stage of life and think differently about what needs to be written. I used to use the joke in my head about a David Lynch movie. I saw a movie called Eraser head. I found it mentally and emotionally disorienting. I liked it, but when I walked out of the dorm room in which it had been shown I felt slightly out of my mind. I said to myself that they should have left some bread crumbs, meaning a path to get back to your sanity. This is how I wanted to be sure that I was writing. Things were happening to me that were unusual to what had been usual to me before. At one time it meant a lot to me to be considered sane. I feel less troubled by that need now. I think it's important to just write the truth and not to censor myself. If something is funny or crazy, that is how it should be put down. I'm not doing this to look or be any certain way. It's beyond that stage in my life. Now the only thing important is to tell it like it is. There isn't any value in anything less than that. A lot of what Jonah thought of my writing was that it didn't sound like us. The real stuff is the funny stuff anyway. So, unapologetically I go forward in digging toward the art of truth. So again, I thank him for giving me the permission to just be myself.

This is a comedy he said. When we've been in the desert before, the desert was laughing. Everything that was alive was roaring with laughter. Walk this whole road like a comedy. Do work, but don't take shit. Stop trying to control the writing of a book. Start with your trip across America with Swami Jonah. You're hooked on your guru's body. You distract me. I love you in my own weird way. You're not the kind of woman I fall in love with. You think it all has to do with looks. We get along tremendously. We're buddies. Buddies are better than lovers. Love sucks. Fast. Fasting will make you too tired to think. It will show you how much energy it takes to keep the self-talking. You'll only have energy for the real you. Not the inner dialogue which we call the self. Listen to your body. If it says rest, then rest. That's not what you've been told your whole life. We stay outside the circle that presses upon people. We don't abide by preconditioned beliefs. Don't worry about copying Carlos. He didn't make up this stuff. Don't let people stretch your luminosity. Even the people that love you. Let them know that there's a line. Don't worry what people will think when they read this story. Enjoy. Hang out and enjoy. Laugh. This is about being a very happy person. Carlos never saw people so happy. He thought it was strange. Other people will be happy right along with you. Don't worry, and be happy. No concerns, no thoughts. Get in good shape. Eat good food. That will close the mortal gap. Seeing is a personal thing. Acting is the first step out of the quagmire. Get involved in some theatrical stuff. You can be whoever you want to be, whenever you want to be. Let the stuff fly. You can play with this stuff.

You can master and develop intent. Ask and you will be given. The day grew warmer. We traveled in silence for a few hours. Our energy was just enough to quietly drive and observe the scenery. I wanted to jot down some things about how to stay in touch with power and this path, for when things got back to normal. That would constantly happen. Nearly all of the time that I was in Jonah's presence or on the phone with him, I would fall into a state of heightened awareness. That was by far one of the most outstanding features of our association. First of all, to stay in touch with power was to get into great physical shape. You are always looking for energy and power outside of you, such as through music, people, art..... but your power comes from inside you. The kingdom of heaven is inside you. You have to get inside your body. You have to bring your awareness back inside your body. To do anything on this path, the first step is extreme good fitness and health. You should only eat healthy food. Then, there should be a full recreation of the body. Aerobics and weights are good. You have to burn hard. A little, getting by, having an ok body for someone your age, is not acceptable. You must make a warrior body. That is the only state of being that will withstand the world of power. So.... eight glasses of water a day, little fats, a lot of vegetarian food and workouts. He also told me no makeup. Don't mess with yourself. Stop picking on yourself. Let the body heal and do itself naturally. Let the body alone. Let it breathe. The more cosmetic fuss, the worse the result.

We stopped by the side of the road. The traffic was light. The sun was setting. There was a magical peace in the air. It was as though the real thrill of life existed for the first time. The whir of crickets, the gentle wind, the scent of life, in its strongest moment. These were the points in time that being with Jonah meant the most. The beauty of the earth would be there without him, but he brought something extra to the picture. Power would follow him. When I was with him in the wilderness, the world would brighten around us. A feeling of ecstasy would come from the magnificence around us. Each sunset was a medallion of honor of the enchanting earth. Nothing could be more precious to me then how it is, to behold the passion of the earths display. Respect the earth. Treat it with the love and dignity that you would accord your parents. If everyone was conscious to respecting the earth, the planet could heal itself and its creatures. It's as simple as... it is the job of mankind to tend this garden. The earth is all we have. Without clean air, water, trees and natural resources, nothing means anything. Presidents, technology, industry and money, cannot exist in an environment that does not support life. The earth is what is supporting our life. Destroy the air, water, and forests, and nothing else matters. All I knew was that the earth was vibrant, magical and alive. Jonah pointed out that this was a WAKE UP CALL! This is for the corporate systems that are systematically destroying the earth. My eloquence may be limited, but this I about making people aware that this is a worldwide emergency. The major focus has been on terrorism, and understandably so. Eco terrorism could wipe us all out also, and everyone needs to lobby and devise ways to use alternate sources that do not harm the ecosystem. They have to figure out another way. May the people in power be given the heart and knowledge to address this in whatever way they can. Otherwise, the earth will wash us off of it, like the menacing parasites we have b

13   COLORADO

The green foothills rolled by on either side of the highway. The scent of nature was strong and virile. One could not help but be enlivened by passing through this kind of place. I felt more alive there then almost anywhere I had been before. The other place of such extreme beauty that I saw, was Switzerland. The people were robust and energetic. There was a sense of harmony between the people and their environment. I felt strong and healthy just being there. There were beautiful natural wood houses sprinkled along the road. There were ski communities and mountain towns of various sizes.

We were climbing higher into the Rocky Mountains. We stopped at a supermarket to get film and sandwich food for dinner. We also got soymilk, avocados and tomatoes. We found a lookout point that was also a truck stop, in the mountains. It was freezing cold at that elevation. It was a

bizarre contrast to all the hot temperatures that we had

recently been through. I was feeling slightly out of my mind

from all the pressures Jonah had put on me coupled with the

wear and tear of such a trip. It was not in any way like being

on some normal type of excursion. He was knocking my

awareness around like a ping pong ball. One minute there was

the mystical enticement of nature, and the next he was

harassing me mercilessly for being a pitiful attempt at being

an apprentice to a warrior. He attacked my personality on

every conceivable aspect. If I did not see with my own eyes,

the absurdly unique manifestations of nature, the shock of

heightened awareness which was for the most part pleasurable

and the innumerable amounts of wisdom that he kept pouring

out to me, I would have fled from his attacks immediately. I

also felt... that the severe ass kicking he was giving me, had to

be part of some method to actually make me a warrior.

Something to do with making me strong enough for anything.

The truth of the matter was that anytime, anything a little out

of the ordinary would take place, I was not down there

amongst the diehards. I was running like a jackrabbit out of

hell. So I could tell right away that he wasn't kidding about this warrior stuff. It's kind of a novelty until you see how real, real is. He also claimed that he was not attacking me, but the bullshit of my false self, that wasn't really me, but was like, negative outside garbage that I had to "get off my island."

That night in the car, on the mountain, a type of purge took place. Jonah encouraged me to let go of horrible feelings I had accumulated about my father's death. I was wailing and screaming and imagining myself going into a grave with him unless I got up and got out. Then I jump out of the car and I threw up. It's extremely cold so I am trying to be quick. I lose my balance and hit my eye on the corner of the open hatchback door on the car. I now have a black eye, but I suppose I'm lucky considering how hard of a hit it was. If we had looked like a strange traveling team before, we now looked worse with my eye. Nevertheless, I now felt lighter emotionally for that particular night on the mountain. The experience seemed intense in an odd way. I also felt that I no longer had to die along with my dad, to commemorate him. To celebrate my life was to celebrate the life he gave me. I would begin to dream of him so much that my feeling was, that he was just on another frequency. It was like he just had another address. I didn't even feel the pain of mourning him any

longer because it seemed like I saw him where I saw him. I
lost a contemporary recently and I am going to try and apply
this same type of healing. I do see this girl on some sort of
dream level, and it's odd how we continue where we left off.
However, she was very useful right here in my waking state. It
is a real charge to feel the continuance of the band on another
plane of consciousness, but I still could use her around here.
At least the pain is less, because on some level I do feel like I
am seeing her somehow.

The mood is more jovial the next day. Most of the day is
spent doing really natural Colorado outdoors activities. We
speak to a lot of enthusiastic healthy people. People that live
very athletic wholesome lives. We went to the Colorado River.
It was spectacularly beautiful. It's rather cold even though its
august. We talk to the people with the kayaks. We are acting
casual, but I know Jonah always seems to be doing something
with some intent. I get the impression he is trying to show me
how to approach and interact with people. He said in the past,
that I don't know how to talk. I wasn't really sure what he
meant by this. I somehow get the impression that I'm
supposed to be watching how he makes conversation with
people. I never ask him about this so I could be wrong. I try

not to be overly analytical about what is just normal living,
however, every time I'm just sort of going along on my happy
way, he says that I'm not paying attention to what I am doing.
After wading in the river we get back on the road. Next we
stop in a town where there is a beautiful craft shop. It's fairly
high up in the mountains. We walk through the shop. A thin
attractive older woman is selling jewelry in the front. He
engages with her for a while as I browse. There are rain sticks
there. We went next door to a restaurant. For some reason
there is immediately an issue going on. He gets into... how
dare I think I am worthy to learn his knowledge. This might
have been the conversation where I said, I want to know what
you know, to which he had an immediate and virile response.
There might be some things that I could learn, and you're
here, which is something, but to consider yourself a sorceress
of any power at this point is below laughable. Again I feel like
crap, and wonder why someone so dull, such as myself, is
involved in something like this. We're back on the road, and
he decides that I should go naked in the river to see if the river
can make me strong. He tells me that my mortal gap is open,
and that I must close it to be strong. It's getting colder out and
I'm feeling somewhat not inclined to be getting naked and

going back into the river. But... to be given a chance, perhaps once again, to get in his good graces, I consider doing this. I feel a little apprehensive about getting naked in public, but I feel the road is far enough away. We walk into the water. He is saying to dunk myself. I finally am dunking myself, beginning to relax, when I feel something suck on my leg. I run screaming from the water. We are on the road again in much better spirits. I do feel invigorated and refreshed. In fact, I feel myself swinging into a state of extreme pleasure. I suspect this is partly due to the subsiding sun in its ferocity. The dusk immediately brought me into a relaxed exuberant state. The fields looked darkened and the fire red sunset hung thickly in the distance. A crescent moon glimmered. Jonah lit a cigarette. Normally I hate when people smoke in a car. This was vastly different. He said that tobacco was an ally of his. The smoke gave him energy to talk. He was so prolific and relaxing when he smoked that I felt anticipation when he would smoke and talk. It was not like a typical manner of conversation. He would become the other Jonah. He would become the Nagual. Conversation would come through him that he said, was not necessarily him talking. He didn't know where this was coming from. It didn't happen immediately every time he lit up a cigarette. I just knew that the potential was there, when he did light the cigarette, that he would relax enough to allow the dialogue to come through him. So, consequently I became conditioned to feeling excited when he lit a cigarette, because so many times a gesture with power would occur when he did that.

We drove in silence for a while. He often chose that we would be silent for long periods of time. He generally didn't want to chit chat as he called it. Certainly not for a three-thousand mile ride. He repeatedly told me to shut off the inner dialogue to reach awareness. While I lived in his presence, we lived with a certain type of mentality and a certain mode of behavior. That meant a lot of times just shutting up and trying to be more conscious of my surroundings. It meant things like following directions, so that, things could happen in front of you. For instance, if you go into a canyon, you're going to be totally quiet and tune into everything around you. He was constantly telling me to shut up so that I could tune into what was around me instead of listening to my rambling inner dialogue.

Around twilight the next day we got to the border between Colorado and Utah. Jonah pulled over suddenly. We got out of the car. There was no sound on the highway. There were no other cars on the highway. We went to the back of the car and looked behind us. There was a spectacular sight there. There were two awesomely huge rainbows. One was a little smaller and dimmer then the other. Jonah quietly said...

"That's an omen." He had talked about omens before. He had said that the earth would communicate with you. He had also said not to interpret things. It is what it is, he would say. The omen seemed uncomplicated to me. It seemed to represent us, and how much personal power, we had developed. Jonah's being bigger and brighter than mine. Jonah said that that was for us. I asked him how he could assume that. He said that because we were there to witness it and because he knew it to be so. The feeling of being on that wide open highway with the stillness felt very ethereal. You could feel a sensation of power in the air. I was starting to recognize an electrical current that would seem to be in the atmosphere at certain times. I believed him when he said that the rainbows were for us. As crazy as that sounded, he was so extremely grounded that I had to take what he said as true. In acknowledging this it felt extremely priceless to feel that the universe could actually be talking to me. I found it extremely difficult to believe that the universe was going to communicate with me. Who was I? No one to my knowledge, that I should have the blessing, to be communicated to by the universe, nature, or whatever you would call it.

We drove away, but this was far from over. The sun began to descend. I started seeing visions in every direction. The sky lit up with inconceivable displays of color. This did not resemble any kind of sunset, no matter how gorgeous. This was the earth becoming completely psychedelic. Murals of vivid colors and patterns began to transverse through the sky. In each direction that I looked was a different array of colors and a different scene. I was one hundred percent mesmerized. Jonah said nothing. He too, was watching the show intently. Everything looked surreal. All of the colors were glimmering intensely with illumination. The sky kept changing like it was some incredible movie screen. The beauty of this was in a sense absurd. It felt absurd because it was totally outlandish. It was like...how...could this possibly be happening? This was not natural to anything I had ever seen before. This was a full fledged living techno color vision, show. I was completely deluged in heightened awareness. The electrical power I felt in my body was enough to make me pass out. I didn't pass out.

We rode in silence for several hours.

We drove for about five hours. We were starting to feel the fatigue. We were getting deeper into desert country. I considered that we were missing seeing fantastic land by traveling through Utah at night. The crickets were loud and the night was still and clear. Thousands of stars could be seen in the sky. Jonah thought he remembered a nice rest stop with a view. He was determined to stop at this place. We looked for this place for hours. We were steeped in exhaustion. Finally, we took a lone dirt road. It took us off the highway, and put us on the side of a road that ran alongside the desert. It was a small road off the main highway. We were as much in the "middle of nowhere" as you could get. There wasn't a town for miles. As soon as he stopped the car, I started shouting... "Stop, stop, we're rolling backwards." He insisted that I was hallucinating. It was so definite of a feeling that I could not believe it. I felt the car roll back at least five to ten feet. I was amazed that he was claiming that it didn't happen. After trying to make sense out of this, we set up our little makeshift car camp. That essentially consisted of putting luggage on the roof, throwing a huge mosquito net over the car, and putting up shades on the windows. I was fearful of waking up with my face baked to a crisp in the desert sun. We put the foam pad and the couch pieces he had brought down. I got the thin pieces. I didn't want to be weak or ill spirited, it was just that my back was slightly aggravated. Being he was doing all of the driving, he certainly deserved the good foam. I wanted to drive at night but he didn't want me to drive his car at night. I had to go onto the night desert to urinate. The way he had been speaking was as if the desert was alive and watching us. I didn't exactly understand what he inferred could be watching us. Nevertheless, when I got out I felt outstandingly nervous about dropping my drawers in this strange wilderness environment. I had already experienced feeling awkward peeing in front of a moose, now I felt funny in front of a mountain range. The thing was, I didn't feel alone out there. Jonah, having suggested that there were spirits, allies, or something watching us, made it feel as though it was so, for me. I did realize that this was somehow nonsensical, but then I did feel something tangibly alive in the desert. There was a very intense feeling of some sort there.

Then... the laughter began. I had no idea what was so funny. We both started laughing and laughing and laughing. My body felt totally at ease and joyous. He commented that the Indians were with us and were laughing tonight as well. I

think he was referring to the sorcerers Don Juan and his cohort

Genaro. He also seemed to suggest that it could have been any

of the sorcerers whose essence was alive in that area. I found it

terrifically alluring to even imagine having something or

someone there that we couldn't see. Something out of the

ordinary took hold of us. We were belly laughing and couldn't

stop. Jonah said that this was a gesture with power. He said

that Dan and Kathy probably felt us laughing in L.A. For at

least forty-five minutes this spell of hysterical laughter raged

on. I couldn't even imagine what we were laughing about.

Something took hold of my body and all that I could do was

laugh. I felt really good. I felt probably as good as I had ever

felt before. I was fascinated to hear Jonah break down from

his stoic self and hear him carrying on. Eventually this

subsided. He said that the sorcerers from the area were

laughing with us. It was like having a party on another plane

of awareness. I have since become a bit more aware of what

other planes of awareness are like and I would have to say that

it seemed like our normal daily life in the car and yet it was

more like heightened awareness then like being in a state of

dreaming. The desert night looked usual, but there was an

intangible energy there, that you could cut with a knife. We dozed off for a little while. It was about four a.m. in the middle of nowhere on a lonely desert off ramp that was not connected to a town. I hear a truck rumbling up alongside of us. Jonah wakes up. For some reason the Ace hardware truck seems very funny. Within minutes the place becomes like a circus. Every five minutes a vehicle passes. Then a large truck stops in front of us. They are about twenty feet ahead of us. They have music coming out of their truck. Jonah says to be quiet and still. A big man with a beard and a belly walks out onto the desert. He comes back and takes an oil barrel a few feet out into the desert. Now I'm starting to wonder if I'm watching something that I'm not supposed to be seeing. The whole feeling in the air is very surreal. Jonah is intimating, as he sometimes does, that this perhaps is an irregular event. This whole charade could potentially be a joke that power is playing on us. At this point this seems almost reasonable, because this is far too much activity at five in the morning out in nowhere. The laughter fit starts up again as car after car comes out of nowhere. Finally, to my relief, the truck with the oil barrels, leaves.

The air was cold in the Utah desert when we woke up. I

was happily surprised. We drove to a rest stop. An Indian family had beautiful jewelry for sale there. I walked into the rest room. An older Indian woman was washing a pot in there. Her eyes hit me like bullets. She had a deep presence. I was disturbed that she was there. I really wanted to be alone in the bathroom. I felt inferior, that I could not be so natural, as to urinate in the morning around such a spiritually evolved woman. I was irritated and disturbed at having to hold in my bodily functions. As in many portions of the trip, I suffered from massive internal tension. Jonah didn't help. His mood had me in extreme stress for many a mile.

He commented that the older woman had a lot of power. To me, it was yet another example of my inability to let go. We finally got to a restaurant where I could get myself together. The desert country in Utah was spectacular. The cactus and the landscape could not have more sharply compelling.

At some point Jonah began laying into me again. When he would get super pissed off a strange fear would overtake me. I was horrified that he would drop me as a friend and an apprentice, let alone the lover part. I also knew that he had to throw an emblazoned fit to get my real attention. He was insanely angry that I hadn't developed properly since he had seen me. I somehow thought that his dramatic display of anger could not really be about something I had done. I mean we were just riding along, and all of a sudden... I'm guilty. I'm so guilty it would have seemed that I had murdered his child. He made me reflect and reflect and examine my behavior. Of course he was right. Here I was witnessing the earths very blessings, literally blessings from heaven, being given power, straight into my body from Jonah and who knows from where else, and I'm still living the life of a slacker.

Somehow his anger would snap me into heightened awareness. I was no longer able to talk or think normally. A strange buzzing seemed to be in my head. I felt numbed by a form of spiritual and psychic electrical current. Jonah did this to me at will. A state of being would overtake me where I was extremely aware, conscious, and understood everything that he said. I couldn't think back a moment before. I could only have perception of the immediate moment. It was very much as though an electrical current in my brain was being amplified.

When he figured that he had tortured me enough to have an open mind, he tapered the aggression in his mood. He asked me what I wanted? I told him I wanted this, pointing to the earth. What do you mean you want this, he bellowed crankily? I just want the earth was all that I could sputter out. I'm thinking that I meant that I wanted to be in touch with the power from the earth.

Well that's the only right thing about you. You recognize the earth, and the earth recognizes you. I told him that I wanted to support the earth because that was the only agenda that I had. The earth will wipe out its antagonists eventually. His softening of mood indicated that I could still participate with him. It was unclear what I was participating in. It was clear that when he wanted, he could shine the light right on me, and I desperately knew that nothing else could ever compare to the feelings he evoked in me and the states of consciousness that would occur for me in his presence. Rationality paled compared to this. The miles stretched on and the evening beckoned. At twilight, we drove through an area rich with Jericho trees. The land showed us many moods of light and wind and essence. It was a radiant beautiful day. I was in ecstasy driving along with Jonah over the spectacular land. This was what it was all about for me. To feel the peace as we drove through the wilderness. This was why I could drive three thousand miles.

At some point we went through a small corner of Arizona. The rock canyons were immense and gorgeous. It was another hot day. I saw white mountain goats perched on a mountain ledge. There were two of them leaning towards each other nose to nose. It was a fantastic sight. Another fantastic sight were the wild mustangs. They were free and beautiful. At the moment that I saw the goats, the thought flashed through my mind...One could never have the time to see all the wondrous things in the world. It reminded me of Don Juan saying that.

We drove through the mountain highway. The canyons were huge and outstanding. As we came out of the mountain we pulled to the side of the road. There was a large canyon stream that raged through the canyon and then filtered down along the road. It was about forty feet down from the highway. It looked far too steep to go down. Jonah thought that we could do it. What if he's wrong, I thought. The rocks had been covered with a type of cement that provided tiny footholds. With much caution and anxiety, I edged down the precipice. When we got down there, there were smooth beautiful sandbars. I soon found out that they sank. The mountain river stream water was fairly cold and relatively quick. We took off our shoes and edged in gently. It felt like an area that didn't get a whole lot of human company. I felt like I was finally being an adventurer. It was just amazingly beautiful to be there. As free and as wild as I felt, was also as nervous as I felt. I was holding to big rocks for dear life because the rapids were fairly strong. In the spirit of sportsmanship, Jonah maneuvered another little challenge. Nothing could ever just be peaceful with him. For me, scaling a canyon that went almost straight down was warrior enough for one day. We're sort of wading near these big rocks that go over a small dam. He yells grab the stick, referring to the walking stick. At this point the issue of trust is weighing heavily upon me. "Come on." He challenges again. The concept of the dutiful apprentice is paling rapidly to my incumbent fear. I grab on anyway. Now I'm really living. A man is dangling me over a dam in strong rapids. I'm holding onto one side, he's holding onto the other. He's laughing slightly maniacally. He thinks my fear is cute. I'm wondering if I haven't made a terrible mistake. Either way I'm getting a hell of an adrenaline rush. For those few split seconds I get keyed into another level of awareness. While I am clutching that stick, I am totally alive and totally aware. Every ounce of concentration matters at this point. He pulls me to a safer rock to hold on to. I'm a little turned on by the whole thing. He goes climbing up the wall like some desert reptile creature. I try to keep up, and again there's not much time for reflection. At the top of the canyon, by the road, a car full of rogues pulls up. I say rogues because I am just not used to seeing this type of men. They're super healthy, have shaggy natural hair and are just shining with an unusual vigor. They too had apparently just climbed out of the canyon after a good swim. Jonah and them engaged in a boisterous chat. I stood there winded, smiling and wiping the mud and water off my face. I had grabbed Jonah's underwear, wet it, and stood wiping my face with it. After they pulled away, I realized, how it must have appeared slightly odd that a woman should be standing there cooling her face with men's briefs.

We drove off high on nature and the natural abandon so precious in life. Later on as we drove toward Nevada, Jonah started refreshing me on some points he had made all along. I needed a lot of recapitulation because I seemed to forget a lot. A lot of times when we talked I would drift into a state called heightened awareness. In this state it seemed that I couldn't remember much only moments after something had been said.

He said that everything that had ever been done or said between us was stored in my memory. He said it was stored in my body. My body remembered everything, he said. He considered the whole body to be sort of a brain. The feeling of heightened awareness was like a supernatural kind of high. I felt adroitly perceptive and yet wired with an extreme force of current.

Thinking is listening, he said. You're being your own audience. To meditate, sit with your head like a ball on a pin. You're listening to your inner dialogue when you think, which is in the English language. People call it thought. Don't discuss self. It takes intelligence to be quiet, to not discuss self. When you meditate, the Hindis call it the self, (the inner dialogue.) Thought also comes from food irritating the body. The whole body is a brain. Clean the body and you will lose negative dialogue. The body is a thinking mechanism. You can will disease out of the body by controlling thought. When you're meditating your listening to another channel, your own channel. Humans claim their thoughts. I don't pay attention to my thoughts. Warriors separate themselves from their thoughts. When you meditate you listen to something besides yourself. God put the birds and things around for a reason.

Listen outside yourself.

Take your mind off thinking. The better shape you're in, the more you get the shield going. It closes the mortal gap. Get healthy, so that when you meditate, you hear other stuff, other than your own thoughts. You listen to the outside. When you get into these states of meditation, your body heals. When you shut off the inner dialogue, you get off your own little island. You actually do get off your island. You leave your body. When you shut the inner dialogue that's when things get interesting. Dreaming is leaving your body. The Indians in those books perfected their dreaming body to where it could be seen. When they die, their dream body goes on.

My spirit awakened by degrees as the enormous power and beauty of the land began to fill me. My heart opened and the land reached in and took me. No more words were needed. A feeling from seeing the land set us at peace. Jonah was astutely aware of my moods. He could read whether I was peaceful or agitated. When we looked at the land it was if time stopped. The heightened awareness that I would experience, when he chose, was magnified intensely by the presence of the earth. In super subtle ways it was as if the earth perked up and started to communicate with us. Little things like a flight of crows at a particular moment in time. The flocks of birds, the scenery, changed fast. The temperature, which could have been tragically hot, was overcast and magnificent. Jonah mentioned that he had willed the weather to be this way. Late in the afternoon a tremendous storm came up. Jonah said that this was all for me. It was as though we had dropped into a magical sphere or time. The air was crisp with electricity. My ecstasy heightened as the rain pummeled us in a vibrant cascade. The storm clouds rolled by making a world of beautiful grey shadings. I believed that the storm was for us because I had witnessed the earth come out to be with us in the past. At first I could never understand how the earth could possibly be talking to us. Weren't we just there? And the earth was just doing its thing? How could that be proven? In a completely logical view it couldn't. The power of the feeling at these times seemed to speak for itself. Jonah seemed to speak, and the rain followed his request.

After the elaborate visions of beauty, the earth had shown us in the past, it became easier to associate the marvelous visions as having the possibility of sharing a connection with us. The rainstorm and the thunder raged across the plains. I got higher and higher as though in an ecstatic trance. At this point, by my level of heightened awareness, and sensation of ecstasy, I was certain that power was present with us.

Jonah would always hasten me to be quiet when he believed power was present. This rainstorm is for us, he said. I wished for it. As he said this, the torrential downpour mediated its flow as if in response. I had the feeling that this was just truly awesome. I know that that is an overused expression, but that was really the deep sense that I had. The feeling that I would get out in the natural world was so far beyond anything I had ever experienced. To smell the scent of the earth, and watch the clouds and shadings of the sunset, made me realize that paradise is right here. There's really not so much to search for. Lying on the ground to absorb the earth's energy could be tremendously healing. I felt very privileged to be in the presence of nature and feeling it's magnificent essence.

14   REFLECTIONS FROM VEGAS

I almost never made it to Vegas. The sun bore down

mercilessly as our Mazda without air conditioning, rolled

through the Mojave. I was obsessed that my fair skin should

not instantly deteriorate in the fatal glare. I was absolutely

determined to completely cover my skin. It didn't dawn on me

that thick denim pants and a jacket would cover me, but cause

other complications. I never really noticed anything was

wrong, I was just sort of fading away into the heat. My mind

became dimmer and dimmer. Jonah was throwing wet rags

from the ice chest on me. We finally got to Vegas. I was

falling into a heat induced stupor. I went into the casino, onto

a long line in the womens room. I felt exceedingly heavy,

worn and just generally sick. My mind felt like a fried haze.

When I got to the sink I had a lot of work to do. I just looked horrible. I struggled to cool down. I put cold water on my face and hands. I tried to get myself together but I felt like I wasn't all there. I felt mentally numb. The casino ruckus barely seemed like stimulus. I felt like my speech was slurred. I went back to find Jonah. The casino was packed. We had drifted accidentally apart. I had horrific thirst. I bought a big cup of iced coffee thinking that maybe that would revive me. I wasn't particularly concerned with finding Jonah, I wasn't particularly concerned with anything. The air conditioning was soothing. The carnival of bells ringing and people milling around just seemed absurd. I sat down in a corner and waited for my mind to cool off. I felt as though I had had a lobotomy. No thought, just being. I was probably the closest ever to those states of mindlessness that Jonah coveted.

Jonah popped out of nowhere. He seemed to think it highly unusual to find me so easily tucked away in a corner, in this menagerie. He took the coffee out of my hands and threw it away. I was unhappy to lose my coffee. He had been consistently on me about quitting coffee for my health. It seemed so difficult for me to believe that coffee could be that destructive. In this case, he said he did not take the coffee because of general health. He said that my physical condition

at that moment was gravely in danger, and that the
dehydrating effects of caffeine at that moment could be
devastating. We went to the next event, which under the
circumstances of my frailty, was ludicrous. He decided that
the roller coaster might lessen my impending heatstroke. I
didn't really notice how sick I was from the heat until I
realized that I really couldn't talk straight. My brain and
speech were actually slowed down. I was slurring.
Nevertheless, Jonah being as challenging as he was, opted for
this blood curdling rollercoaster. Admittedly it some kind of
reviving effect. He absolutely loved this rollercoaster. The
pictures that came back had him looking robust and beautiful.
I have taken some bad pictures but I think that was the worst.
It had an almost straight twenty-two foot drop. In some ways I
liked it a little. I sort of liked it afterwards when you could
relax from the big rush. I despised the ascending part. I really
felt scared shitless, and the bodily sensation of that drop was
excruciatingly unnerving to me. Like a lot of things that
transpired in his presence, some things were actually
terrifying.

We had a blast in the casinos. I found a wallet on the bar.
I promptly returned it to the bartender. I didn't dare look in it.

I expected to be congratulated in my fine morals. He was livid. He said that power left that for us and that there could have been any amount of money in there. It could have at least been our gas money back to Hollywood. I was shocked. I was perturbed that this man of great power, knowledge and honor could consider lifting a wallet. He told me that I was an asshole, and that anybody leaving their wallet on a bar deserved to lose it. He told me about a story of him returning a wallet and not even receiving a thank you. In retrospect now.... I see what he meant about the wallet. But then, I never would have imagined his reaction, in fact had I done anything else I would have feared serious reprimand.

One of the most outstanding difficulties, I felt with Jonah, was that I was often walking on eggshells so to speak. I was always wrong and he was always berating me. This was a problem because I never knew what to say for fear of reprimand. The flip side of this was that sometimes the scenarios around us were extremely hysterical. Sometimes I was really laughing, being intensely real, and having a great time. Sometimes I would be in heightened awareness, which would be a totally amazing feeling. I vacillated between ecstasy and horror, constantly, in his presence. At times I felt ashamed of the appearance of the relationship. I of course

knew we were far from what would be considered a couple.

Our association was one of me being an apprentice to a

sorcerer. That may sound strange, but nothing could be more

true. There were elements of being friends, of being a man and

woman, but by and large this was a far more peculiar situation.

I would normally not allow someone to act in public with me

as he did. As a sorcerer's apprentice, not only was anything

virtually acceptable, the gold of the good situations, made

anything that came with it, something to be tolerated. Needless

to say, this quest built on tough love was nothing short of

horrendous. This was not all his doing. I was uncomfortable in

the sun until I learned how to protect my skin. Still this was a

trip into nature with a bona fide Indian sorcerer and I was

going to cover myself comfortably so that I could have a

natural encounter in life like this. The truth of the matter is

that I could never say enough prayers and thanks to come

close to seeing the blessings of nature. As difficult as I found

the weather and his rough temper, was as fine and excellent

the feeling of power, energy and the sacred interaction with

nature. I love Jonah, and no matter how extreme his nature,

the energy coming off of him I revered. There's no level of

thanks I could ever give him or nature for the bounty of their blessing. The way nature would behave as we drove by were the moments of a lifetime. If everyone could feel the sensitivity of the earth around us there would be no war. To have such an extraordinary planet around us is a blessing beyond imagination. What could anyone want when they feel the spirit of the earth befriend them? Man's foolhardy destruction of nature is at an extreme crisis point. What insanity proposes that it is for us to kill the earth? It is unbelievable what is being done. Our rivers, forests and air is being ruined. Civilizations have lived here peaceably for millions of years with respect and consideration. Is this modern progress? Two hundred years to destroy a planet. What god or messiah is anyone looking for when they are defiling their own home? I am not a corporate power and I am not a politician, I am no better than the typical American consumer. For some reason the earth saw fit to shine in front of me. I can only say that I hope to god that this destruction can be stopped and reversed. All that is holy and sacred is right before us. Cleaning up the planet should be a world team effort, so that there might be paradise for all.

The feeling between us in Vegas was frictional at times.

One night in the hotel room he became viciously confrontational. He was basically aggravated that I hadn't followed his instructions to any worthy degree. Sometimes in the midst of his disagreeableness, he would choose to talk. Such was the case. "Leave yourself alone." Get out of the mirror. He said other things as well. The way in which he was speaking implied that he didn't know where this was coming from, as he would put it. He said that often when he spoke to me he didn't know where it was coming from. It was like he was channeling someone else. He felt like a listener. He didn't use the word channeling, but that I think is a word for what he was talking about.

He said he had known Jesus in a very personal way. He wouldn't tell me exactly what he meant by that. He alluded in some way, that he had had contact with Jesus.

He was very hard on me. He wanted to emphasize that our togetherness was not a wasteful conversation, and that I had better become a warrior or leave his party. I wished desperately to please him, and yet a strange inertia seemed to penetrate me, preventing me from ever doing all of what he asked.

That night we went to dinner. There was a long line for

the casino buffet. We walked in the back entrance bypassing the line. We sat down and then went to the buffet table. I was horrified. I couldn't figure out why he was doing this? I felt very nervous that this was actually a crime and that there could be an arrest. His walk and demeanor indicated that I was to pull off an act, and not act like a spaz. I considered that this was a lesson in how to be an actress. How to stalk. I thought he was crazy. I thought he had taken this whole thing too far. It wasn't that we had cut in line, it was that he had circumvented the meal payment, and not without notice. Finally, the manager came over and he started double talking. We eventually paid and left. He said that I had done an ineffective job of acting in such a case.

We drove to Los Angeles the next day. The desert was gorgeous. I loved the road. It was tough but it was beautiful. Entering Hollywood always completely excited me. It felt like coming home. The apartment building still felt like my home. We were exhausted when we got in. It was fun to be back in the city. Jonah and I got along. I felt every moment we spent talking was valuable. We would sit on the couch after dinner and he would talk. Sometimes I would again go into heightened awareness on these occasions. I would feel a strange feeling in my head. It was like a thin current of electricity. I would feel great. At that moment everything in the world would feel supremely perfect. I don't know how this would happen. I would be acutely aware of what he said and how he felt.

15 HOLLYWOOD

I always felt immediately at home returning there. I tried to stay in town long enough to talk to his benefactor Dan. I had had the privilege to talk to Dan a couple of times. His engaging nature and intelligence were the event of a lifetime to be around. He was very business minded. A couple of times that I saw him, he seemed pretty much professional in his interaction to me. Other times he had been more engaging and spoke in a more familiar context. I had looked forward to meeting his wife whom he spoke highly of.

Later Jonah again spoke to me in a more serious tone. He said that humans were supposed to be caretakers of the planet. It was not their right to hurt it. The earth will take care of itself. The dinosaurs messed up as well. They were gone quick after twenty million years. He said that a pen is an effective tool against tyranny. Being responsible for the planet meant dissuading ignorance. He also said that if I wrote it would be enlightening to me.

While Jonah slept I went out to a restaurant. In the evening light Hollywood looked more worn down then I had recalled. After a few days there the old sparkle returned. It was a town where glitter and grit were often ground together.

Jonah arranged for us to go to dinner with Dan and his wife Kathy. I was a little nervous. Jonah had acted like I was being prepped to meet Kathy for years. I was never introduced to her because I wasn't "ready yet." I wasn't really clear what ready for this meeting would mean. Jonah had intimated that she was an extremely organized impeccable warrior, and that to be around her I should be the same. He once said while we were in the middle of the desert and my nails were dirty, that she would notice that. It's a better life to be as he described her. Organization will service creativity. Productivity can best occur in a disciplined and organized way. Sometimes it would seem that art or magic would occur in a state of mental abandon, but actually a clean and orderly backdrop for creativity seemed more powerful. I guess the same would go for health and nutrition. Clean food makes for clean power.

Once back in Hollywood I reflected on several experiences that occurred on that trip. I kept remembering different things. Things I had not necessarily put in the journal.

One evening we had had a light dinner in a country inn. We returned to the car in the late twilight. The sky was an outstanding blue. Jonah commented that people were blind to power around them. The hue of the sky definitely looked specifically superior to an average sky. At that moment a man who looked like a vagabond appeared out of nowhere and crossed the parking lot in front of us. He's a sorcerer, Jonah whispered. I sat in awe wondering why this guy was a "sorcerer" and not some vagabond. Then we left. Several miles down the road Jonah said... "Death is out here. You have to be extremely alert while driving." Seconds later we passed a horrible accident. A car had jumped a barrier and hit another car head on. It was clear that there could have been few survivors. We drove in silence. I felt stunned at his precognition and sad for the people.

On another night there had been an unusual evening in Utah. I remember after dinner getting some fruit juice. The effects from the sugar were pronounced to me. I had an uncomfortable feeling that I generally attribute to my sugar raising and then dropping. We drove for a while before finding a rest stop that overlooked a great canyon. It was already nightfall. Jonah took his walking staff and one of the lounge pillows from the car. He made a show of himself walking with the staff. We walked to the cliff edge. The place was immensely gorgeous. Even in the darkness the sense of beauty was apparent. We sat down on the ground. Then we both laid down on the couch pillows. We were sort of crunched together on one. He told me to be absolutely still and silent, and to listen. The dirge of the crickets flowed in an even murmur. We stayed in this position for some time. Somehow a violent restlessness came upon me. I knew Jonah would be livid if I so much as moved, and disturbed the ambience of the situation. It became somewhat apparent that this was not a casual meditation. There were odd noises coming from the canyon. I thought I saw some rather large shadows cruising by. He told me that this was a gesture with power and to be absolutely still. I felt like my blood sugar was extremely low, and my skin and body felt like they were itching with horrific restlessness. I tried to stay still, but it was harder and harder. My body made a little jolt to restlessness. Jonah jumped up, grabbed me by the arm and pulled me toward the car. Get in! He shouted. As we drove off, he bitterly denigrated me, and told me that when we got to Los Angeles, he would put me on a plane and that our association was over. I probably never felt more horrible in my whole life. He told me that I was a horrible failure as an apprentice, and that this path was not for me. I felt that the itching restlessness was from a blood sugar drop from the fruit juice that I had had after dinner. Truthfully I didn't know what had happened back there. I did experience hypoglycemia all the time and unless I ate in ways that satisfied it, I was ill all the time. He said that it was not a blood sugar problem, but that something back there was making me feel that way. He said that it was probably a good thing that he had grabbed me out of there, because that feeling meant that you were not supposed to be there. He said that there were definite allies there that had come to check us out, and that had we been able to stay, anything could have happened. We could have crossed the gates of eternity for all we know. We could have crossed over into other dimensions, and you... couldn't handle it. We will never pass this way again and never have that chance again. That was a huge real life gesture with power that you blew. There was a part of me inside that I couldn't account for. There was a little voice that had kept making jokes. It kept saying let's come back later, while we were out there. Jonah kept raving on about all I was good for was a Hilton Hotel and a T.V. set. I felt crushed that I could have ruined such a thing. There had been shadows of huge birds flying around. Almost like what you would have imagined in prehistoric times. There had been an immense energy of power there. I had behaved irrevocably childish. I should have forced myself to be still, but I just couldn't.

After two hours or so, he decided it was best we had left there. If I wasn't ready to be there, there was no sense in endangering my life there. He said we could have possibly left this life forever. I didn't know what he meant. I wasn't looking to "never come back." What did that mean? I realized that whatever I was made of was not much of a warrior yet. Whenever this stuff got real, I was a scared baby. Somehow many miles down the road it was apparent that I was forgiven, and that I wasn't going to be sent away as if in exile.

Another example of what a novice I was, occurred back in Hollywood. We had dinner at a charming outdoor Italian Bistro, that was near the Hollywood Hills. After dinner, we drove around Mulholland Drive, to take in a bit of scenery.

Jonah pulled up to a woman in the neighborhood to inquire directions to a particular lookout point on Mulholland. I had to stifle my laughter when I heard his approach to her. He spoke as though he was exceedingly wealthy, and devoutly ostentatious. I marveled at the nuance of the reflection in his voice. She apparently found nothing unusual in his manner and instructed us on the way to go. As we sped away, he commenced in a grotesque banal utterance, that one had to make people comfortable with you.

We came to an area to park the car and got out. We sat on a tree log that was lying in an area that overlooked the hills. It was a warm beautiful night. Jonah began talking in a manner that indicated that reverence and attention would be in order.

Out of nowhere a white Toyota pulled up. A thin wiry man bounded over and started a conversation. He was extremely fit and chipper. He told Jonah that he was from Ohio, Gypsy Lane. Jonah had told me that that was a unique place to him. The guy said he stopped because he saw Jonah's license plates. Something was strikingly bizarre about this man. I looked back at the car from which the man had emerged. There were three people standing in front of the car.

They looked really weird too. They were attractive with long black hair and expressionless faces. The guy rambled on about Gypsy Lane for a while, then he said good-by backed up the hill and went back to his car. Jonah said… let's get out of here now!" I was deep into heightened awareness by now. That guy's energy had stunned me. Jonah whispered… "He, wasn't real. That was a phantom." Jonah had talked about how there were beings here that looked like people, but they were really allies, phantoms, or something else. I was terrified. It didn't seem farfetched that this man was somehow out of the ordinary. He more or less had come out of nowhere, and had started saying personal things to Jonah. Things… any normal person would just not know. The thing about Gypsy Lane was entirely personal, Jonah said. To top off an already freakish meeting, this guy started chasing us down the hill. Jonah sped up and he sped up. Jonah drove into a cul de sac, in a neighborhood, this car followed. Jonah was driving fast. He went zooming around the winding roads down the mountain and this white car was right behind us. We get out of the mountains and go to a gas station on Sunset and La Brea. Just be quiet, he says. He often says that when something's going on. At some point the white car had simply left. I look at a couple of biker guys that are walking around. I'm thinking...

this is absolutely unreal. Here we are back in Hollywood and

the world is just going on. It seemed crazy that moments ago

we were in the hills dealing with god knows what. I was

becoming hysterical. This guy had scared me badly. I wasn't

just getting over it. When we got back in the house I quickly

put on a nightgown, washed my face and teeth and jumped

into bed. I actually hid under the covers and tried to relax. I

realized once again that I was a complete baby and that this

stuff was not normal, and was a lot more then I bargained for.

I was scared. After a while I joined Jonah on the couch in

front of the television. I was afraid those people might have

followed us. He seemed nonplussed and wouldn't talk about it.

He told me not to dwell on it. Sure I thought. People who were

not really people, that had chased us, were insignificant. At

last the terror subsided.

All this weird crazy stuff would keep happening, and

then I would also be around old friends. I couldn't tell my old

friends that well.... I'm having a rough day. Phantoms are

chasing us and I'm trying to adhere to this... apprenticeship.

No .... he's not my boyfriend.... it's just this kind of unusual

association. My friend, who was the quintessential Barbie,

might have understood. But, I wasn't supposed to say anything so I wouldn't. It was just somewhat difficult to act normal under the circumstances.

While I was in Hollywood, I waited to see if I could see Dan again. I stayed around a couple of days to see if he and his wife Kathy would have a break in their schedule. I had met Kathy only once. It had been only briefly, several years before. It was great being in L.A. I worked out, went to the beach, and almost felt like I had never left. I tried to stay with Jonah as much as possible, because his conversations and energy were where the juice was. There really wasn't anything anymore exciting for me than that.

Jonah arranged to meet Kathy and Dan for dinner. Now for some reason, Jonah had deemed that it would be ok for me to meet Kathy. Dan spoke of her with great florish and magnificent esteem. Seeing Dan was always an event to me. Never had I ever, met someone of his intelligence, stamina or wit. He had energy to talk for hours. Jonah had told me that he had once driven from Ohio to Los Angeles without a sleep break.

We drove to their home in the Valley. They invited us into the apartment. It was nice to see Kathy after almost running into her for so many years. Their apartment sparkled

with cleanliness, order and purpose. It exuded a blend of warm

creativity, and polished corporate decor. I was a little edgy at

first. These people were like normal people, and then again

they weren't. From all indications, these people were clearly

brilliant visionaries, real ones. Not the make believe variety. I

knew that these were private professional business people that

didn't invite inquiry into their lives. I knew it was considered

dumb to act as if anything unusual was going on. The

emphasis on them being normal folks had been stressed to me

for years. Certain conversations were simply fascinating, For

instance.... Dan had once said... I know what the tenant

knows. The tenant was supposedly a Nagual whom had

maintained life for two thousand years, by somehow obtaining

energy from each successive Nagual that came along in the

lineage. It would be natural to say, that this was a little

mysterious. The way Dan had said it that time, seemed to

indicate that he knew on a deep level what the tenant knew. In

fact, I believe he had then said... that he was the tenant. At that

point my mind had almost exploded. I didn't know if he was

speaking metaphorically, or literally claiming before me to

have existed for two thousand years. Another time, Jonah had said over dinner at the Italian Bistro, that Dan and him had a long history together, perhaps two thousand years. He would not be specific when he would say things like this. Did he mean reincarnation? How could something like that be? He would usually indicate when he would talk like this, that what he told me, he told me, and that anything else was not my business, and was not open to idle inquiry.

The point being... that although Dan and Kathy were normal people, they also had rarified intelligence, which led me to feel a little self- conscious.

We talked about some of the art that they had, as well as traveling and family. I immediately felt very comfortable with them. I forgot about my curiosities in mysticism and just enjoyed their company. Kathy was extremely gorgeous. She was very delicate and beautiful looking. She seemed warm and energetic in personality. She seemed very complimentary to Dan. They were both powerful, but in a connected way. They didn't seem to be competitive with each other. I felt healthier just being around her. To even converse with them required me to uplift and invigorate my more sedentary state of awareness.

Earlier in the week I had gone to the same Italian

restaurant alone with Jonah. It had a lovely outdoor patio surrounded by large old trees. One felt just a bit out of the city there. On the occasion with Jonah, I met someone very interesting. He was our waiter Bryan. Bryan had known Jonah many years ago. Bryan too, had developed a mentor relationship with Jonah. Jonah said that Bryan had just gotten everything immediately. Not like me, who was a procrastinating doubting Thomas. I was not fully clear to what extent Bryan was told what I was told. In the past Jonah had said that he had told no one else of his situation. I felt that I was told very little of Jonah's tales of power. He told me I had to have my own tales of power anyway. His were not as useful to me as my own would be. I thought somehow his had to be better. Bryan did seem to have all the characteristics of a complete warrior. He was bright, efficient, charming, healthy, and bounding with positive energy. He was a man with flair, and looked equipped to handle any job put in front of him. He was of an oriental persuasion. Jonah introduced me as a friend of his, but yet there was a knowing glance from him that there was more here than meets the eye. Jonah said that he was also an apprentice. His energy and charisma were titillating. At one point, Jonah said to me "I would like some desert." As though on cue, Bryan swooped down a piece of cheesecake. It was ridiculous the timing. Bryan could not have heard him. Likewise, it was a long drawn out dinner, and it was not particularly time for desert to be served. I was startled. Jonah started laughing. See, I told you, Bryan is very up on things.

Bryan was our waiter again when we came in with Dan and Kathy. The restaurant was filled with an attractive ambient crowd. We were able to get a good patio table immediately. It was Bryan's first opportunity to meet Dan. Bryan seemed to understand immediately that Dan was Jonah's benefactor. Bryan had probably been told about Dan years ago. Bryan mentioned that he had ambitions of acting. Dan had been, and still could be if he wished, a master actor. This was a major forte of his, and he was bountiful in information for Bryan. Bryan seemed fully receptive and ready to digest what Dan talked about.

I had private concerns that I did not appear to be progressing on a warrior path because of my lack of fitness. I proceeded to tell Dan and Kathy how the energy of N.Y.C would surely propel me to new heights of fitness. It was a walking community and I was ready to hone my body to the bone. I was excited about New York, and spoke at length about how the pace and culture could only hasten my progress in life and healthiness. Dan had told Jonah that New York was a writer's town. Dan said that I would do well there. Jonah said that because he had said that, that it would be true. I never forgot that, and actually it was very true. I was not rolling in money, but the continuity of meeting my obligations seemed like an endless stream of last minute miracles.

Kathy talked about how they made salads a lot. She looked extraordinary. Her skin seemed angelic and translucent. Health and fitness had always been a core issue of the things that Jonah talked about. There could be little success in cultivating awareness in a sluggish body. Dan had once said that the body is a lazy piece of garbage unless you make it move. I felt that was essence was dim, and that these people could clearly see to what level I was taking care of myself, and following the instructions that Jonah had been generous enough to give to me.

On the other hand, Dan was very energetic, but had habits that would generally not be considered health bearing. I reminded myself that I could not compare myself to Dan because he was born with unbelievable energy. He did drink coffee and smoke cigarettes. Jonah had referred to substances as allies that would work on you. He said that he didn't write much anymore because he used too much tobacco when he did.

I was having a good time at the dinner. It was really exciting to be around really sharp people. I began to slip into heightened awareness right at the dinner table. This was subtly indicated by the way my attention started to be drawn more toward Dan, Kathy, or Jonah and the restaurant began to fade behind me. I didn't specifically notice this while it was happening, I was just talking and listening to them talk. I was an eager audience to listen to Dan talk. Listening to and watching Dan talk was not only a show, but a gift. Jonah said that when he spoke to people at times, it cleaned their awareness. It brightened up their luminosity. It energetically could rewire your brain, in a way where you were healed, of the bullshit in your mind. His energy would sort of burn off the bad energy that you had accumulated in your travels. You were closer to your spirit, closer to your higher self after being cleaned in this way. You could say that it was like being shined up to be closer to the real you. Jonah claimed to not know how this would happen. It just happened in Dan's presence.

Then an interesting thing began to happen. I was all of a sudden hearing two conversations at once. In my eagerness to be attentive I was listening to Dan and Kathy at the same time. They both began to talk to me simultaneously, and I was actually able to talk to both of them at the same time. My mind was having two entirely separate conversations at the same time. I didn't actually notice this. I just felt like I was going into a more extreme heightened awareness. We carried on the rest of an enjoyable dinner. Bryan, the waiter was also having a gesture with power. It was his opportunity to meet Jonah's benefactor, the Nagual Dan. He had heard of Dan for years. Dan discussed acting with him, in a way that could change his whole life from that one conversation. Dan put his force on him in a manner of speaking. Bryan was ready. Bryan was a sharp straight shooter that had it going on already. He was the type of individual that perceived immediately. Not like me.... that wanted proof. I didn't consciously disbelieve. Jonah always said.... I am disguised in everyday life. He was disguised very well, because somehow I always took him to be this guy, that was brilliant, but he was no different than me. I really made a gross oversight that this guy was a normal guy. A normal guy that you could take what he said with a grain of salt. In hindsight that comes upon me now. I should have been taking note of his every instruction. For him to have to tell me the same instructions for seven years, because I am an ignorant arrogant person weighs on my conscience now. Even with this I still feel he wants me to try harder and succeed. The inertia of my inattention scares me. To have the lords light of wisdom shining upon me, shining in my eyes, and for me to feel.... what does he know that I don't know, is unexplainable. Fire should have burned beneath my feet for me to propel his wishes. I see that lack of appreciation in some people today. It' amazing to me that sometimes I can forget. The gifts of magic and nature, and the magnificent forces that have opened themselves before me. How almost an amnesia could make that seem a little distant. Loving life, but not seeing the power that played itself before me. Falling back into a routine and not remembering anything. To some extent I think this is the effect of things happening in heightened awareness, that are not on the surface of your mind when you come out of it. For this I should not denigrate myself. Whatever happens naturally, I think you should just be positive and grow from it. Jonah often said that the magic is in everyday life. Continuously I would be woken up, and I would fall back asleep to the feelings and lessons I had had. Jonah would say.... your body knows. Your body knows what was stored in you in heightened awareness.

This was by far one of the most tangible aspects of my apprenticeship. In the last ten years I had perhaps hundreds of conversations that would have a distinct and very real occurrence in them. Jonah and I would be talking. Slowly I would just enter into a trance like state of mind. Something would change in the energetic feeling of my body and spirit. He would say that what he was doing was cleaning off my island. This was a phrase to illustrate him shining up my spirit. Cleaning off energetically the thoughts, feelings and powers of the world. The part of you that was separate from your spirit. In later years, after the last Castaneda book came out, he called this getting the flier off the island. He considered the spirit to be the real you, that little voice that was always right, the higher self. A flier, it was said, was a "foreign installation" of an entity that fed upon your awareness to sustain its life. It could be called a demon, an ally or a flier. He explained that what we would have commonly considered our own mind, our own thoughts, were actually coming from an entity that would attach itself to a person.

For years I felt stressful by what would normally appear to be someone attacking my personality. He relentlessly attacked my false personality, my self- importance, and anything that did not seem completely in line with my true higher self. Then he would say.... I'm not attacking you. I'm trying to get this scum sucking leach entity to release itself from your mind. What you keep doing is getting your spirit cleaned by me. You feel good for a few days, and then you begin to accumulate refuse from the world and then this flier gets back on your island. You are cleaning your own island better, he eventually said. It was energetically consuming for him when he cleaned off my spirit. He didn't know exactly how the act would happen. He would be talking, and I would slip off into heightened awareness. It was a definite bodily sensation. My mind and body would become very relaxed. There would be an unusual pressure building in my head. I would feel more and more light headed. After a while the pressure would become more and more intense. Sometimes he would talk for hours and I would try and take notes. Eventually when the pressure in my head became too much, we would end the conversation. During heightened awareness, I would only be able to understand what was being said, as it was being said. I could only focus on the present moment. I could not remember what was said even five minutes ago, although I had understood it implicitly while it was being said. He said that I would remember what had been said in heightened awareness by writing later. The information given was stored in my body and could be accessed later. In a way, that is what I am doing now. I'm remembering years of conversations by writing and letting it come out.

After a while in the restaurant, my mind became more and more pressurized under the spell of heightened awareness. The duel conversation had managed to escalate my psyche to a fevered pitch. I was not very aware of what was happening. I did not have an awareness of the split perception act that they had just maneuvered. Jonah said that they had actually split my awareness in two, right in the restaurant. I was not aware of this. I thought perhaps the wine was getting to me. When I remembered it, I did remember diligently trying to maintain total attention on both of them speaking at the same time. I do remember somehow having two conversations at once. I had only one glass of wine. I felt we left at the right time because my head felt so strange. I was very much enjoying talking with both Dan and Kathy, and part of me was aware that I didn't know a thing about life compared to these two. I felt

power pouring out of these two people. I'm not trying to

denigrate myself, it was just a feeling that I got from them,

that was of an odd supremacy. Not like a blind dumb

imaginary supremacy that some people feel about themselves.

They commanded awesome respect regardless of what they

did or didn't say. Don't get me wrong they were acting like

very warm and nice people. Jonah had tempered my natural

arrogance. I was very comfortable with them, despite that

there was something advanced about them.

We went back to their apartment. What took place in the

next two hours will never be erased from my mind. We all sat

down in the living room. I sat furthest into the room in a small

chair. Jonah sat to my right on a couch. Dan and Kathy sat

across the room in big soft business chairs. We smoked a joint.

Jonah had considered Marijuana to be a power plant.

The conversation started out normal enough. Pretty

soon things started to change a little bit. Dan, by degrees

became more and more outgoing. As he spoke, he

seemed to be expanding in some way. His gestures went

from inward and subtle, to becoming more dominating

and aggressive. Smoking something with them, was not

like being with people that were looking to "tune out," or were just partying. They were very serious and sharp intelligent people. This was not a sense that we were doing this to get stoned. It was more like an aid in awareness, done in a small dosage, done with care and moderation. It was not like people trying to lessen their sensitivity. It was not unlike the Indians when they used peyote or other substances to explore and enhance awareness.

Dan continued to speak, and I continued to listen. He cascaded through topics effortlessly and dramatically. I hung onto every word for understanding. I began to go into heightened awareness. In that state I could implicitly understand the statements of the moment, but could not concentrate on any prior moment other than the current one at hand. I had a few hits of the joint that was passed. The feeling of heightened awareness did not seem to be of the same nature as the effects of marijuana.

I began to get nervous at Dan's outburst of expression. I looked at Jonah and thought that he must have guts of steel to deal with this man. He was simply telling stories, but his dramatic demeanor was throwing me into a chasm of fascination and fear. I had never seen anyone act this way. He stood up and he sat down, he elucidated personality after personality, as he told various stories. Sometimes they were angry stories and I was terrified. I didn't even want him to walk to my side of the room. An intense pressure kept building and subsiding in my head as he spoke. I was enamored completely by his depth and expression of character.

I stared on as he continued his display. This was surely a display of power if I had ever seen one. I knew enough to be attentive, alert and to keep quiet. I knew I was having a gesture with power and that this was not a casual conversation. The energy of his power was immense. The energy I could feel from him could be felt in waves. It could be cut with a knife. I was conscious of trying to appear intelligent. This was a concern of Jonah's that he had about me meeting his warrior party. He was concerned that I would not act intelligent. The strain to appear intelligent under the onslaught of cosmic energy was useless. Somehow Dan must have been cognizant of my reticence because he didn't advance too closely in my direction. Kathy looked on, alert and interested. She was indelibly impressive to me as well. She appeared literally perfect. Not only was she delicately gorgeous, but she seemed to glow angelically. She was perfectly nice and relaxing to talk to. She seemed unusually together.

Then my marbles really started to scramble. As I'm watching Dan talk, he starts changing faces. Face after face after face. Small imperceptible differences turned into completely different characterizations. My father's face even seemed superimposed on his at one time. I stared at him desperately trying to see if I was really seeing what I thought I was seeing. He kept changing and changing and talking and talking. I was beside myself. I knew unequivocally, that the man in front of me was some kind of superior being, or to be modest, as he would be, would be to say that he had some kind of superior ability, because what I saw was not natural to anything I had ever seen before. Soon he began to tone down. As if by degrees he faded more and more into the simple Dan that we knew. I think he would find being called a superior being inappropriate or perhaps inaccurate. He clearly said on one occasion that we or he

are no better than anyone else. Because he has had the
grace and fortune to be exposed to different experiences
didn't make him feel that he was better than anyone else.
That is all well and good, but what he did was ......
rather unimaginable. However regular he liked to be,
there was nothing regular about that. "Not in these parts"
as they say. He was sensational and magnificent. The
staggering energy in my head began to ease up, as if like
an airplane coasting down....... into a semblance of
normal awareness.

The conversation flowed onto normal events and it
seemed as though nothing particularly out of the ordinary
had taken place. I realized that the protocol was to act as
if nothing had just happened. We thanked them for their
lovely company at dinner and left the apartment. I
wondered if Jonah had seen Dan change into a thousand
faces. I was too mentally high to get into a discussion
about anything. Jonah seemed joyous that Dan had
shared with me, like that, and that I had finally gotten to
see Kathy again. I was overjoyed as well. As intimidated
as I had felt, I felt extremely positively energized. In
retrospect I have to say that that was a moment of

extreme happiness, as we left their home. Their energy breathed the fire of happiness. The intimidation was from knowing that I was just not as smart as these people. They were operating from some other perspective. They knew it, and I knew it, and I knew that they knew that I knew it. So while I tried to "act intelligent," I still felt a little dumb. I also knew that I couldn't expect to be on their level of awareness. I wasn't even quite sure what I thought that they knew. I felt that it was on my behalf that I should even know that they were people of real wisdom and power. This was my little trump card of pride in the face of their awesomeness. In retrospect, if I had had less self-importance, I would have realized that it was ok to be inexperienced.

Still and all, in spite of their natural attributes, the most overriding feature of who they were, was that they were normal people. Not asleep normal people, but bright alert business people.

Jonah said that Dan had rewired me. He said that the rest of my life would be different from having been cleaned off, and in essence, blessed by Dan. I felt different. The topics he had discussed were all somewhat

usual. Writing, acting, creativity, business, people, etc....
but the energetic feeling I had gotten from him was
completely extraordinary.

When we got back to Hollywood we remembered
the details of a day we had had in Utah. It was another
situation where things were anything but usual. It had
been late in the afternoon. It was perhaps in the vicinity
of four o'clock. The small hills and valleys of Utah were
a phenomenal sight. We passed a lot of Jericho trees.
Somehow the conversation took a turn for the worse.
Whatever I had said or done had, had spiraled Jonah into
a fit of unabashed fury regarding my shortcomings. He
called me idle, inattentive, dangerous to a party of
warriors, unproductive and fit for garbage. I couldn't
deny that I had forgotten a lot of his instruction, my
blood sugar problems affected my attention and that I
was sort of exhausted from sun and travel. I had learned
to shut up when he would start screaming, because to
even question him, would redouble his fury. I really felt
bad when he would scream at me but I knew and hoped
he would snap out of it. I knew that probably an hour
from now, things would be fine, and that we would be

having an equally joyous occasion. This was not to say that I took what he said lightly, or felt he didn't mean it. He wasn't wrong in what he screamed about. He was actually dead on. This was why I tolerated being spoken to with such violence. He was generally right. No matter how harsh he sounded, which was extremely discomforting, the knowledge of his observations, were uncanny. Where could you get an education like this. No one could look at someone and give them a rundown on the situation with that fortitude of candor. His observations were so brilliant one could never hope to have someone give them such knowledge and clarity about themselves. Its' comical to even think of how this person would have been as a psychologist. He got my attention and pointed out areas I needed to improve. I am thankful for him straightening me out. A lot of people never get that kind of instruction that will make them live better.

On this occasion he added a new twist to his dialogue. He said that he was going to erase himself and his knowledge from my memory and that I was just going to go back to my old self. This was terrifying because I knew he could do it. I felt that he could do anything. My body distinctly felt his energy and knew that logic was blown out of the water with him. He could do things that would defy logic as it is commonly assumed today. I had no doubt of this. I didn't want my mind "erased." I had sworn to myself to always be respectful and diligent in the area of his and his warrior party's privacy. I didn't want any knowledge that I had accumulated to be taken away from me. I didn't want to be a failure.

The other aspect of his miserable floggings was that he professed to be performing a feat called… "cleaning off my island." This was an act of energetically emptying my head and body of the negativity I had picked up in the world. He later added the idea of something that Castaneda had termed… a "flier." This was in essence a demon of sorts. It sustained its life energy by draining ours. This "demon," would cause the chatter bullshit of the mind. So… when he addressed me in that vicious maniacal manner he sometimes did, the idea was that he was trying to chase the 'flier" off my island. My island being a metaphor for my body, spirit, mind etc.… He was not really attacking me, he said. I should not take it too personally, although the instructions to act better should be taken very seriously. He would use his power to "clean my island." This was an indelible force that, I felt to the utmost extreme, physically. He healed me from total physical sickness and aggravated mental anguish on countless occasions. For this reason alone, I would do anything possible to help this man, no matter how he had screamed at me. He cleaned off my island when I was feeling bad, as well as when I thought I was feeling relatively normal. It would occur almost unconsciously. We would be having a normal conversation, and then I would drift into a state of heightened awareness. This was like a very soothing light trance, where everything stood out with great clarity, and concentration seemed focused on only the present moment. I would go from a normal state of awareness, to a glowing sense of bodily health and elation.

He told me that it took a lot of energy to affect me, because the "demon," or "flier," that I had on me was very bad. So… we're riding through Utah, and he is cursing my ineptitude blindly. We pulled over to a huge overlook canyon. At this point I'm becoming very unnerved. I start to imagine he's simply going to kill me. He seemed so mad and fed up that I began to fear for my life. I try to tell myself that this is ridiculous. I become wired with fear that something like this actually could happen. Maybe this guy is just bats, and here it is, the end. The total desolation of the location is undoubtedly spurring on some of the fear. I'm not used to being in environments away from humanity. Something about this canyon felt like it was worlds away from humanity.

He is now bounding down the canyon. He tells me to stay in sync behind him. He tells me to walk exactly in his steps. I engage myself in the quick accurate walking and temporarily abandon the idea of ... where are we going and why are we doing this. He had great agility in getting down the canyon. I climb and run behind him trying to maintain my leverage. Finally, we take a break. There is a father and two children below. The children are tossing large rocks. Jonah comments that he is surprised that the father doesn't just keel over dead from disrespecting the land like that. We pass them and go a bit further down. We go as far down as one possibly could without careening to one's death. The view is gorgeously awesome yet terrifying because we are too close to the edge for any kind of inattention. This has my attention. This has my attention in a strenuous way. I am scared to death of falling. We sit down in a way that is ok. We're still a little close to the edge for comfort.

I remembered suddenly the thoughts I had had about Jonah's mood and behavior. I thought again of whether or not this was a demonic lure to isolation to kill me, or "erase my memory" of him and his knowledge. I tried to get reasonable, but I felt a strange current of fear. His mood no longer seemed to spew such vehement venom.

I relaxed with my back against the rock with my body as far from the ledge as possible. He said to be very still. We watched the approach of dusk for a while. We sat in silence for a while.

All of a sudden we had two magnificent visitors. They appeared to be two sparrows, only there was something odd about these birds. They looked like some kind of variation of a bird in the sparrow family. The thing was… that they weren't really acting like birds. In a wide open vast space, as vast as the open canyon, they came directly right up to us. They flew down onto a rock about three feet in front of us. Jonah said to be still and watch carefully. They were more red then a typical sparrow. They began to act very strangely. They seemed to talk to us through a strange little dance that they did. They danced around in a way that was very precise, and so orchestrated as to seem like a form of conversation. I was enchanted but a little fearful. They did not have the presence of birds. They seemed more directly interested in us then birds would normally be. They continued this little bird dance for about five minutes. They were riveting. It occurred to me that these were what Don Juan referred to as allies, although I did not have a definitive concept of that either. I just knew that these did not act like birds. They danced for us in a very sophisticated way. Then they left. Jonah said "let's go" and began bounding down the canyon. The dusk was setting in, and we had a distance to go to get out of there. I was glad the apparent purpose of going down the canyon did not hold malevolent intent for me. Jonah commented that they, meaning the birds, had come to check us out. Stuff was always coming to check us out. That was why Jonah even talked to me. He made it apparent that I was generally not his cup of tea otherwise. Somehow, our combination in the wilderness created a stir.

His pace was furious. He used the gait of power to get out of there. I lunged behind him to stay in his tracks as he requested. As an apprentice I was constantly in the position of trying to prove myself worthy. Often my urbane state of princess culture interfered with my rustic athletic fortitude. This type of trip and his company were challenging and invigorating. I knew it was meant to "toughen me up," but he was rather maniacal. If he was some normal guy I would have chewed him up in a second., but I knew who he was. No matter what he did or said to me wasn't going to alter the fact, that this was an out of the ordinary experience, that required out of the ordinary patience, strength and endurance. At some point he commented… "Those were not birds." I hadn't thought that they were.

On the way out of the canyon, we stopped to meditate on the canyon. We stopped and looked and listened for about forty minutes. The night sounds poured

forth. I had to cough which I tried to stifle. He said it was

rude to be disruptive there. He told me to thank the

canyon for the gifts of power that we had received there.

I did. The place had an extremely reverent feel. It

occurred to me that nothing manmade was in the canyon.

It was a totally different world then the one I was used to

living in. This was God's country as they say.

Our minds returned to the fact that we were in

Hollywood, in his apartment. Just talking about the trip

had a sense of bringing me back there. Our conversation

wandered back to other events that had happened when I

used to live in Hollywood. I told him about the time I

experienced an unusual wind in my sleep. I had gone to

sleep a little after midnight. Toward morning I had felt

an incredible wind come and attack me. I was still

asleep. I felt it was trying to kill me. I mentally screamed

for Jonah, thinking perhaps in some way he would be

sensitive to that. I felt as if the wind was trying to drown

me. I thought to calm down and look for my hands in my

sleep like he had told me to do. I thought I had woken

up, but I couldn't see anything but an amber fog with a

purple light in it. Moments later I was awake in my bed. I was scared to death. I wondered what I had just fought off and survived. I didn't move for a few minutes, then I kept the light on for a while.

Jonah said that this was the most important thing I had told him, since we had met. A few nights later something else had happened. I felt as if I was awake in my dream. I saw a wall covered with green vines, with sunlight pouring through the vines. Then someone dropped a utensil next door and I woke up in my bed. The vividness of being awake while still in a dream set it apart from a usual dream.

Jonah said that the amber fog I had seen was in another world. He said that there were other worlds right before us that we sometimes had the energy to see. I was amazed about the amber fog place because I had felt completely awake. I felt that I had already woken up from my dream, but yet, where I was, was not in my room.

While I visited in Hollywood, we again spent a lot of time talking. He would talk about all sorts of things. He would cover a whole subject in one sentence and then continue on with something else. Oftentimes I would slip into what he called heightened awareness. I would understand what he was saying with an intense clarity. Learning is doing. The body is an animal body. Power is in your body. You feel your will from something like tentacles that come out of the stomach area. There is the world of the thinking and the world of the doing. Thinking and knowing something intellectually is not doing. Knowledge is to be passed down. Your body can develop a dreaming double that can come out and appear the same as your body.

"Do what you're doing, when you're doing it." That was another idea about focusing on exactly what you are doing. There were many practices in aiding you to become a warrior. There were practical exercises to train your awareness.

One thing he constantly spoke about, was to shut the inner dialogue. This was the random thought, voice, in your mind that rambled on all the time. This, he said, could not necessarily be claimed by you to be your thoughts. He said... How do you know where these thoughts are coming from? Shutting off the inner

303

dialogue is going to help you develop awareness. In meditation, you should listen for the silence. Listen for a slight hissing noise that seems to be in the air. This he decided to call "the tuner." This was the hissing sound of the universe, to listen for in meditation. What he was teaching me was the study of developing awareness.

There were many angles and aspects, to him passing on his knowledge. He had many suggestions. He said that I should observe everything with people. I should see what is going on with them. The whole body was like a perceiving brain. I should listen to the thoughts and feelings from my body just as if it were a brain. To be intuitive he felt, was natural to the body and that we should pay more attention to it. Build and develop a shield. No one gets over on you for anything. Not being at the mercy of other people was not being stalked by the world. The world was predatory, and he felt that one should not make themselves available to other people's dominions. To develop a warrior body, was very important, he stressed. A warrior body will develop awareness for you.

He said that acting was called controlled folly. To

act was to open up many freedoms. I was terrible because I didn't want to be phony. He said that people couldn't stand it because I acted so lousy. I looked like I should behave powerfully and yet I always acted with inordinate politeness, which looked phonier yet. People hated my false modesty. Acting was stalking, and that was an art form. His benefactor Dan was the actor of all actors. He had placed a great deal of importance on that to him. I eventually realized that if Dan said it was ok to act, then it simply was. I didn't have to go to school for it to give myself permission to explore simply the act of doing it. I had never perceived myself as an actress, so I hadn't really thought the conversations on acting could pertain to me. As if by magic, I one day had a different sense of what they were talking about. It occurred to me that acting in a sense was just like playing, and could be done without great seriousness. In fact, it seemed that everybody already was "acting," and that was considered normal. It seemed more unusual that for all these years I had never loosened up enough just to act naturally. Just be myself. In other words, all of a sudden it just seemed natural to act. It seemed like great fun as well. All of a sudden you could play with any situation and be anyone whom you chose. It was especially fun in social situations and in musical situations. You could act as crazy or intense as you wanted and it was ok because everyone knew you were just fooling around.

We reflected on another trip we had taken. There were actually four, across the country, journeys that we took. He told me I looked well. That was a big deal being that progress as a warrior had a lot to do with fitness. My feelings about seeing him were that, it was usually the best and worst of any sort of encounter that you could have with someone. The conversations and experiences I had had with him were by far the most thrilling and fascinating things that could have happened to me. Often around him a feeling of heightened awareness would slip over me. I would feel less able to speak. Everything would intensify around me. I would feel great, but I was still very much afraid to say the wrong thing to him. I always had to believe that he had good intentions beyond his extremely vicious demeanor. I could relate it to a method of psychology they call tough love. I don't know the specifics of that. He called it cleaning off my island.

Cleaning the bullshit off my island. He at times did it in a very scary manner. It was in essence to clean off the negative brainwash I had accumulated in the world. He would be obscenely forthright on every point. He would sometimes concede to solace me that he was not attacking me... but that he was attacking my bullshit. The logic and haunted house of old baggage that I had accumulated from every passerby I had met on the trail of my life. From parental judgments, to school, to adolescent angst, and all the other authority opinions one gathers through time. He attacked all the preconceptions I had learned in life and taken to be fact. He challenged my worldview on every front. He called the everyday world, the world of the black magician. He said... It's how everyone gets together and agrees on stuff... And then they consider it fact. He called this, the people's "tonal" getting together and forming agreements. He referred to the "tonal" side of man, as the everyday state of consciousness. He referred to the higher portion of a man's consciousness to be his "nagual."

One such agreement made by the "tonals," was that you have to die at a certain age. People drop off at a certain point because they program themselves to. People of earlier time lived vastly longer existences. They knew how to shut off the stresses in the body. One of the most basic premises he made about challenging the world view, was that everyone acted as though they knew. They knew how everything was. How the world was. He said that a person who knew they didn't know a finite synopsis of existence was ahead.

We drove away from the Pittsburgh airport. Early evening in the Ohio Valley was perfect scenic hills. The Indians had been free. The white society were slaves to western thought. The white man hated that the Indians were free. The Indians had no knowledge of how to deal with these people. They should have confined them and not let them go back to their people, he said.

That night was essentially a horror. I was uncomfortable in the car, and my movements disturbed him. Jonah considered it wasteful and for sissies, to stay in hotels, so on this occasion we parked in a hotel lot. I don't recall whether they were full, or he simply preferred the car. I wound up resting on the lawn in front of the car. The police ran a check on me. Jonah thought this was amusing. I was becoming exhausted and traumatized by degrees.

The next day was beautifully overcast. I loved the serenity of that type of weather. It deeply relaxed me. I started to feel better. I tried my absolute hardest to be positive with Jonah. He was not like a boyfriend whom you would strangle if he treated you to any sort of inconvenience. He was never like a boyfriend, even when some years of our association were more personal than others. There was not room in this warrior apprenticeship for the complications of love. That sort of association never came up. Not that our association wasn't excellent in every manner, it's just that while it was of a personal nature, it didn't contain the mentality of a couple association. No level of our association was any more important than any other aspect. The apprenticeship aspect really would have been the overriding factor. It was just, a very well rounded apprenticeship. His spirit of love coexisting with not claiming ownership of each other was actually really cool. Let's just say, his love for me was more about the deeper me. He probably felt I was attractive in a nice way, but I wasn't the muse he was going hang off a cliff for. I was in awe of him. The guy was magic. Honest to god magic. At times we may have appeared as some type of couple, albeit a strange one. It was an elaborate deception that was not lacking in humor. I quickly put aside the discomfort of last night so that I could soak up the joy and the privilege of the present. Enjoying the countryside was an ecstatic adventure. Jonah's company was extremely exciting. The land seemed to cater to his arrival as he drove through. Storm clouds loomed, and rains came and went. It was as though the earth danced for our benefit as we drove on down the highway. There were rainbows, fog and mist. It was very pretty in an ethereal way.

We pulled into a truck stop. We were now in Indiana. The sight of a large school bus of scientology students struck us as very funny. It was a colorful sight, for what seemed like the middle of nowhere. Their bus was brightly painted different colors.

There was a huge rain toward sunset. He told me to stare at the windshield and let my eyes relax, and to cross them slightly. We stared into the rain in silence for an hour as the sun set. He used a rain remover called Rainex, instead of the wipers. As we drove, the feeling of power descended all around us. Jonah said to be quiet and to shut off the internal dialogue.

Late the next afternoon we saw a crop duster airplane. We pulled over to the side of the highway and got out. The guy did all kinds of sweeps and swirls. He came down and flew right over our heads. The fields were beautiful and he was very playful. He gave us a show for the next ten minutes. Right before he flew away he did a sweep that almost went straight into a truck. We flipped out. Thankfully the near disaster did not occur. Then another big rain came up.

We got to Colorado a few days later. The birds are there for a reason. I don't think he was referring to the ones in the canyon. They're very important. We rolled towards a Colorado sunset. We had been in the habit of observing cloud formations. Often it looked like there were pictures and faces evident in the clouds. On this occasion there was a cross eyed face. He said… "It asks you why your spirit is sad?" I felt ashamed that something "out there," could think that I was sad. I mean what could I possibly be sad about. The way nature would seemingly light up around us was only something to be extremely joyful about.

He asked me why I was a devout disbeliever? He asked me if I wanted him to perform magic tricks for me? We were at a table in a diner. I said no. He then rolled up a piece of paper from a straw, put it on the table, made three circles around it with his pointer finger, and made it fly across the table without touching it.

Over dinner we got into conversation. He told me to practice meditation. He said to stretch with my legs back. Sit in a half lotus position. Prop the back up and get real relaxed. Give yourself instructions in the form of a mantra. The brain is a garden and whatever you plant in it will grow.

We listened to the band Rush as we drove. I found the singer Geddy Lee to have a very pleasurable voice. He talked about my move to Manhattan. Let Manhattan unfold for you. I have something pending, apparently you do to. Don't cling to me. Dan can open the crack between the worlds and I'd be out of here in a N.Y second. I feared him leaving. I thought I would have to be mature about it. Be a warrior about it.

The next day on the trip was his birthday. He said…. We're in the most beautiful place in the world on my birthday. You're the only one invited to my birthday party. He got into a conversation about doing. Do meditation, writing, stenography, good food, exercise, music and recapitulation. "Mimic the master." Be in control of what you are doing. Control means doing. No control breeds anxiety. Don't interpret omens. Nothing means anything. If things visit you, nothing means anything. I wondered what he imagined might visit me.

We stopped at the Colorado River. It was a beautiful treat. We left when it began to rain. The little lake where we had camped last year looked cleaner. This felt positive. The year before the stream had seemed sluggish and had reminded me of my health.

As we drove he spoke. You have to be in warrior shape. You have to treat yourself with respect and responsibility. You have to treat the earth with respect and responsibility. He said that when we had gotten to the bottom of the canyon before it was like a benefit. Nature had illuminated around us like we were honored guests. He changed subjects. Don't fixate on the mirror. Stop picking on yourself. Stop the inner dialogue. The inner dialogue is in the English language. The inner dialogue is also in pictures. A warrior is a master of absent thought.... He said. The mind is flash pictures, which we call memory. Pictures are subtler than thought. The inner dialogue is easier to notice. The Nagual says that pictures are travel. The spirit travels across the universe in a second. Daydreaming could be traveling. As we get older logic sets in and we are told what is possible and what is not. Our beliefs even dictate when we are going to die.

You must rewire and reprogram yourself anew to overcome the mental manipulation that has been fostered upon you from childhood. Living extremely organized and disciplined is essential to keeping your mind clear. There will be a great release of energy when you know where everything is. Put everything back where it belongs.

Real learning takes place at a slow rate. He ran down different subjects randomly. A borrower or a lender never be. No handouts. The more generous, the more they interpret kindness for weakness.

The warriors of Don Juan's party prepared to leave the earth. When they died they could take their awareness with them. They could enter another world where their awareness could not be taken from them at death. This is the warrior's quest. If you don't do anything with your gesture with power, then it is meaningless. To mimic the master means to act up. My benefactor was a master actor. He was just like the Nagual Julian, whom was the teacher of Juan Matus.

Lose your personal history. Surround yourself with a cloud so that people can't pin you down with personal history. Track power but don't indulge in it. You don't realize that what has happened to you is very rare. You have to wake up your animal body. The body and it's feeling is the nagual.

You can master and develop intent. Ask and you will be given. He reflected back to something Dan had said about acting. Acting the subtext is the key to acting. Don't just act the lines. Act out the inner self of the character. The people want to become close to the character.

Jonah reflected back to the dinner we had with Dan and Kathy. We were talking about our parents passing. He said he was disturbed to hear of his brother's illness after it was already too late. He was robbed of the opportunity to seek solutions. I told them how when my father had died there was a big smile on his face. He said... it doesn't end. It's going through a door. Life never ends, he said. Some old seers, he said, had managed to retain their awareness. Nothing human would want to go near them. They were cacti in the desert. Something very powerful kept you away from them. All of the other cacti looked worn and frayed. Not these though. They were all as if untouched by time. If you don't go through that door you can hang around earth. That's what ghosts are. They refuse to go on and they hang around earth.

A man of knowledge can learn to slip out of his body and go through the crack between the worlds while he is alive. He can develop his body to the point where he can gather the totality of himself and go back and forth. Then, because he had developed the conscious ability to do this, he can take his awareness and slip to the other side with his awareness, when his body dies.

His body will die, but he has developed the vehicle for his consciousness to reside in. He can "slip by the eagle." He can, not have his awareness become "food for the eagle," when he dies. This takes a lifetime too perfect. This takes good food, rest, meditation, recapitulation and intense exercise.

To act in an extreme intense manner is to focus extremely hard on the will. The will comes out from tentacles in the stomach, he said.

As we drove on I noticed that when I was with Jonah, I felt distinctly detached from society. When we were on the road it was as if I was in some other world. It was his world. We would meet and greet the world, but it was somehow not a part of us, or so I felt. The natural world began to seem more real. More outstanding, more present. The trees stood out more. The scent of the air was strong. People faded out and the environment began to hum. The crickets bristled in the night. The wind became a noticeable presence.

16 CONVERSAIONS AND NOTES

One of the years that I was in Florida I made a list of conversations and subjects that we had discussed. Here are some of the conversations that transpired at that time.

He started by saying…. You can ward off diseases on the mental and spiritual level. Stop thinking. This will stop disease. Disease is waiting for a weakness to get in. Thought is disease. Stop the internal harassment and the internal thought and you will block out disease. Think, concentrate on your work, then cut the internal dialogue and be at peace. Be in harmony with yourself and the earth. The earth can boost your health. Tune into the subtle vibration of the earth and you will quiet your mind, quiet your body, and quiet your spirit. You will become in tune with your body and therefore in tune with your health. Calming the mind, shutting off thought allows the stress to be taken out of you. Stress causes disease. Thought ages you. Worry and stress age you. They age your looks and your internal organs. Meditation can cure you. For meditation he said, relax and shut your eyes. Relax your throat and tongue, this will help you still the mind. When you still the mind… the self of "personality" forgets about itself. Forget you…. Tune into what's around you. Forget your personality.

There are ways of keeping your awareness when you die. You can even take the shell if you want it. Don Juan did. He's not buried anywhere. Start out by taking gaps in your thinking process. Take naps for short periods to drop thought. All thought has an effect on the body. Thinking causes stress on the body. Good thought, bad thought, violent thought. No thought is the healthiest. Thought causes reaction in the body, such as a stiff neck etc …

I stand behind the peacemakers… I don't need to

think violently... but don't mess with me. He was adamant about not letting people get over on him.

Jonah told me that he was trying to drag my awareness up to his, but that he was not going to muck around in my chaos.

Read the Desiderata when I am not there. Read it, commit it to memory and even chant it. Thought effects body. At least put cleansing healing thoughts into you. The Desiderata will help you judge people around you. The ones saying that they're this and that have nothing to offer you. The quiet ones may have something worthwhile to say.

Meditation will take you to a level where you will be listening to things and you can write them down. For example, with music, you can get to a point where you will hear music in your head. That is what Mozart, Bach and others have done. They became quiet, enough to transcribe the music they heard in their head.

Turning off thought rejuvenates you and wards off disease. Lay down for a sleep state for five minutes. Your body could be totally stresses out, but if you hit the sleep state for fifteen minutes you'll be totally recharged.

Tell yourself to turn off the darn mouth inside your head. Shut off the head. Be gentle to yourself, give silence to the head.

These were told to me and I tell them to you, he said. Sorcerers realized that the internal dialogue was bullshit. Turn off the English and just perceive. Allow your eyes to cross and focus on the arch of your nose, with your eyes crossed and shut. You will see light refraction. You will become quieter. Your voice and dialogue will eventually disappear, and other dialogues will be heard. Very interesting dialogues will be heard.

There are two types of thought. Random thought and controlled thought. Get rid of the attacking inner thought, which is random thought. You can have controlled thought be telling the random thought to shut up. Controlled thought is when you have dissected data, or applied yourself in a focused way on whatever you were doing. Nothing is absolute all the time, so you don't always have to control your thought. Enjoy your imagination, just don't become prey to your thoughts. You control them, they don't control you.

Let yourself be free. By stopping or controlling

your thoughts you actually will become relaxed and feel free. The fruits of your imagination will run forth. By controlling the thought and telling the English language to shut up, you are shutting the internal dialogue, which is cutting off the random thought.

The random thought that is always rattling inside you is what you may consider you, but it is not you. This doesn't mean don't function normally. Don't meditate while you are driving. Stay alert. Just relax your mind, stay calm, and at given opportunities turn off the language inside your head. This is shutting the internal dialogue. Shut the mind up for optimal health and to reduce stress.

Always be calm if you can. When you have opportunities to lie down and get clear, do it. This doesn't mean to walk around in a state of total meditation. Be normal, but cut stress in daily life. Meditate deeper when you can.

When you look at the arch of your nose and see light refraction, you will see light emanations. This becomes perception. It becomes interesting. You perceive when you have no thought. He then said something about how I had met my match. I am humbled by my benefactor, he said. He said my stupidity and denseness shielded me from become too energized too quickly.

To relax, you lie with the head and feet propped up. Go into a light sleep where everything leaves your mind. Your body is not bothered by the ego, which is the internal dialogue. The self leaves. When the self leaves the body, then the body is left alone.

Save the body. Allow peace to come into the body and heal it. He continued on… a wise man doesn't grieve for the living, or for the dead. I asked him, "why not?' He said… because then they're not being wise. It accomplishes nothing. There will be a hole in your life when someone dies, but the hole will mend. You can't save someone. Save yourself. That will save others. Save your body. Disease is waiting for a weakness, an opportunity. Don't give it one.

Reverse the aging process. Heal and save your body. When you relax, listen for other voices, when you are in meditation. Each day is new. Each moment is new. Don't keep repeating the same old same old, day in and day out. Realize that each new day is a new opportunity for new thought and new action, new progression. Each new day is unique. Break ruts. Topics were continually changed as he spoke. "The genius is quiet." You can reach the genius inside you by being quiet. If you can read and write music, you can get to a deeper level of meditation, if you can plug into it. Divine voice will allow you to perceive music, and you can write it down.

You can get to a creative state, by going to a deeper level of mediation, where you can shut the mind. Once you shut the mind, stuff will come to you. You catch it. You write it, play it, paint it, diagram it, invent it...

He then moved onto the topic of Taoism in sexuality. He had a book call the Tao of Love. It was a book on Chinese sexuality. He said that it was better to have the woman climax and for the man to save his own energy. Women, he said, never lose their drive. Men feel threatened, because they know that once they climax, they are history, and they know that past a certain age they are not necessarily as they were. The way to satisfy a woman is to not climax all the time. This will give the man energy and the woman pleasure. A man can climax, but realize it is energy spent.

Warriors are disconnected from the concerns of the world. The do not allow weakness to penetrate them. I was taken out of this world. I was the first person in two thousand years. I was put back here. The only heaven is here. We're standing on it. Religion is right here. Jesus shifted people to another world. Naguals used to do that. They would shift the assemblage point of a whole town.

Jesus shifted people so that man could use our potential to be at peace with nature and with the planet. There's going to be a chemical accident, and when there is I suggest that you get out of the way. Everything is happening now. It seems like it is normal because we were born into this time in history, but that is not the case. This is not the way the world always was. We are too close to it to see it in relation to the history of man. It's only the last hundred years that started to destroy the earth.

You cannot save the world. Save yourself and you will save the world. Save yourself through meditation. Each day is unique. Be on to better days. Don't misuse wealth. These people run around saying they are witches and sorcerers. Whoever is effecting your thoughts is the one being the witch or sorcerer.

The object of the warrior's path, Jonah said, was to gather your totality and leave. Not going back to the human egg pile, the cycle of reincarnation.

Be the best you can be. "Do what you're doing, when you're doing it." Cut talking and be peaceful. He continued... lay down and take naps to rejuvenate you. Things are chaotic in the world. Take a beat. Be at peace.

Watch the world but don't go up and down with it. The best thing that you could possibly do is to leave the world a better place than when you got here. You will have accomplished the greatest task, by leaving the place a better world here.

My story is different than yours. Everyone looks at a Monet and sees something different. Everyone who reads the Castaneda stories sees something different.

"We're on our own. There's nothing but the earth for light years. The cosmos is right here."

Mozart and Bach tuned into another level of existence that dictated their music to them. They were master transcribers.

You are dead mentally when nothing is interesting. Don't lie, cheat or steal. Have a mind of your own. What you think of yourself doesn't matter. I told Jonah about being nervous in school one day, and how my glasses fell off my face seemingly of their own volition. He said that it was an agreement from the earth. The earth is everything around us. The Indians were in nature, so they got communication from the earth, but even with technologies, everything around us is still considered the earth. The glasses shattering could have been to say shut up to the inner dialogue. I noticed it because it was like I was feeling this inner anxiety about a teacher, and the way they fell seemed like they moved by themselves, but it seemed in response to my inner nerves, not a physical movement. Your nervousness was a reaction to the inner chattering dialogue.

"You are... where your mind is at." You can be in a different world out here. That's why you stay in total concentration when you walk around or are driving. I'm expanding your awareness. I won the cosmic lottery ticket. The Nagual knew of me before I knew of him.

We are radios. Most people are on automatic pilot.

They are running on instinct. They can smell power.

They can smell another person's essence on you.

17   CONVERSATIONS WITH JONAH

I dreamed that my dream body was flying. I
dreamed that I had gone back into my body. I thought
that I had woken up and was writing about it. Then I
woke up and realized that that had been a dream also. As
I was flying I passed an aunt. I saw her eyes greet me. I
dreamed I saw an old boyfriend. I dreamed my parents
were together in our old house. When I see my father I
always appreciate seeing him because I always
remember that he's usually dead. When I see him in the
dream, I still remember that in another place he's dead.

Jonah said that if you're doing something imperfectly, you're wasting your time. Everything should be done perfectly. I told Jonah about the dream. His statement was… "be on your toes." Don't go through this like a butterfly on an acid trip. I told him that I was concerned that my account of this would sound perhaps crazy. He said… You care too much what people think. It's a detriment to your whole life. They are all limerick sorcerers. Sorcerers of language, that get their energy on you. Other people's energy gets on you and weighs you down. That's why you have to clean other people's energies off your island. What I do for you in heightened awareness, you have to do in the exercise of recapitulation. Recapitulation gives you back the energy you gave away to people your whole life. Only this will enable you to assemble enough energy to perform dreaming, develop a dream body, and succeed at getting past the eagle, which is a maneuver to continue your consciousness after death, in another realm of existence.

I told Jonah about the female dancers I had met at the gym. He became emphatic that I needed to strip to lose my self- importance. I never could. The idea was completely mortifying. I now think that it wouldn't have been the most horrible thing to do. I secretly hope that at some point I would feel so confident and comfortable with my body that I could go to some amateur night and do it for the emancipation of losing self- consciousness. As of yet I haven't managed this. I will say the idea makes sense now. When he first mentioned it I was really shocked at even the idea of it.

I told Jonah that it annoyed me that sometimes people would just treat me as a gender and not an individual. Some people will always look at you as a "woman," he emphasized the word. They will fail to recognize you as a human being, and will always consider you as "one of them." We laughed. He talked about the deterioration of society. Egypt was good because they had street punishment for offenses.

The Tonals are hooked on their own bullshit. They get together and agree on things and take that as solid fact. Their worshipping the god they created. Limerick sorcery is language sorcery.

I remembered how he told me that I spent all my time skimming stuff, hanging out and never producing anything. The fact that I had never produced anything should be alarm bells that your life is going by. I thought it was ok because I knew how to find the really talented people, but I never produced like them. I just got around them to check out their energy and their work. Musical performances fed my mind, body and spirit to the point where I didn't need anything. I didn't feel like I needed to produce anything, and for years at a time it could even replace sex.

I acknowledged that dealing with accomplished people was invigorating and inspirational, but that you still had to do your own work.

When you get emphatically crazy about something, it's called indulging. If wisdom doesn't teach you then life will. Warriors don't worry about anything. They are right down the middle of the road, meaning moderation is the warriors way.

What does it take to wake you up? You're acting and doing things teenagers do. You're overindulging and living wrong. You can't go back to the life that you had. He said this after I told him about a night of drinking.

There are places if I walk into a room people will

kiss my feet. I don't indulge in that because we realize that we are just men. But you don't listen. You don't listen to anybody. You puzzle me. Don't talk about or dissect power because it dissipates. Why are you so afraid of boredom? Remember I told you not to take food from strangers. These people are phantoms. Those "children" at the party could be like demons. They think it's funny to drop acid in a keg of beer, or piss in it. They're self -destructive with no brains. They are angry and stupid, and have no consideration for the planet or anybody else. I told him I felt sick. You better lie on the earth. You better not take my presence lightly.

You're neurotic, don't worry. Warriors don't worry. Remember what I said about not picking on yourself. Do you listen about staying off of yourself? Change your behavior, but don't sit around criticizing it.

The warrior's way is no wasted moves. No wasted energy. This path is about energy. Dreaming is a whole other track of awareness.

I was here before. There was evidence that popped up. There were puzzles about my existence. Large factions of people brought theories of reincarnation to light about one thousand years ago.

When I met my benefactor, things clicked when he showed up. The evidence for me is astonishing. It's phenomenal. I'm not a self- made phenomena. I had nothing to do with it.

I didn't have anything to do with what happened in my life. Decisions were made before I was born. Death is inevitable. I know reincarnation is a fact. It has nothing to do with religion. Enlightenment has to do with the way that you live.

I'm light years ahead of everyone, he said. There should be honesty. Don't lie, cheat or steal. Take care of yourself. Be responsible for your actions.

Society is unnatural and messed up. It's hopeless when you look at the family of man. They will self-destruct, and what they will take with them is tragic. The only thing that you can do is take care of yourself. That affects other people. All the religions are trying to save everyone else. We don't give a fuck. Nasty people are disguised well. The people polluting the oceans. The politicians raping forests.

"Ignorance is no excuse for breaking the laws of

nature." The president should be cleaning the planet. I continued over time to take notes of some of our conversations. This is a loose synopsis of a group of conversations that took place.

We don't care about things. Caring about things zaps time. The Indian, (he refers to Don Juan Matus) is up to freedom. "Freedom is what I am up to." The Castaneda books will explain what we are up to. If you follow the path, and become a friend of the earth, the earth takes care of all your needs. Humans are the hardest to become friends of the earth. When the earth loves you, things come your way. It isn't luck. Do right, and right comes back to you. If people get hip to this, politicians will be fired. I try to substantiate this to you to give you faith. Why believe me? To believe me is getting with it. Knocking down walls that the black magicians built up. Knock down bullshit. Free yourself from that. Getting you to not be a skimmer is a task. Education disturbed your spirit. See lies for lies. There's potential that you can get to. Read the Art of Dreaming by Carlos Castaneda before you go to sleep.

Catch yourself before you go to sleep. You'll see

things in dreams. You'll realize your asleep. You'll get clear on dreams. When you see things bring them into focus. See things, recognize them and then move the focus around. You'll see it when it happens and then you will recognize it. I'm a dust gazer. I gaze at dust in the sun. Gazing is for finding things in your dreams. I can pick you up in your dream, then don't freak out. Don't fall into a deep sleep. Try to wake up in sleep. Eventually it will work. Then, there's a new world.

I've taken journeys with Dan. Dan is like Don Juan in a lot of ways. Genaro is his benefactor. Get off the occult crap. Don't idolize. Jesus said follow me, not worship me. The unique people, who have real knowledge, are anyone to get to the real side of knowledge, are anyone to get to the other side of the universe.

Indians call it Maya, the illusions of the world. Rock stars, gurus, it's all scam. It's all bullshit. You shouldn't be impressed. It's about life. It's about survival. If you can't lay a rabbit trap, what good are you? Magic is in everyday life. Be good and good things will come to you. Don't kiss ass to anyone. You are on another level of awareness because you are not asleep.

18. RECAPITULATION

Recapitulation is an exercise for regaining the full energy and power of your dreaming body. This takes back the energy spent in the world. Dreaming is developing a perception. Recapitulation is how you clean yourself off to prepare for dreaming. Do slow deep breathing in privacy and meditation. You should be breathing deeply on a regular basis.

Inhale as you roll your head to the left. Exhale as you bring it back to the right, then sweep it left to right again. Think of someone or something as you do this. Breathe deeply. Make a list of everyone you have encountered. You can do a formal recapitulation of an exact list as well as doing a random recapitulation. Random would be to recapitulate whatever comes to mind. A daily recapitulation is good too, for the events of the day. Do this consistently. Do this systematically. Set aside time daily, as if you were doing a meditation practice. This theory and practice is well delineated in the Carlos Castaneda stories, as well as the books written by his other apprentices and Don Juan's other apprentices. This is to erase things clinging to you. Two of Castaneda's apprentices wrote excellent books. Their names are Taisha Abelar and Florinda Donner. Taisha wrote "The Sorcerer's Crossing. Florinda wrote.... "Being in Dreaming, The Witches Dream, and, Shabono. An apprentice of Don Juan named Ken Eagle Feather wrote... "The Toltec Path, "Traveling with Power" and "Tracking Freedom". He wrote some other things on different topics as well.

Recapitulation is to erase things clinging to you. Doing something nine times in a row forms a habit. The head is like a haunted house on your shoulders. Clean out your head. Keep belongings to a bare minimum. This will actually clear out your head and give you more energy. Don't let belongings become weight on you. Neat, clean and organized has the most energy. Keep only necessities. Focus on awareness. Dreaming is the ultimate goal. No obligations. You owe nobody anything. If you owe anybody anything, it's me, and I don't want anything. I've saved your life. I've saved more than your life, I've saved your soul and I say you don't owe me anything. We canceled out you owing anybody anything. You can take this as casual conversation. I noticed you act like your obligated to people. I've seen people play you like you're a piano. The whole world finds it hard to be honest. The honest one is so independent it's scary. I told him I saw a part of him in my dream. He said I should have touched him, and he would have felt it. "Look at things, don't look too long, look around." He recommended I take naps, as needed, to renew energy. Moods, he said, have a voice. Everything has a voice. Bad food has a voice. There are thoughts with the body if you pull a muscle. The body is a brain. It thinks from different areas.

To quiet the inner dialogue and for meditation, focus on the tongue. Tell the tongue to relax. Focus your eyes on the bridge of your nose. Cross the eyes lightly. Then turn off the inner dialogue. You'll get to a level where my voice will come in. Whatever you saturate your mind with will continue to linger in your mind. Just relax. Relax the tongue. Relaxing the tongue will relax the inner dialogue. Let it go. Feel detached while you meditate. Listen to your thoughts. He told me to stop feeling bad for my father who had passed. Stop entertaining thoughts. It's stupid to feel sorry for a dead person. He changed the subject. It's good to blend in. It's a freedom. Other people like attention. This is about getting your attention off yourself. There are a lot of levels you can get hooked on. The tenant lived over two thousand years. "This is to not lose the totality of yourself." Carlos made roadmaps of aspects of discipline. Be prepared, stay awake to opportunity. Hook onto opportunities and cultivate them. It takes a while for all this information to settle down in you. The path will present itself. Everyone got bits and pieces of this thing. I believe because I lived it, he said. I'm humbled by my experience. Warriors stay in the middle of the road. This path expands on contemporary view of the possibilities of the human condition. What we are really capable of doing. The real challenge is not showing it off, but keeping it quiet.

I'm in my benefactor's realm. I don't go through the changes of fellow men. I'm not affected by other people's opinions. I act up. I'm a stalker, an actor. I can exist here without being a sorcerer. I live here as normal. If you would have a mirror in front of you when you were out living, you would act better.

People invent you. They see what they want to see. I decided to get off the phone at this point. I was feeling almost high in a way, as so often, our conversations made me feel. This was an intensely literal feeling. Not like a mood, but like a serious euphoria. I asked why Jonah why I was scaring people? He said that I had to act and behave better. It's ok to act. To be a stalker you have to fit in and act.

All of these books in the new age bookstores are trying to get you to go outside of your head and see what's outside yourself. See how far you can go outside the self without getting lost.

19 THE VOICE OF THE EMISSARY

Jonah told me that a Mexican man from the neighborhood had asked about me. I went to sleep and had a bad dream. I dreamed that I had seen a shootout on television and that later, I found myself running for cover trying to get out of the way. It seemed like it was four am and the participants were there for entertainment. I demanded five dollars from a friend for causing a flat tire on my car. I was tough and people seemed mad. Childhood friends were there. I woke up out of that dream and I was a little scared. I thought at that moment about how Jonah had told me about the Mexican man from across the street, whom had sent his regards.

At that moment, the compassionate sensual voice, of a Mexican male, said hello in my head. I became alarmed. I had been awake. The voice was closer to a thought. It was not spoken into the room, but I heard it in my mind. I started groping around for the lamp to turn on the light.

I thought it was odd also, because I had been wondering about something Dan had said. He had said that Don Juan and Genaro had come inside his body. I had wondered what that meant. Then it made me wonder about Jonah mentioning the Mexican man in LA who had asked about me. I couldn't jump to any wild insane conclusions except that a very warm clear voice had resounded in my mind when I was seemingly awake. I wanted to call Jonah, but it was three thirty in the morning and I doubted he would consider this newsworthy, were he asleep.

He was going away for a month or so. There was talk of me driving back with him from the East Coast to Los Angeles. I was a little concerned that while he was away something bizarre would happen that I would want to confer with him about. I still thought that he could help if there was some kind of emergency in dreaming or something else outside my abilities. I didn't want to call him about my personal life melodrama.

I called Jonah to tell him about the voice I heard. I said to him... I hate to lose my credibility with you, but do you have a moment. Yes, go on already, don't take all day, he said. I told him that I had a dream where people were partying and shooting guns. I told him I woke up and was thinking about the Mexican guy who had spoken to him about me. I told him that out of nowhere, on the level of thought, a very rich voice with a Mexican accent had said hello to me. He told me that it could have been the emissary, the voice that had talked to Carlos. He told me not to make more of it then it was. He told me that I didn't have to report back to him like a cub scout leader. Then he said... if you get communications its ok to tell me about them, but don't become jarred by anything that you see or hear.

We are observers. I observe a lot of crazy things here. Things are not as you have grown up to believe. Now you're getting a taste that things are different. Like the thing about the aliens, they're trying to become known slowly. I didn't stop him to question that. Just don't interpret. Don't be an expert. You're demonstrating a higher level of expertise by acknowledging that you don't know where this stuff comes from. People get bits and pieces of this stuff, and then they're convinced that they're talking to god and that they know everything. At least Don Juan and the warriors say that this is in the unknowable. He seemed concerned that I would become excessively frightened by the experience. I told him that I was not disoriented, but that I thought it was worth mentioning. I actually felt like a wimp when it happened. I realized that this stuff was bigger than my imagination and that perhaps I didn't have the guts for this path.

I didn't have the pompousness to imagine that Don Juan or Genaro, would have any reason to greet me, but I thought of that as a possibility, because that was supposed to be on some other level, and this was not a call on the telephone. That even occurred to me only because Dan had said, that they had somehow come inside his body.

In our next conversation, Jonah said…. Everything is equal. Daily life and dreaming are equal. What you seek, is within you. Perceive outside yourself.

I took a walk in my benefactor's dreams. You make this professional or you lose it. This is not a love affair. There are two ballparks to play in. The everyday and the Dreaming world. Recapitulate bad feelings until they fall off your body. Don't be a bottom feeder. Stay away from slime. If I tell you my tales of power, then you better learn how to write. Stay out of office gossip. Be professional, organized and impeccable. The tenant has the only game worth pursuing. Eternity is one minute after the next, forever. I have a strange knowledge and I have a normal life. Life was supposed to be very wide open. Over the centuries things that were common knowledge became unknown again. It became radical to discuss other natural aspects of life. The con artists, constructing today's society didn't want to be found out. It threatened them to lay down the real information that would expose their lack of perception. Seek and ye shall find. Seek the real stuff, not the fake stuff that appears to everyone in their travels of life. Don't be afraid to be your real self. Be quiet and watch. Trust your real self. Trust your instincts, and talk only as your real self. Don't engage in stupid conversation. You were dead before because you had no job or career. You screwed up, but you can get on track. He said that dreaming and the emissary were natural parts of the human experience. So why was it that anytime anything of this nature occurred I would become bodily frightened?

The world of heaven is within. Seek within the kingdom of heaven. Stop looking outside. You have to go inside of yourself to get out of yourself. I thought to myself … stalk that guitar, and the door slammed loudly. There was dreaming and stalking as the cornerstones of becoming a warrior. The dream world with its mysteries, and the act of stalking your everyday life into a state of impeccability.

I woke up feeling as though my whole life I had been subtly pursuing the Nagual, the higher awareness and experience. I had let the Tonal wither down to nothing. I forgot to get the normal stuff in life right. The most flagrant example of that is the pursuit of something for the love of it with no financial return. It's fine to do things we love, but I put a lot of effort and time into guitar, without the use of it for anything financial. I began to get paid, but it was only after I was financially devastated for years of focusing on an avocation.

Another serious topic that was discussed endlessly was the idea of cleanliness, order and organization. He was maniacal about this. He said that the mess outside you, is a reflection of what is inside you. Clean up the mess outside you, and it will heal and clean out your head inside you. This was a lifelong relationship with order. Put everything in its place. Clean one corner at a time. Clean an area and then keep it clean. Have only necessities. Things can own their owners.

When I talked to Jonah everything would clear up. If I was depressed, lonely or paranoid, talking to him plugged me into joy, laughter and potentialities. It was magic itself.

I dreamed I was walking through the ladie's room of the Roosevelt Hotel. There were built in pictures of Jimi Hendrix. I walked past a couple with a baby. The father sort of resembled Eddie Van Halen. The child was crying and could not be consoled. Finally, they put an electric guitar on it and it played the song eruption. He was still in his mother's arms, couldn't walk or talk, but he could play lead guitar. I woke up feeling very dissatisfied with my guitar playing. Just as I thought this, the earth chose to punctuate this by changing the speed on the ceiling fan. I realized I had to work on it a lot harder.

I dreamed I saw my father. His afro was tall and he was wailing on a pretend guitar acting like Jimi Hendrix. I laughed because he was making a joke, but I cried because I knew he was dead or dying and was just trying to cheer me up.

I'm keeping your stuff together. I don't even know if it's good to be laying all of this on you. You know more than ninety percent of the people on this planet. Get into training your body. Just talking to him made me mysteriously and totally happy, peaceful and content.

My benefactor is like an ancient seer. Carlos and Don Juan are like modern day seers. You don't know normal guys. You know transient types. He again mentioned recapitulation, dreaming and impeccability.

Be your own best friend. The real you, is the best possible you. Be yourself. Get outside your head. Tune into the world around you. Stop the internal dialogue, which is the chatter in your head. Learn by doing. When you stop thinking, you will tune into awareness. All the mantras are to get you to be quiet, and to shut off the mind. They are to bring inner peace. To learn effectively, break everything down slowly. Doing something nine times cuts a groove. Do things nine times in a row to set a pattern.

The world is full of sorcerers. They're all sorcerers trying to bend you to their will. We call them limerick sorcerers because they use words to draw people into them. Whoever is getting under your skin, and is on your mind, is a sorcerer. Not the people with the incense and the rituals.

Being professional is where it is at. Being professional means having everything exactly organized. Nothing extra added. Your closets should be professional, cleaning your room should be professional. Being professional is having everything running smoothly.

Your mind and your life is comparable to an island. Everything on your island should be cleaned off. Your connection to spirit should be cleaned off. The bullshit cluttering your mind should be eliminated. Cleaning your mind and life, makes you more accessible to spirit and power. People connecting to spirit have emptied their minds and life of excess baggage and crap. Cleaning up your body strengthens your link to spirit. Relaxing the throat will help still the thoughts in the mind. Stop thinking and listen. Thinking about someone else is their karma on you, if you're thinking about them in a negative way. Control random thoughts. There's random thinking and constructive thinking. Constructive thinking is when your studying. People can make you feel good or bad. Deal with bullshit or it kills you. Under subconscious thought is consciousness. Be conscious of your subconscious. Observe your thoughts. Thoughts influence body. Positive thoughts help heal the body. Negative thinking and feeling tear the body down.

Power is a feeling. Power is in places. There is magic in life, if everyone was free. The warrior's way is to be free. Get yourself impeccable, with your stuff together and you will feel free. Follow the path of heart. Make it simple. Watch what the animals do. Most people are not what they look like. Get along with the human race.

The planet will heal itself. People will do a complete turnaround if they realize, that if they take care of the planet, that is the shortest distance to the planet taking care of them.

If you heal the planet, it will clear the stage, and life will reward them. There can be peace or war. A benefactor is a Nagual, who is a container of knowledge. Knowledge is passed on from generation to generation. To live healthy is to relax. To relax as you work, to relax as you live. Chaos grew with the population and the life span shortened, Dan had said. Everyone can be creative. It's a matter of developing a method to achieving creativity. Create a formula to doing something, and then do it. Writing brings you into a state of perception. Writing inadvertently expands awareness. Work on seeing what's around you. Sit down and write what is around you, and expand your perception of what is around you. Sorcery is training in awareness. There's the world inside your head, and the world outside your head. You have to go inside to get to the outside. You have to listen to the inside to hear what is outside. When you entrench yourself in something, ideas start to be created within you. If you listen to a lot of music, then music will begin to brew inside you. Thinking is hearing. Hum it the way you hear it. Draw it out of the ethers. Get silent to hear stuff below the conscious mind. Shakespeare and the real creative, practice the art of listening. They listen to art that comes into their mind. They have an idea of form, but then the creativity comes into the mind, of itself. The individual has the skill, the mechanics, but the muse comes of its own volition.

Food has a voice. What you put into your body comes out of you in the way of your thinking, mood and feelings. It speaks through you. To have the mood of a warrior, a feeling of power, eat healthy good food. Bad food brings negative thoughts and feelings.

Discipline stops negative mental ranting. Discipline, faith and patience are the only ways to redeem yourself. Jonah continued.... Work for the earth. The raw truth rules. Mother nature presides. Wise men are learning that our place is to have dominion over the earth and to tend this garden. To treat it with the infinite care and respect that it deserves.

"Cleaning the earth is a universal priority." The leaders are small time. They can't do their thing without the planet.

Dreaming is knowledge. It is learning how to go from one level to another. The spirit moves at the speed of light. Astral projection is the spirit. Some worthwhile pursuits would be.... Living forever and healing the planet. Seeing a better world is a slim chance. The planet will prevail. The planet will collapse back. Jonah continued.... Taking care of yourself is the first step. Taking care of the thought process is number one. Try not thinking. Slow down. Don't rush through things. Do things calmly and accurately. To speed things up, slow things down. Doing things thoroughly creates progress.

To organize a project, writing or otherwise, make a rough draft. Outline topics of conversation. Get organized. If you look at a whole job, nothing gets done. Do it one piece at a time.

We started talking on the phone two or three times a week. Sometimes we would talk for hours.

It's possible to go from life to life and retain your consciousness. If you master a certain type of wisdom, you can go from life to life with your awareness intact. With the knowledge that he had been given by his benefactor, he only had one main desire. To leave the planet in better shape than when he got there. To help the human race, you had to believe that the potential was possible. The planet will heal itself. People have to realize that if they do a turnaround and take care of the planet, then the planet will take care of them. Taking care of the planet will be the shortest distance to reach the potential of clearing the stage, for what could be man's natural inheritance, of what could be heaven on earth. Where everyone was fed and clothed, and got by in a peaceful and productive manner. If everyone could be their true selves, and do what came naturally to them, the world would take care of itself. People could choose peace.

A warrior's knowledge is like any other discipline, be it science of mathematics. It is a body of knowledge passed down from generation to generation. To live well and to live long it is important to relax. To live in a meditative way is the way to health and peace. Today's lifestyle is stressful to the body. Shutting off your inner dialogue brings you closer to your senses. To feel the peace and freedom within is the warrior's way. Watch what animals do, because they go with their instincts. They are intuitive and always alert. They use their senses. Humans could do that more if they made themselves more aware to.

The chaos grew when the population grew, and as the population grew, the lifespan dropped. People used to live to eight hundred or so when they used meditation daily. I had a natural skepticism when he said that. That was not a believe that I had grown up to consider as a possibility, but neither was lucid dreaming, so I don't know.

He began again…. An artist is a sorcerer. Someone to tap and bottle the source, and to effect people either negatively or positively. The hardest part about creativity was slowing it down. You don't write a book, a song or a screenplay. You write a sentence, a hook, a riff…. A theme. Rome wasn't built in a day and creativity could be approached the same way. Learning could also be approached the same way. Learn in chunks. Don't try to digest everything in one sitting. Do it piece by piece and then put it all together. To look at a whole work and try to recreate it could be very intimidating. Do small pieces. Start slow and go on. He told me that the doves were outside on the window ledge by his bed. He always fed them.

Get over the hump of being alone, because everyone is really alone. Then again we are social creatures. It's alright to have company, but it should be good company. Company that has a good effect on you. Nothing means anything. Don't interpret things, just be an observer, a witness.

20   THE LIVING WIND

I told Jonah about an experience that I had. In my

sleep, a wind had come and attacked me. I felt that it was

trying to kill me. I had mentally screamed for Jonah. I

felt like I was being drowned by a wind. I thought to

calm down and look for my hands like he had told me to

do in my sleep. I thought I had woken up, but I couldn't

see anything but an amber fog with a purple light in it.

Moments later I was awake in my bed. I was scared to

death. I wondered what I had just fought off and

survived. I didn't move for a few minutes. Then I kept

the light on for a while. Jonah said that this was the most

important thing I had told him since we had met. A few nights later something else happened. I felt as if I was awake in my dream. I saw a wall covered with green vines, and sunlight streaming through the vines. Then someone dropped a utensil next door and I was awake in my bed. The vividness and the texture had been clear and as if in a waking state.

You start conforming to your surroundings. You start meeting your parent's expectations, and then the whole world becomes like your parents. You become messed up by bending to everyone. Do your thing. You are in control of your behavior at all times. People interact with you on your terms. You are where you are at all times. You invent what your preconceived attitudes are. Stop thinking to stop disease. The bad health will be taken out of you. Thought is disease. Thought ages you. There are ways of keeping awareness alive. Take gaps in thinking process. Thoughts have an effect on the body. Having no thought is the healthiest. I stand behind peace, he said, but don't mess with me.

People are in a state of sleep. They are unaware of the potential to expand their awareness. Get quiet and get totally organized. About the self, a warrior realizes what an inept clod the self is, and leaves it in the dust. That is one of the great challenges of becoming a warrior. Consistency wins the race. Put your life on a metronome. The metronome of life. Stay paced, but moving. Don't get ahead of yourself in the learning process. Repetition creates good real learning. Go slow.

21   JONAH'S BENEFACTOR DAN

His story, Jonah said, was that he had been living close to a college campus when he met his benefactor. He was going to meet a friend at a restaurant one day. The friend showed up and brought another guy. Then for some odd reason, the friend started sputtering inanities and walked off the scene. He left him with this guy Dan.

Dan started saying stuff, and before he knew it, "his jaw just started catching flies." He was just amazed at how this stranger knew him. It didn't take long for him to want to know what this stranger was about. He had a

strong presence. "No woman could resist this energy."
He would visit Dan in his apartment which also in the off
campus vicinity. A group of people would just go over
and listen to this guy rap. That was all that they could do.
Shortly after he met Dan really amazing things started
happening in his life. He wound up buying a tavern with
no money down. The scenario of his apprenticeship took
place in an old English Tudor style large gorgeous
tavern. They did a great renovation on it. At the
beginning of an apprenticeship, everyone is drawn in by
the interestingness and the coolness of it, but as it goes
on it gets really hard, and most people try to take a
vacation or escape from it, as such. One time he just
hitchhiked away to be with friends. His assemblage point
had shifted.

I'm waking you up to things that are unknown to
you now. This is about how to wake up in your dreams
and how to live in your dream state awake. Stop hassling
and restricting yourself. Let yourself be free. You go too
far to be normal. Do not judge yourself by how other
people judge you. Be your own best friend. Look for
your hands in your dreams. The Indians knew a lot about

knowledge and existence.

I would get into a trancelike state just by talking to Jonah. He called that heightened awareness. It happened with him and his benefactor. He said that it was a gesture with power.

Art is thievery. It is to observe, to chop apart, and to recreate. The path with heart is where the feeling is. Pursuing the unknown. To interpret what you see, is to call yourself an expert. That makes us talk above our heads. People who give explanations are making it up. Gazing is doing something meticulously. Staring at something and recalling it in your dreams. Gazing is focusing and then dreaming about it.

I told Jonah how I had been waiting for soup at the deli. I had been absentmindedly looking at a large chocolate cookie as I waited. I later dreamed vividly that cookie.

Cut the starving artist bullshit out of your existence. No more, hippy dippy bullshit. You need strong survival skills. I told him about a peculiar vibration I had felt at our corner rock and roll pub, in Hollywood. He said that he had probably left the vibration there when he had lived and worked there.

"I'm an Indian," in spirit. My spirit loves the earth. The earth is God. The path of heart is an Indian warrior path. We live in a world of sorcerers. It's hunt or be hunted. The whole world has that game going on. Sorcery is the power to influence someone. Clean up your own act and you will be able to heal others around you. Shut off your inner dialogue. The endless chatter. When your mind is talking, then you think it is you thinking, but how can you be sure that it is you producing these thoughts. What if these thoughts are coming to you from somewhere else? It is better to be aware of the silence inside, then the nonstop barrage that comes from you or from who knows where. To be present and not lost in thought, is a better place to operate from. Like an athlete who must perform a function without thought.

Allow the natural ability to flow without hindrance of thought or analysis. If there was no consciousness of self, there would be no self -consciousness. People's proficiency would soar. Children ride this crest. They worry about nothing and just blow through things until inhibitions are taught. Watch animals. They are in their intuitive state at all times.

Function in your own element. Be where it feels comfortable for you. Do, what feels right and be with people that feel right. You attract what you seek. Thoughts were like magnets. You attracted a sorcerer because that is what you sought. If you still have desire for something, then you can achieve it.

I thought about the time I had planned to go upstairs and give Jonah the rent. I had gone in the bathroom and looked in the mirror. I told myself... "You look good without makeup." After five minutes in his house, he looked at me, and in the inflection of voice that I had just talked to myself, said... "You look good without makeup." It gave me this strange electrical charge. I picked out your thoughts was what he said later about that. He continued talking.... Learning is doing. Moving is creativity, forget about thinking. Normal is relative to yourself. Fair and honest is impeccable. Never let an asshole run their shit on you. By that he meant, that a lot of people will always try to control you for whatever their own interests are. You have to be wise to that and make sure you are living in accordance to your own values and interests as much as possible. Too many people let other people just come in and boss them and it's just simply unnecessary. Make sure you protect yourself from that. Clean up your life and get professional. I see it when I believe it. Believe something and it will more likely come to be. Jonah continued... Listen for other voices. The genius is quiet. It's like reading music. Plug into the divine voices and transcribe the music in your head. In sexuality, the secret of Taoism is to satisfy the woman first, because once the man ejaculates, he is history. Have no weakness. Warriors are disconnected. Relaxed, detached and at ease. I was taken out of this world, the first person in two thousand years.

The planet is heaven. We're on our own. Religious stuff is right here. Jesus shifted people to a different world, so that we may use our potential to have peace with nature and the planet. Everything is happening now. We were born into it so we don't see the magnitude of the destruction. We are too close to it. Save yourself through meditation. Save your health. Every day is unique. Don't just keep having the same days over and over. You can be on to better days. Whoever is affecting your thoughts is the witch, or the sorcerer. The idea is not to go back to the human egg pile. To take the totality of yourself and leave. Be the best of yourself. Do what you're doing when you're doing it. Stay present. Cut the inner talking. Be in meditation and peaceful. Lay down and take naps to rejuvenate. Things are chaotic, be at peace. You have accomplished your greatest task when you leave things better then when you found them. Everybody sees something different. Everybody sees a Monet differently.

Mozart and Bach tuned into another level of existence that dictated their music to them. They were master transcribers. We're on our own. There's nothing, but the earth for light years. The cosmos is here.

A wise man does not grieve for the living or for the dead. It is not wise. It accomplishes nothing. The hole in your life mends. When meditating, relax the neck and tongue. Tell the body to have no cancer. Relax the tongue chakra, which is the inner dialogue. When the body is not bothered by the ego, which is the internal dialogue, the self leaves. Save the body by shutting the mind. When the self leaves, the body is left alone. Shut the eyes and you can see light emanations. It is like a big screen right behind your eyes, where they tell you to imagine that the third eye is. Translucent light becomes perception. When thoughts shut off, we are free to perceive. Lie with head and feet propped up. Go into a light sleep. Everything leaves the mind. Control your thoughts. Tell thoughts to shut up. Stop the English language. Stop random thinking. Focus on the third eye. Shut off the head.

22   SHUTTING THE INNER DIALOGUE

We took up again the next evening. Be gentle with yourself, he said. Give silence to your head. Random internal dialogue is garbage. When you turn off thoughts you can just perceive. Turning off thought wards off disease. The maturity of man never got past the twenties in most people. You see adolescent people in old bodies. They reach a certain plateau and they kick off their learning process. They go into a sleep state. Henceforth you have people closed in a pattern of some sort and they have little interaction with the world outside of them.

Keep the island clean and the spirit will talk to you.

Make progress every day. Don't worry about the whole

picture. Take time but don't let up. We could become

extinct like dinosaurs. There could be a freak accident or

a meteor. Man created God in his image. There is a god.

A positive creative force here. I pay attention to the earth

and my allies because I pick up interesting things.

Coincidence can be taken away. The Indian Juan Matus

took coincidence away. My benefactor took coincidence

away. It's not a big deal if the earth wants to

communicate with you. Raise awareness to what's

possible. Instead of killing nature, take care of the earth.

Everyone could be rich. The rich are afraid of everyone

becoming rich. Religious stories stood the test of time.

There are more modern ways to say things. Modern

stories are aimed at saving the planet. The white man lost

track. Places have feelings. We stay where we suffer

sometimes. Go somewhere else. Mental and spiritual

health has to do with places. Warriors don't get overly

involved with people. That is closer to being a seer. You

get out of the human band. He went on... don't be

responsible for other people, being a warrior is enough.
Sorcery is a level. There are levels above sorcery.
Sorcery just deals with influencing people. A real man of
knowledge is a jumping point. A man of knowledge
knows that knowledge, is where the highest point is.
Warriors are independent. Independence means not being
impressed with celebrities or possessions. They are just
flashing their wad. They are the world of the black
magicians. They are all playing masters and slaves. To
me, he said, it's all boring bullshit. I'm not inside that
circle that presses upon people. Happy means not having
to worry. An artist.... They are invisible people doing
their thing. No public image. America is a concept. It is a
word.

We took a break and then I called him back again.
He took up again. When you don't know anything,
you're closer to knowing something. A clean room has
energy. Going out alone depends on what you are going
out for. He said that when I used to say I was shy to
music bars or concerts alone. When I realized that really
all I was looking to do was enjoy the music and the
company of being around people, I was not longer shy

about it. It might look like I was looking to meet people just because I was alone, but in reality I really was there for the music. Socializing could be an added bonus, but the reality was that the music was what satisfied me and made it worth my while.

You can ward off disease on a mental and spiritual level. You can write about anything that you see. I took notes as he rambled out information.

We were talking and out of nowhere Jonah mentioned.… "a man biting tires." This set me off into hysterics of laughter. I had once witnessed an odd scene in the Bronx. I was fascinated that Jonah could conjure a memory from my head. I had seen a man chasing a truck, and the image reminded me of a man acting like a dog would. There had been a creepy feeling at that scene. It was just crazy to me that Jonah would seemingly pick something like that out of my mind.

We then touched on the subject of the sorcerer on the airplane. That had been a real fiasco. A gentleman had asked to sit down next to me on the plane. I said ok. He was highly unusual. He was about 6.6 in height. He had large features. He had a resounding voice. He spoke

six languages, played five instruments, and seemed
unusually intelligent. The problem was that his energy
was paralyzing. During the airplane layover I couldn't
even summon the ability to leave the plane for a break. I
was mesmerized in a somewhat uncomfortable way.
After I returned to Florida I kept in touch with the man.
He visited my school to inquire about the program.
When I told this to Jonah, he was somewhat fanatical. He
was even more incensed when I told him that he had
someone with him. He came to my town and I met him at
the train. By this time, at Jonah's instructions, I was on
the lookout for any shifty behavior. When he was in my
car, he seemed interested in the items in my glove
compartment. At that point I took him to the train and
got rid of him. Jonah said that he was a sorcerer stalking
me, possibly to kill me. He said that these people have
accomplices. He said that I was carrying around
awareness that didn't belong to me. It will attract
weirdness, he said. "He probably wasn't a real person," I
was fascinated by what he could possibly mean by that.
The guy had been exceedingly unusual. Aside from
resembling something like a handsome Frankenstein, he

possessed an unbelievable presence of energy. When he visited the class, the whole room was in shock. They didn't say it, and the teacher was professional, but you could somehow feel their fear. Jonah just said, he flashed on it, he could see the person. "He was going to kill you." I wanted to press further for why he would make such a huge assumption, but he seemed adamant not to dwell on it. He then changed the topic. Parents are friends and they don't have almighty power over you past a certain age. They can drag you to their graves with them. Get professional, get organized, he said. You have met two of the most important people in the history of mankind, he continued.

To be naturally thin and healthy is not what you do, it's what you don't do. You don't overeat. That's it. It's nothing extreme. Eat only till you are not hungry. Don't be hungry, just don't eat when you are satisfied.

If I told you what I know, your assemblage point would leave your body and maybe never return. To shut the mind is the key to other experiences, meaning perception. Everyone is in their own little world, when you're thinking of someone, you're not thinking of anyone else, so you're in their world. "I know human character." I told Jonah that I had dreamed of someone, and they responded to me that way the next day. We are perceivers, he said. He felt you dream about him.

Jonah said that he was the first person in two thousand years to go out of the world and to be put back into it. He was born into it. Parents do not have the artillery to handle this.

You have an anxiety about learning, he then said. It shows because you act that way. You make it detectable. At school, the others learned and you didn't. Your mentality is dead when nothing is interesting anymore.

When Jonah spoke, oftentimes he would go from topic to topic. I understood his manner, so I jumped along with it. Each sentence could be about something different. Often I would just jot notes.

He continued.... We all have cancer unless we ward it off. "Get off your own back." Leave yourself alone, stop picking on yourself. Be your own best friend. When you stop self- doubt and self- hatred, then you can do what you're trying to do. The only way to learn something is to go slow.

Music is in the ethers. Quiet the mind and listen. Absorb culture and then let it flow out of you in a quiet moment. Save the earth. Our species could become extinct in our lifetime. Clean up your own spiritual environment. Pollution and overpopulation, which is pollution, are the bomb. The environment is diseased.

Develop your dreaming like you do your guitar playing or anything else. Program yourself to look for your hands before you go to sleep. The dream body can live in the world. There is no life or death. The dream body and the physical body coexist in the world. Don't grieve over parents or friends, they're going to their dream body. They'll get another chance. If you have not gained the totality of awareness prior to death, then your awareness will be "eaten by the eagle." If you have developed a functioning dream -body, then it will be a vehicle for your consciousness after dying.

If you are going to know people, then have meaningful relationships. People effect the way you think. Disassociate yourself from people that you don't want to think about. We are a fragile system. Be careful who you are running into. Warriors don't buy the bullshit. We look at the world and nature, what God created, and we see a perfect world that is being environmentally destroyed. The potential is extraordinary, but the people that hate life are destroying the planet. The Christians think they are going to heaven. There may be no recourse but for the planet to fight back. The planet will retaliate. The bubonic plague took 80% of the population in Europe. My fooling around days are over, he said. Parents have kids so that they don't grow old alone. The seers that I come from, are top of the line. They are the best.

Knowledge is dreaming. Do all business accurately. We're about business. Stop thinking too much. You're a morbid person. I cheer you up. I cheer you up more than anyone. A good sorcerer will walk away with your soul. They'll do it tactfully, so that you think that it is you, that had made up your mind. I'm a sorcerer. But I'm a regular guy, because I enjoy a regular life. You can do all of your mantras, but basically it just means shutting off your inner dialogue.

Don't think, do. You've been a hippy living on false dreams. You've lived well on nothing. There is knowledge to that, but it is not a way of life. Be professional. Be a business person. Being a business person is a whole lot better than being a hippie. A rag in the wind that is controlled by whatever force blows by.

You're the only thing that matters. Keep the shield up. Once stuff is sorted out and you have organization down, then learn music. Enjoyment of learning is about a lifetime. Writing and music and art are about a lifetime. You were a borderline transient. Shift gears. Don't let the past hang on you. We deny. We deny that we do nothing. Get busy with life. Get the shield so that nothing in life bothers you. It is called impeccability. Focus on money, learning and creativity.

The planet needs help. Problems need confrontation. The planet will erase the species. The bible stories made it through time. The bible stories were word of mouth. Art gets to the public. You're up to doing art. There is no time to waste now. Jesus was a warrior. He changed their world. Jesus shifted people to a different world so that they and we could use our own potential to be at peace with nature and the planet. We are born now at the time of the end. There is great emergency and great catastrophe. Ignorance has gotten out of control. Forget saving the world. Save yourself through meditation. If someone is bothering you, then they're getting over on you. Wake up to doing with your time. You're living, but asleep to the spirit. To wake up, everything must be spit clean and organized. In the body and outside of the body.

I'm expanding your awareness. I won the cosmic lottery ticket. The Nagual knew of me before I knew of him. We are on radios. Most people are on automatic pilot, and are on instinct. They can smell power. They can smell another person's essence on you. You are where your mind is. You can be in a different world out here. That is why you stay in total concentration when you are driving.

The earth is everything around us. The Indians were in nature, so that they got in communication with the earth. Even with technologies, everything around us is considered the earth.

Forget your personality. Tune into what is around you. Calming the mind takes the garbage out of you. Reverse the disease process. Heal the body and strengthen against disease.

You can get to a creative state by going to a deeper level of meditation. When you shut off the mind, stuff comes to you. You catch it, write it, play it, paint it, diagram it, invent it... art is a rip off business. Rip off and recreate. The path with heart is down the center of the road. It is where the feeling is. The path of heart is pursuing the unknown. There is the known, the unknown and the unknowable. You can get to the unknown when you shut off the mind.

To interpret is a pitfall. To interpret is to be an expert, which is bullshit. People who explain phenomena are lying. It is what it is. Gazing is focusing on something and then dreaming about it. Find a place to orient yourself in your sleep. Then wake up inside your life. Some people call it enlightened. Organization is the key to success. Seeing is personal, Kathy had told Jonah. Nothing means anything. Be true to yourself. Keep learning. You won't age. The beauty is, that you keep learning. People get locked in. They stop growing. Stay organized. If you're not using something put it away. Have only useful things. Toss out excess baggage. Think about nothing. When you meditate, there is stuff in the air. Everyone is a radio. There is no peace and quiet.

Warriors don't pay attention to the self. Ignore yourself. Go to a quiet place and you can pay attention. You meditate by listening to the outside. Inside is the self. The self is the hardest friend to make. Have peace with oneself. Have the right food. What is in your body thinks your inner dialogue. If you have peaceful food, you will have peaceful thoughts. Let go. When you die, do not return to the cycle of life and death. When you do a job, do it in pieces. Creativity is a piece at a time. Take corners. This applies to everything. There should be no backsliding.

Your own natural self is the best possible you. Stay on the sunny side of serious. It is like a divine comedy. The earth is a living thing. Don't play faster than you can play accurately. You'll know what you know, when you're supposed to know it.

Inner dialogue is called thinking. We think in words, pictures and the English language. The differences between a warrior and a man, is that a warrior observes his thoughts and is detached from his thoughts. He does not claim his thoughts as his own. He observes what he is thinking about. To be a warrior is to never come back. To be a warrior is to be an observer. Don't lose your cool. Observe the world, but don't get caught up in it. Books describe things. Your apartment is a reflection of your mind. Be impeccable. Catch problems as they occur. Do it now. Clean up your life. No mess should be in your life. Stay in charge, be professional. Clean off your island and be what you are, whatever that is. Logic runs interference on creativity. Be yourself... "It's my art." You can hear ahead, and you can see ahead. The body is the spirit. Don't let people get beyond your first base. Watch the animals. Human beings are animals. The body knows. The body tells you. When you are in the wrong place, with the wrong people, the body reacts to tell you everything. Listen with your body. Instincts tell all, like the animals that we are. Jobs kill, Do them on your own terms. No pressure will help you live longer. When you feel a tugging on your stomach, something is making you tense. You can feel thoughts.

23 COMMENTS FROM DAN

I came across an old notebook. I had taken some brief notes from one of the sit down conversations I had had with Jonah's benefactor Dan. Every time I had sat for over five minutes in Dan's presence, my energy and awareness had started changing. Sometimes when I met him at Jonah's apartment, he was just a regular guy. Other times if the mood was right, he would engage in talking. When this would happen, I would almost instantly start to feel minute changes in my perceptual awareness. It was as though he was emitting a cosmic electricity. I tried to be normal, but I was feeling a variety of peaks and valleys in my energy and mind.

He mentioned that he could read people's minds. He proved this very easily, by continually commenting on what I was thinking about. I was thinking about, how I felt that I was attractive, but not perhaps as competitively attractive, as say a lot of other people. He said that most of the world was average looking, and that it was not how you looked, but how you felt. Living in Hollywood gave you more of a sense that life revolved around your face, then say other places. He told a story about how he told his friends not to sell pot now, but they did, and they went to jail. He said that he had warned his wife not to drive the car because he knew that she was going to get into an accident. She did and he felt very badly about that. He talked about how he had traveled to the Masai Plains and to Far East Asia. He said that his secret dream of traveling had come true as a writer. For acting, he said, never show your- self. Have it Be real onstage. He said that he had coached actors that had been on cocaine. He said that they were scattered, but they would piece it together and follow the best. He skipped around like Jonah would. These notes I found

seemed to be just bits and pieces of a conversation. He

told a story about a teacher saying that a child was lying.

The child was making up stuff to deny his pain, he said.

The child was being creative.

About Jesus, he said... Jesus isn't here today. If

you're hearing his voice in your head, you're

schizophrenic. Read his books don't follow his

interpreters.

You don't feel anything when you kill, only when

you come home from war. When there's fear I feel

awareness. Like an animal. I don't know how this

intuition happens but it does. His voice dynamics rose

higher to lower to higher, casual then angry to casual.

His face had different appearances from different angles.

As he spoke, he animatedly sat, stood, walked and

stretched. Marriage could kill creativity. Material things

will own the owners. Life is an adventure. Live it. Don't

wait, and don't lock yourself into what you "should do."

Hear your body. If you get itchy, move. It's human

nature to get bored doing the same things forever, so stay

fluid and flexible. Never stop learning.

Blue hairs and retiree's invaded the island paradise. The tourists and developers were discouraged from staying because they couldn't understand that money wasn't everything. They were obnoxious.

"Who is worth lying to?" "Who is important enough to be phony for?" In sales, tell them about something. If they like it fine. He said that he got rid of clients by disagreeing with them. People all need approval. He mentioned that he supported five children in third world countries. The U.S is starting to look like a third world country. The body is a lazy pile of garbage unless you do something with it. Ask questions. Learn by asking questions. Find out. Develop characters. Have people talk about themselves. When you're the best people always hire you. Tell them that you can do it better, and that you can do it for less. It's ok to be a slow learner. He was a slow learner, he worked harder. That didn't seem remotely possible that he could be a slow learner. Don't let anyone get over on you, even your friends. He was familiar with posers, he said. He stood up in the middle of Richard Dreyfus doing Shakespeare and shouted... "This is the worst Shakespeare I have ever seen." He said his wife Kathy wanted to crawl under the lawn blanket they were sitting on. Dreyfus was doing himself. You couldn't find the character. Stars are weak because they do themselves. They do their acts and their personalities.

Writers get paid the least. Everyone on a movie is replaceable except the executive producer. People believe what you tell them. That is what makes them stupid. They see an actor and believe that he is his part. The politicians are bad comedians, bad actors. They're his favorite characters. People rather be timid and conform then think for themselves. Parents become friends. They are no longer dictators. Energy would come and go during the conversation. Writers do spec work, he said. He had athletic type clothes, whitish gray thick hair, and black glasses. He came off with a sort of New York type behavior. He wore sneakers, jeans and smoked cigarettes. He leaned over in a peculiar manner. He walked around and got his knapsack. He moved like a younger person. Jonah was sleeping, then gazing as he lay on the floor.

My wife does what she wants. Don't try to make a

person what you are. Leave them as they are. He told a story of how he once met a woman who pulled a gun on him. He saw the love in her eyes. Families love to scream at each other, he said. Elders keep each other alive by keeping the fight alive. Question everything, he said. Don't just take the damn bullshit that people put in front of you. He said that the people with the caste system should disown that system. Nobody else's law is any better than your own. Think and act freely. Challenge people on what they say. It seemed that time stood still as he spoke for about three hours.

He went back to the topic of acting. Grab their attention head on. Never be yourself, onstage. Act your role impeccably. People barricade themselves into their own views. Stuff will come out when you write. Don't be gullible. Dan kept recreating story after story. He said that he was an apprentice of Don Juan's associate Genaro. He said that he saw an old Sonora cactus that was an old seer. The Tenant, he said, takes energy from the Nagual for continued life. He jumped around a bit in his conversation. He said that he was once in a theatre, and a man put something on his leg. When he turned around he saw that the man did not have a face. He was

going too fast, and I would have felt it too impolite to

question him on the unusual nature of some of the things

that he was saying. I felt weighted down by an unseen

electrical current anyway. That was extremely real. No

matter how unusual some of his statements would seem,

the bodily sensation created by his presence was entirely

tangible to me, and was equally unusual. He said that he

was a new seer and a dreamer. He said that he saw spirit.

He said it somehow resembled hay. He said that he had

seen the spirit like a cascade of bristling lights on the

Florida turnpike at sunset. When Dan left, I floated back

to my apartment. Never in my life did I feel so high. This

man's energy felt like magic in the flesh. Exuberant

didn't come close to how much well- being I suddenly

felt. I was very happy that he had taken the time to speak

with me. I looked forward to meeting with him and his

wife at another time.

24   NOTES FROM JONAH

Jonah and I picked up our note taking and
conversations. He was very pleased that Dan had
revealed parts of himself, and had so graciously spoken
and given me a boost of energy. Jonah felt that I would
be better off for the rest of my life, from him having
spoken to me. I could believe it. He bore the countenance
of a very special person. A very great man. Jonah went
on to tell me to read and chant the desiderata. Get it in
your mind. When you are alone, shut off the self. The
secret is in the silence. No meaning and no talking. He

continuously told me to look for my hands in my dreams.

There's the known, the unknown, and the unknowable. You can get to the unknown. Be quiet, shut the mind. Concentrate on not thinking. Stop wasting energy chit chatting with people. Be organized. Follow only a path with heart. Follow your heart. Our conversations meandered back to a time when I moved out of Hollywood. I felt a huge tug when I drove away from the building. The place had really grown on me. The song by Eric Clapton, "I can't stand it" had been playing on the radio. That may have been the chorus and not the title of the song. That particular good- by had been many faceted as had been our relationship. Jonah, at that point had worn several different robes to the dinner table so to speak. I thought that it was wise and caring that he sent me back home when someone was ill. The pull of the situation would have been difficult without his caring guidance. In fact, much of my life would have been difficult without his caring guidance. At this moment I can safely and assuredly reflect that his wisdom, generosity and guidance have had immeasurable significance in my life. The blessing of crossing paths with a Nagual warrior and having his energy bestowed on me is a gift beyond any value. I can really say that I wonder why my fortune was such. The only virtues I can imagine that had had some influence, were that I had a true love for nature, and that I have always innately seen the good in people. Other than that, I didn't see any distinct reason for my wonderful luck. Always seeing the good in people has been a bone of contention, to some degree between Jonah and I. He considered my naïve accepting nature to be an invitation for disrespect and potential danger. To some degree I suppose, I have waltzed through life with an unseen feeling of protection. I have girlfriends that wouldn't walk alone at night. Thankfully, without being too unaware of my whereabouts, I have generally felt secure in the world.

On religion, jonah said that it was all the same wearing different uniforms. They worship a god that they created. He moved onto a topic that he read from the female sorceresses. They had a phrase of saying that having semen in you was like having worms. It meant having someone's essence on you. Their thoughts were that a man's semen would somehow feed on a woman energetically and that was part of the way a man would still want to draw energy from a woman. That was partially how an energetic bond was made. They claimed that to have too many people feeding on you energetically would be taxing to a woman. You're picking up pieces of their karmic essence when you sleep with them. Clara, in Taisha Abelar's book... "The Sorcerers Crossing" gave a detailed view of this process. This again ties in with the concept and process of recapitulation. This is an exercise with the intent of reclaiming the energy you have dissipated through all of your interactions with the world. The active practice of a process called recapitulation was found by sorcerers in the past to aid in regaining one's energy. One's energy that could then be reconstructed into developing a dream body. "The double," "The other," or known as the nagual side of man. These were terms for getting to that part of ourselves which is the crux of why and what a "sorcerer" is actually working toward and doing.

Jonah continued... life is a series of picking up experiences and also the habits of others. Try and stay around people who have habits you find admirable or worthy of emulating. The old cliché… "Birds of a feather, flock together." Whoever you spend a lot of time with is going to have some type of influence. You are going to hear them in your head if you are around them long enough. Go with your instincts. Develop instincts. A wanting and desperate person gets sucked into things because they want things and company. They allow potentially negative people to influence them. It's like you have a devil and an angel on your shoulder at all times. Listen to the spirit. There's the big voice and the little voice. The big voice is outside persuasion. The little voice is the spirit inside you. It only talks once so listen for it. You pity people. You empathize with them. You put your- self in their shoes. That's why you are always nice. Well, no good. That's not the way the world is. They don't respect nice. They do not want business or anything from a nice guy. Their rubbish rules them. Don't let them run their rubbish on you. I don't let you run your lies, or falseness on me. You love me for it. By making you be honest with me, I make you closer to your real self. I make you throw out your fake self. Your fake self runs you too. You have to stay on it to keep your own bullshit from running you. Stop being locked into your own bullshit.

Speak up for yourself. Don't take negativity from people. Be fair and professional, but if you don't want to be licking boots, cut out the bad low self-esteem behavior. This needed to be pointed out to you that you go around like Mr. nice guy. People don't respect overly nice or shit licking. You keep putting yourself in other people's places. Don't do that. It's not real. If they look weird, they are weird. Stay the hell away from weird people. You have no business talking to creeps. Protect yourself. Tell me if you feel you are right about something. It sickens me for you to be kissing my ass. Don't allow browbeating. You don't have to take stuff if you choose not to. It's how you run your life. You're in charge. Stop nice ness. Niceness sucks. It means you have a sign on you saying... I suck ass. They see you coming. I was astonished at his perception. I could see how right he was. I was a gratuitous flatterer, but I actually meant it. It was part of that I see goodness in people thing. I could see how it disappointed people to not have to work for my affection. They would have liked me better if I had made them produce the better of themselves, or have me not be so accepting. I could see how people loathed my friendly nature.

I'm a mirror when I reflect your garbage and your real self, back to you. You catch a glimpse of yourself. That's why you can't get enough of me. I tell you the truth with no shield, and you can't get enough of the real you in the mirror. You understand these things as concepts. Now you have to reprogram your old habits and put this to use. There can be no accepting negative or abusive behavior from people. Your mother mentally browbeat you too much, and your father spoiled you. You came out like a babbling idiot, he said. My mother was absolutely correct in keeping me on the straight and narrow in looking for tangible results. She was a perfect business teacher and more generous of an individual than I can ever imagine to be. She was smart and perceptive beyond my capabilities. I was beyond fortunate in parents!

25   LIVING ASSERTIVELY

"You're acting as if they'll reject you, but if you
are nice enough you'll win out. Your mother rejected
whatever you said, but being nice was understood and
accepted by your father. I didn't agree with his comment
on my mother. I felt she was just discerning and watchful
to protect that I was making accurate decisions. Take no
garbage, take no prisoners and kick ass. Be your own
best friend. Be powerful to yourself. Don't blame your
parents. They loved you anyway. When negative people
run their games on you, treat them like little children

acting up. Do not take other people's nastiness. You're in control, be yourself. Speak up for yourself. Don't act polite, be yourself. No being miss nice. Be true to your spirit. No more disciple behavior, be a warrior now. You're on warrior time now. Everything counts. Don't be the garbage inside you. It comes outside now. Don't pay attention or claim your thoughts. When you are annoyed about someone, they are thinking about you. Act up. Act business in the real world. You know it's acting, but act business. Be accurate in business. Be firm and correct. When the Nagual thinks you are messing up he will send the environment to reprimand you. No more me having to clean up the bad energy that you accumulate in the world. It's up to you to clean off your island. Defend yourself. Don't let people come at you with their bull. See through the human race in its costumes. It is not your responsibility to be giving out handouts. Save yourself. The earth is going to shake its bones. Keep out of the way. Don't get sucked into other people's bullshit. If you still worry about what other people think of you, you are being an idiot. Beauty comes from the soul, not from the flesh." I did not agree with what he said about my mother. She was discerning about things, not rejecting.

"You carry around a mirror of what you see yourself as." You've had some of the best conversations of all times. Speak up for yourself. Recapitulate. Stand up and be counted. No more, meek and timid behavior, he said. Be your own best friend. Be forward. No more being needy. Let the stuff fly. Be openmouthed. Jonah continued… "Self- hatred shows." Be aware of hating yourself, so that you can kill that feeling. That feeling drives you to show pain all the time. It kind of was uncomfortable to hear him say that, but what a relief to pinpoint the bad feeling and execute it. I really secretly liked myself a whole lot, but I could tell that half the people liked me and half didn't. I would say that that is probably in the ballpark of true for most people. So… I think I did allow other people's attitudes to influence me in regard to myself. What a relief to pinpoint what I was doing. I wouldn't have noticed what was wrong without him being so precise. I noticed how odd people were to me the other evening. There were men that seemed to have underlying hostility when I got up to perform with them. They actually settled down and I enjoyed myself and they seemed less confrontational, but they were initially subtly rude. I could see that as a woman I get some unwarranted attention as a performer. That seemed to make the more talented musicians irritated. At least in this situation I was not hating myself, but nor was I being anything other than polite toward playing with them. I didn't take over their stage, I waited for the right cues.

Your body knows that this is the real deal. Your body is perceptive to the energy that you feel when you talk to me. I'm inside rewiring your brain. Study habits must be put in gear. Dan had said that everything could get done in a day. You should be able to have a schedule, and there should be time to get whatever you want to get done. Nothing is more important than anything else. Work, art, cleaning, leisure …

Jonah was relentlessly issuing ultimatums. Be a warrior or good- by. Clean everything. Get busy or it's over. I burn energy when I lend you my energy. You use it or leave. The gig is to do all the knowledge, not to just know it.

Some of your emanations are chasing your personal

death. You speed up too much. I am the real deal. You are like the "Last of the Mohicans getting help."

People are in a state of sleep because they are unaware that they are listening to the internal dialogue. We are looking to master the art form of being detached with ease. Detached from the inner dialogue. Not thinking. Thinking is tiring. It stresses the body. Not being pulled by the inner dialogue is being awake. Awake to the fact that there is an inner dialogue pulling us around. Most people are asleep in their inner dialogue. Moods are just the inner dialogue getting free rein and going off. Bad moods could be unused energy building inside you. You want to be independent, you're an artist. You should have been learning from the beginning. People are unaware to the forces that are working on them. The food, the earth, people, these things contribute to the inner dialogue inside you.

The planet is a living planet. The Indians were right. Thousands of years, and they didn't damage it in the least. Western culture and industrialization has nearly destroyed a continent in two hundred years. This is not successful. They made slaves and now they have a problem with blacks. Karma connects. Slaughtering the Indians created deep karmic trouble.

What is creative and ingenious is being successful. Chip away at it every day. Every day I learn a little guitar. The odds are against us. Having my back up against the wall is the only way. Let's see what I know. There's a nightmare on the way. Learn how to get tough and survive the elements. Learning to survive is a great art form. Tell a story and get through to people. Jonah continued... I have opinions on how things are. The bible is real. I found Jesus in a way that is unquestionable. I'm not a religious person. It's about the planet. Dan looked into writing. Do it right. If you do it right, the right way, doors open for you. Slow down and don't let up. Keep the hocus pocus, garbage off your island. If you keep your island clean, the spirit will talk to you. I know. Make progress every day. Take time but don't let up.

Raise awareness to what's possible. Something to take care of everybody. Instead of killing nature, take care of the earth. Everyone can be rich. The rich are afraid of everyone being rich. We'd be harvesting greatness.

I called Jonah and told him I was thinking of him. I told him that for the first time I was feeling really relaxed. I was more used to chaos. I asked him if he didn't find the word warrior a tad strange? "corny?" he interjected. I said yes, that's it. He said there really weren't too many other fitting titles. If you could become a warrior that could see, you could become a man of knowledge. He said that the term swami of yogi could apply on some occasions, but warrior was just the phrase being used. A warrior is free of the self. Forget about the self.

I told him I felt some feelings of frustration when I had lived in Florida. He said that my feelings were from feeling out of control with money and letting people step on me.

Talking to Jonah washed out all of the bad feelings that I had. He said I was a lovely talented person that had an outstanding command of the English language and a good sense of wit. You want to be a writer, then write. Just don't write yourself to death.

26   COLLECTION OF MISCELLANEOUS NOTES

I found a collection of notes. Some of the stuff was mentioned a few times so that I would benefit from the repetition. White man lost track. Places have feeling. We stay where we suffer. Go someplace else. Mental and spiritual health has to do with places. I'm teaching you as an apprentice to do something. Do not overly involve yourself with people. Christianity is the other end of the spectrum with being selfish. Being a seer is closer to reality. The closer you get to being a seer, the more you get out of the human band. Don't be responsible for other people. Being aware is enough. Sorcery is a level. There are other levels above sorcery. Learning is doing. Moving is creativity. Forget about thinking. Be in your own groove. Normal is relative. You are not your art. Fair and honest is impeccable.

When you're starting a canvas, make a sketch. Make a rough draft. If you look at the whole job, nothing gets done. Do it a piece at a time. A real man of knowledge is just a jumping point. A man of knowledge knows that knowledge is where it is at. When you don't know anything, you are closer to knowing something. Watch what the animals do. People agree about things, and then it is accepted as the only reality. It's like America, which is a concept. It is a word.

Some of the most surprising times with Jonah, was when he would make comments about things that he could not have known anything about. I made some inane comment about something and he comes out with… "Like what? A man trying to bite the tires." Now that was a seemingly disconnected nonsensical thing to say. I was spun right into a spasm of intrigue when he said that. I had used that exact phrase to describe a distinctly strange circumstance that had occurred in the past. It was not an overly important occurrence, but even at the time, there had been a dreamlike quality to the situation. What had happened was that, as a teenager I was riding around with some friends, in the Bronx, where I wasn't supposed to be. It had the reputation of being a dangerous neighborhood. We had just finished eating at the White Castle, easily known as the evilest of all junk foods. Even in the White Castle the energy was surly with vigilant overtones. The men all seemed different, threatening yet exciting. We drove away down the street. We're fairly attentive due to the unfamiliarity of the location. First I saw a thin muscular man running down the street at breakneck speed. Then I saw a man chasing him with a spear. I realize this sounds utterly ridiculous, but this is what I witnessed. Who knows exactly what he was carrying and why. I know what I saw was real. One man was running for his life. We kept driving. Seconds later a man runs out into the street and begins to act like he is a dog trying to bite the tires on the truck in front of us. He is jumping up and down, barking and chasing the truck. This was behavior I hadn't seen in New Jersey, not that it couldn't exist there. I just felt a weird sensation when I was in the Bronx. So when Jonah, out of the blue said... "Man biting the tires." I was dumbfounded. I'm not saying any of this meant anything, but it was like getting your funny bone tickled.

Learning and creating is the world of art. The planet is Mecca. It is heaven. Learning is fun. Learn a thing a day. This apprenticeship is about real life. Rent the movie Fantasia. I was Mickey Mouse. That's what happened to me. It's like living in a circus. Impeccability is having a shield so that nothing bothers you in the world.

The line of knowledge that we are connected to would not be considered religious. Jesus was a warrior. He moved the assemblage point of people. The more things change the more they stay the same. I thought he was quoting the rock band Rush, but perhaps it was Shakespeare. I'm not sure. I don't know what is in other people, he said. You can have an effect on your own life. You can't necessarily save others. If you clean up and do your best, that will energetically and positively affect the people around you. All you can do is write books and leave something behind. You can better people's lives that way. I used to indulge in my own stupidity by capturing the attention of people via Dan. Writing has staying power. Look at what Carlos Castaneda and Don Juan Matus, left behind. A roadmap to achieving higher awareness, dreaming and enlightenment.

Jonah continued talking to me. You're the only thing that matters. Keep the shield up. Get busy with life. Once you have organization, then you can set about learning. The enjoyment of learning is about a lifetime. Writing and music is about a lifetime. You were a borderline transient. Shift gears. Don't let the past hang on you. We deny. We deny that we do nothing. Get busy with life. The world needs help now. It needs confrontation. Get to the public via writing. Art gets to the public. The planet needs help. The welfare of the living earth is priority now. Never let an idiot run their game on you. He reiterated this idea vociferously. Apparently I looked like the consummate naïve person. Clean up your life. Wake up and get professional. I repeat these types of comments to illustrate his instruction to me. Many people reading this undoubtedly will have a lot of this accomplished. This is to the wayward disconnected teenage type that feels starving for art is ascetically virtuous. He's saying… Being able to be professional and levelheaded is paramount, especially when dealing with power, spirit and art.

Stop thinking. Random thinking draws energy. I'll see it when I believe it, not I'll believe it when I see it. Listen for other voices. The genius is quiet. Read the music in your head. Plug into divine voices. Transcribe the music in your head.

He changed topics again. He started telling me about the study of sexual Taoism. The secret of Taoism is to have the woman orgasm first. Women are threatening to men on the sexual battleground because they seemingly have more energy. The male is less energetic after orgasm. Many relationships could be more nurturing if people understood the energy factors typical to men and women. The woman needs to be satisfied first, so that she is not left wanting after the man has had an orgasm. It goes past the sensual realm. She may interpret his lack of energy to represent a lack of affection. Taoism promotes a retention of sexual energy by the male. It promotes sexual activity without release, so that the male stores his potency and energy. It doesn't say never to ejaculate, but to be conscious that it is ok to stimulate the energy without releasing it. It gets more complex than that. Then there's ways to transmute the energy by sending it back into the body without ejaculating.

He felt that this was the overriding fear of women, that caused male insecurity and the impetus toward dominance. They were afraid to be rendered impotent by the female. They were afraid that her energy was more, and that they would appear weak. Obviously not all people fell into this category, and these were some basic principles of physiology. The Taoist idea was to have the woman finish first, so there would be an equality of stamina and desire.

Warriors should have no weakness. Warriors are disconnected. I was taken out this world, the first person in two thousand years. He would not particularly elaborate.

You start conforming to your surroundings. You start by meeting the expectations of your parents, and then the whole world becomes your parents, and you become messed up. You begin bending to everyone. Do your thing. You are in control of your behavior at all times. People interact with you on your terms. You are where you are at all times. You invent what your preconceived attitude is. Consistency win's race. There's never enough time. Do it right the first time, but there's always time to do it again. Real learning takes place at a slow pace. Don't get ahead of yourself in the learning process. Repetition gets things good. Go slow. The tortoise wins. Play the musical scales flawlessly perfect.

On the subject of the self, the warrior realizes what an inept clod the self is and leaves it in the dust. It is also a challenge to stay "outside the ring that presses upon people." That sort of meant being not susceptible to the effect of situations around you. Participating in the life and daily affairs, but not allowing the world around you to disturb you, too deeply.

People are in a state of sleep. You're learning to expand your awareness. Get quiet, and get totally

organized. I'm trying to drag your awareness up.
Thinking causes happening. Thoughts are energy. No
thinking is the healthiest. To stop disease, stop thinking.
The garbage will be taken out of you. Take gaps in the
thinking process every day. Do meditation every day.
Thoughts have an effect on the body.

You don't write everything at once. You write in
parts. Creativity and learning can be done in chunks. To
look at a whole work and try to recreate it is too much.
Break things down into sections and parts.

Each moment in time is unique. You can change
anything at any time. Each moment is its own. The
possibility to continually progress is available, when
each minute is a possibility for entirely new realities. An
artist is a sorcerer. To effect things negatively or
positively. Someone to tap and bottle the source. The
hardest part about creativity is slowing it down. You
don't create works all at once. You break it down.

Find a work element that feels all right. Hang with
people that feel natural to you. Basically do what comes
naturally. Listen with your body. Your body has good
natural instincts, if you listen to it. Self- importance is an

enemy to people on this path. You attract what you seek.

Thoughts were like magnets. Being yourself at all times,

was being the best possible you. Being here is all it takes.

Being present to realize. Get down to brass tacks and

clean your head.

Function in your own element was a concept I

found comforting. It meant to be where you like it.

27   A REVERIE FROM THE PAST

We started talking about the past again. There had

been one time where I had run into him about three miles

from the apartment. We were across the street from a fast

food health food restaurant. I commented on how I had

heard that someone had been shot there. He said that he

had just been thinking that some act of violence had been

committed there. Occasionally we would get onto the

topic of cleaning off your island. He said that slowing

down the inner dialogue would help in cleaning off your island. He said that the path he talks about is an Indian warrior path. He said that he is a sorcerer, but that he really doesn't do much as a sorcerer. He prefers to be a warrior. We live in a world of sorcerers and its hunt or be hunted, and the whole world has that game going on. Sorcery is the power to influence someone. I started to notice people's persuasive bents all over the place. I ran into Jonah at the oddest moments. When we ran into each other a few miles from the apartment we started talking. A bum approached us and tried to join us. Beat it, he told him. We're talking. He was never overly polite. I wondered that for someone with so much knowledge, that he wasn't seemingly more gentle. He was hardly the kindly wise man. This path attracts geeks, he said. This is one of the worst side effects. He didn't actually mention that Hollywood was full of characters to put it mildly. Stay away from creepy people. He kept mentioning a path, or "this path." He said that his spirit was Indian, and that because his body is not "Indian" now, doesn't mean anything. He loves the earth and the earth loves him. This path can tap you when you're out of sorts. When you are somewhat out of it, like staying up all night. Jonah thought my odd sleep schedule was conducive to having shifts in your mental assemblage point. After Jonah mentioned that our conversations were a gesture with power, I observed again that I would run into him at odd moments. Coming home at two am he would just be in the hall, or down the block at midnight he would just be there. At restaurants, out of nowhere he would just be there. He said that once his benefactor had disappeared right before his very eyes. He said that he could do stuff like that, but that I would start throwing up and go into shock, because my body would be scared. The phone would ring, and he would say there's my agreement if it jived with the timing of what he had said. He talked about the earth communicating with you in funny ways.

The difference between a warrior and a man is that a warrior observes his thoughts and is detached. He does not claim his thoughts as his own. He observes them. He says that he does not know where they are coming from. It's as though thoughts are simply on a radio wave, and you can't be sure where your thoughts are coming from.

For some reason I could feel Jonah's presence when he was in the building. He seemed very friendly with the other tenants. It seemed like he was the king of the clubhouse. The tenants seemed friendly toward one another as if bonded by knowing the landlord. I heard him walking around a lot. I assumed that this was why I thought of him so much. Initially from our brief conversations I had thought that he would come around and drink tea and talk philosophy, but we never really got together like regular friends. Each time we would talk, it would be particularly interesting. We'd have brief conversations in passing, but they would always be very cool. He talked about specifics, not the casual rhetoric so often used in just passing conversations. My friends thought he looked warmly eccentric since he didn't act the part of the Hollywood business cutthroat. He would appear in a funny moose hat carrying enormous sticks of incense. Something about him often just cracked me up and I didn't even know what it was. He just brought joy to me when I would see him. In our initial meeting he had seemed extremely serious and businesslike. Not like the guy in the moose hat. So he really could display a plethora of moods and characters. I thought it particularly odd the times I saw him meandering in the yard in his white bathrobe. To me this was much too urban to be seen in a bathrobe outside. I thought it was comical that this was a city street and this guy had no more inhibitions then had he been on his back porch in Idaho. I said, ok the guy is not inhibited, I guess that is a good trait. Occasionally when I was paying rent we would get into these esoteric conversations. One day after numerous thought provoking sessions he said... "hey you ought to jot this stuff down." I thought it was unusual that he would want his thoughts jotted down. I saw him as saying very interesting things, but it seemed pompous to suggest that his words deserved paper. If I took these notes, even one word about a thought, I'd remember it when I saw the word. At this point I thought to myself... Aren't two people having a conversation here? I wouldn't think to write down my thoughts, why would I think to write down yours?

He referred to our conversations as a gesture with power. He said that our conversations were not idle conversations, and that some heavy knowledge was being transmitted if I would just pay attention. What I could conclusively admit, was that I was entirely absorbed by him somehow. During these conversations, a loll would fall over me as though time was completely suspended. Later he would refer to this state as heightened awareness. Some energetic force would palpably hold me until the end of a conversation. Then, as though the air was removed from a balloon, the energy in the room would lessen by degrees and once again everything would feel normal. He said that I should weigh what he said against my own experience. While he had knowledge to transmit he wasn't looking for followers, slaves or disciples. People who say they are a guru or this or that, or that they know, usually don't. If I wanted him to discuss this path with me, I would need to stop letting people control me. It didn't mean that I had to impose my will wherever I went. To avoid confrontation, I went along with a lot of stuff in general, and that was not the way of being impeccable. By this time Jonah had really grabbed my curiosity, though I wasn't thinking, oh I have to talk to this guy. These conversations would just unravel. There was innate esoteric knowledge. He even said that you could continue consciousness from life to life, which I found fascinating.

We got on the topic of altered states of consciousness. Our neighborhood had a lot of irrational people. I asked him what was wrong with them. He said that their assemblage point was, in what was referred to in sorcery terms, as the left side of awareness, the junkyard of consciousness. It was innovative to explore the mind in acute states of anxiety. In other words, stress could occasionally access areas of strength and determination that might be weaker without the extra pressure.

I went up to talk to Jonah during the LA riots. He was kicking back playing guitar. I couldn't believe it. The television was on and he was just hanging. By the time I left his apartment I felt as though the war was over and I could get a good night's sleep. There had been a lot of concern regarding buildings burning and gunfire.

What he was passing on to me was his benefactor's knowledge. He said a warrior's knowledge was like any other form of discipline. His benefactor told him that to live long and to live well it was important to relax. To even relax when you work, because to be in a meditative way was the way to peace and health. Today's lifestyle was too stressful to the body. The chaos grew when the population grew. As the population grew, the lifespan dropped. He claimed that the people used to live to 500 or so when they meditated daily. There's magic in life that could be everyone's if they tuned into it within themselves. For everyone to be free, to feel the peace and freedom within is the warrior's way.

People are wearing different uniforms. Christian, Buddist ... The Tonals get together, and agree on stuff. They're worshipping the god they created. It's all limerick sorcery. That means language sorcery.

Overtime I started having a variety of experiences. I was thinking about a certain guitar player and how stupendous his playing had been. I was dosing back to sleep after popping his tape in around seven a. m. I had the distinct sensation of my ears popping and it was though my head had changed channels. I knew immediately and without a doubt that something was happening. I heard a voice that sounded like Jonah's say… "Get comfortable." I told myself to stay in my

body. I was feeling a little sick, and didn't feel ready to

fly. I continued to doze, and then I tried it. I think I was

asleep. I felt the sensation of flying. When I landed there

were people clapping. I saw the guitarist I had been

listening to sitting at a piano with headphones on. It was

apparent that he couldn't stop playing. It was as if he had

to let the music out because it was burning inside of him.

He had to release it. I then flashed on feeling very good.

I dreamed I was approaching a house. Some pretty and

cool black women were walking behind me. I was so

exhilarated I was skipping. I couldn't get in to the front

door of the house. Five dogs then approached me. I had a

lot of eye contact with the dogs. I felt the analogy of

seeing the guitarist play was just about letting the

creativity out. Outside of the flying episode everything

felt like normal dreams. Not like doing dreaming or

waking up in my dreams. The one distinctive feeling was

that of having direct contact with frogs and little turtles. I

felt like I became part of the prehistoric amphibian world

in one particular dream that had had the sensation of it

being in dreaming.

In retrospect, I began to differentiate entirely between a normal dream a dreaming experience. Learning how to do dreaming is a cornerstone to what this whole apprenticeship situation is about. At present, my dreaming experiences are more than anything else, the validating factor to this whole situation.

Jonah said that eventually, a lot of the unknown will become known. What is unknown to you now will grow into becoming known. The unknown will become controllable. Then there's the unknowable. That, he intimated was better to not concern oneself with. Mold your own destiny, he said. A lot of people know that, but they get into the master/disciple thing.

Being anonymous is the art of the warrior. A warrior can do anything, but should be strategic. The world isn't what it was. Everything changed two thousand years ago. The world is more lost now. Maybe good exists when evil sleeps. Don't subject yourself to crazy people. Pent up energy creates moods. Do what the body wants, your striving to be independent. The older you get the more you have to get it together. People don't know the inner dialogue. It dictates to them what to do. A person's karma gets on you. It can run interference in your life. You're afraid to assert yourself, he said. Lay off yourself. Release your energy. Use common sense. Run your jive on someone else. I was one with my jive until I gave it up. Write down your goals and deal with them.

So here is somewhat of a summary… he started out… Be real and intelligent. Develop the time which you live with no thought. Slow yourself down. The universal priority is to take care of the planet. The world leaders can't do anything without the planet. Learn how to do dreaming. This is going from one level to the next. The spirit goes at the speed of light. Astral projection is the spirit. Not thinking will heal the self. Writing brings you into a state of perception. Writing inadvertently expands awareness. Work on seeing what's around you. Sorcery is a training in awareness. There's the world inside your head, and the world outside of your head. You got to go inside to hear outside. Hear music, what you want to hear. When you're entrenched in something, try to hum something in your head. Thinking is hearing. Hum it. Hum it the way you think it. You draw it out of the ethers. Shakespeare was really creative. Practice the art of listening. We are receivers. There is an infinite amount, of things to listen to. You can hear positive and negative things. Don't identify with what you hear. Don't claim your thoughts as your own. Food has a voice. Good food produces good thoughts. Discipline stops negative ranting. Discipline, faith and patience are the only ways to achieve a feeling of redemption. Work for the earth. Tend to this garden.

Most people are not what they look like. Get along with the human race. Find wisdom to immortality. Getting out of here alive. Taking your consciousness with you. That's enlightenment. Help human race. The planet will heal itself. People will do a turnaround if they realize that taking care of the planet is the shortest distance to reach the potential of heaven, and prosperity for all on the planet. Healing the planet will create a clean stage. It's a magic life if everyone was free. That is the warrior's way.

There is power in places. Don't let power run you. Power is a feeling. Deal with energy blocks or problems so that they don't disturb you. People make you feel good or bad. Detect it. Don't talk your mind. Not to yourself or out loud. Try to meditate. Try to listen. Your thinking is random thought. Thinking about someone is their karma on you, if you're thinking about them in a negative way.

Trust is in letting go. Good things will come to you if you do your homework, so to speak. Let things flow. Be firm and correct with people. Never let them step over your line. Stop being Mr. Nice guy. I don't trust Mr. Nice Guy. Mimic the master. You made a bid for power, and now you got it. You hit the big time, now you can do with it what you wish. Don't talk to me about your personal plans, he said.

You support you. You're the most powerful person in your life. You're looking to everyone else for the emotional support of approval. You are the most powerful that there is for you. Trust yourself. Trust your instincts. Read the desiderata. Light incense, relax. Make yourself happy. Stay clear of energy vampire people. Stay clear of the difficult ones.

Do what you have been taught. Reread and organize everything you have been taught. Your feeling panic because this is death, death of the self, death of the inner dialogue. Death of the phony bullshit person that never got anything done.

You were chosen for this path, now you have to walk it or go back to the bullshit world you had of nothing. You had nothing. Now you have everything. This is not about changing who you are. A leopard cannot change his spots. This is about being your higher self. Ye of little faith. You act like such a believer and yet you are not. You don't believe things will come to you. You don't believe this is real. Pray for things, they will come to you. You're meant to be in the world of daily life. You're not meant to be in the Himalayas. You would scare nature. Your body knows what kind of friend I am. You are a container of knowledge. I have bodily stored this knowledge in you.

Knowledge is power. I have knowledge, so I have power. If you do your work and don't indulge, you are going to be successful. I put my warriors word on it. It will happen because I say it. Your body knows that that is true. Get over your desperate clinging personality. Let that, fourteen year-old, part of yourself die. Clinging is like an empty box. You'll always want and there's nothing to satisfy you. Leave clinging alone. It won't get you anywhere. Clinging causes pain. It keeps you in pain. The earth is your gift of life. Love it and it will love you. Love the spirit and the cosmos, and it will love you. Hate life and it will hate you. Clear your head and do recapitulation.

Make good relationships. Have quality things. Join the gym. Don't lose yourself in me. Lose the self. Be your higher self. Laugh like the Indians. Have your soul screaming with laughter.. Be the person underneath the self, that one that taps the source. The one that taps creativity.

The self is insecurity, desperation, pettiness, being lonely and childishness. Get rid of these clothes, be a warrior. Be a woman of knowledge. Relaxed, detached and at ease, in any situation. Be outside the circle that presses upon people. Watch the world go up and down, but don't go up and down with it. You can't keep running to me to clean off your island. You have to do that. When I leave, you won't have me, but you'll have the whole world to play in.

When you are alone, shut off the self. The secret is in the silence, no talking. Be quiet and shut the mind. Concentrate on not thinking. Stop spilling your guts to people. It's like an energy leak. Be organized and stay on the path with heart.

Follow your heart. Listen to your spirit. Your body tells you when something is off. Knowledge is dreaming. People don't want to grow old alone. They possess their children.

The seers I come from are top of the line. They are the best. I see a perfect world that was messed up. The potential is extraordinary, but there are people that hate life and are destroying the world. The Christians think they are going to heaven. I'm an Indian. My spirit is from an Indian Seer source. There may be no other recourse other than for the planet to fight back. The planet will retaliate. The Bubonic Plague took eighty per cent of Europe.

Have meaningful relationships. We are social animals. People affect the way that you think. Disassociate yourself from people that you don't want to think about. We are a fragile system. Be careful about who you are running into.

Old wive's tales become truth. Dogmatic ritual has no spiritual forbearance. Watch the animals. Watch the ant colony. Humans are strange. Don't buy into the dogma. I look at nature.

Do. Be about business. Take chances. Tell the inner dialogue to shut up. Don't get ahead of yourself. A good sorcerer will walk away with your soul. They'll do it tactfully, so that you think it is you that has made up your mind. When I get silent, you get nervous. I hear your thoughts. You think there's a need to fill in with conversation. You've been a hippy dipshit with false dreams. You don't do, you think. Don't just think

28   A GENERAL RECAP

Jonah said that I was awesomely lucky to have met his benefactor, and that it was especially unusual to know that he was his benefactor. He said that I had had the privilege to meet two of the most important people in all of history. He said that I should listen to what he said and to be thankful for every word. I said... how do I know that you are not swindling my mind? There are no guarantees in life he replied. Most of the things he had ever said were seemingly serious and credible. If he told me all that he knew, my senses might be damaged irreparably. To shut off the mind and the inner dialogue was the key to other experiences. To stop the mind chatter, and to not own that the chatter was yours. The monks long ago decided that they didn't know where their inner dialogue was coming from, so they began to practice shutting out the inner dialogue. Supposedly this gave them the ability to receive other information into themselves, other than the normal jibber jabber of the everyday mind.

He told me that I was like a phantom out to suck his energy. He told me that I was of this world. I interpreted that to mean that I was still kissing up to a world that was directly opposed to the mood of a warrior.

We had a long discussion about self- doubt and self- hatred. It seemed to have pointed out that when you stopped doubting yourself you could do things that you never imagined. Absorb culture and let it out of you. Music for example is in the ethers. Quiet the mind and let it out in a quiet moment. Stay the master of yourself at all times. Clean up your own spiritual environment. Pollution and overpopulation, which is pollution, is the bomb. The environment is diseased. Save the earth, it could have our species become extinct in our lifetime.

There are two lines of study. Develop dreaming like you do guitar playing or any other study. Program yourself to look for your hands in your dreams. The dream body can live in the world. Yogis stay alive for huge amounts of time because their physical bodies sit in a cave and don't endure wear and tear while their dream bodies live out in the world. There is no life and death. The dream body and the physical body coexist. If you are not in the totality of your awareness at the time of death, your awareness will be devoured by what they termed the "eagle." If you have mastered your dream body, you can click into that vehicle for your consciousness when the physical body is done.

Jonah talked about the greatest feat of Don Juan Matus was him leaving the physical world and maintaining life in the astral world. He said that Don Juan had taken his whole party of warriors with him. I wasn't sure of why it was such a good or useful thing to have their bodies, but it did sound incredible. I do know that I did wake up on another plane of consciousness. I really was awake, alive, and momentarily somewhere else.

People used to look for Don Juan. Hoard's of people went down to Mexico to look for him after they had read Castaneda's books. People are on automatic. They're listening to their internal dialogue, not realizing it's their internal dialogue directing them around. Recognize when you are on automatic pilot, going through the motions of not being present, not being awake. Turn off the bullshit. In later books, Castaneda called the internal dialogue, "the flyer." He likened it to a "foreign installation," or intelligence that runs interference in our mind. He wrote about this in his book… "The Active Side of Infinity." It can be likened to the devil in your mind. Just turn off the ranting garbage because it's not your higher self.

Experience the world with your instinct and be in touch with the brain of your body. Your body talks to you and tells you what is going on. Are you tightening up around someone? Are you relaxed and feeling good?

Is your heart racing and your palms sweating, if they are, then why? For example, would you not say that the man on the plane made you feel fearful in some way? He referred to an incredibly odd but intelligent and handsome person that had joined me out of nowhere and had made me exceedingly uncomfortable.

Everyone is in their own world, certain friends of yours have tried to put you in their world. When you are thinking about someone else, you're not thinking about anyone else, so you're in their world.

I know human character. We are perceivers. One time you told me of a student giving you a massage in your dream, and then the next day he did that in class. He felt you in dreaming and responded.

29 NOTES FROM MISCELLANEOUS

CONVERSATIONS 1990-2001'

You've been accepted. You've had a conversation with a Nagual. Not only have you had a conversation but, they know that you know what is going on here. This isn't a little get together, this is a warrior's party. They know you know what's going on, that means you've been accepted.

Put up a mirror in your mind. Remember to have

that mirror when you are out in public. Monitor your act.
Dan and Kathy split your awareness at the dinner table.
You were in two places simultaneously by maintaining
two conversations at the same time. I know you
suspected the wine. My awareness had felt very
heightened.

You can leave your body during dreaming. Look at
your hands, bring them to eye level. Don't gaze on
things, keep it moving.

Keep the weird people away from your life. Walk
away from the creeps that try to follow you. Friends
should be successful. The inner dialogue is a barrier to
perception. The women in Castaneda's books are tight.
They have time for nothing but freedom.

Many are called but few are chosen. Get busy or
you will be put back to mental sleep where we found
you. People are sleeping, they are brainwashed. You are
half awake. Dan and I woke you up.

The education system is messed up. We are fragile
creatures that grew up in debilitating systems. The
American Indians and tribal people had the children with
the old people. The old people could play with the young

and the young with the old. No one was lonely. If you look around you can see that the capitalist system isn't working. It's more isolating then tribal life. It's not living with nature harmoniously. The industry is damaging Mother Nature, and it is clearly not what God intended. If you mess with nature you will be sorry. It's so arrogant of man to say or act like they know more than earth law. There are so many energy sources out there. There is solar energy, there is wind energy.

I am cleaning off your island. This referred to a peculiar occurrence that occurred through-out our conversations for the better part of ten years. A typical example of this would be that we would start a conversation either on the phone or in person. I would feel myself to be in a normal state of perception. I would drift into a state he referred to as heightened awareness. I would feel completely different. My attention would be completely riveted to the now moment. It was as if the focus capacity of my mind would distinctly sharpen. I could only remember what was occurring exactly at that second. I would feel an amazing sense of wellness and joy. He would claim that he was lending me his energy.

We would talk for however long. He said that he was storing his knowledge in me like a container. My body would feel a distinct change in its state of mental and physical equilibrium. Then, like a fog lifting, my consciousness would hover back down to reality. He called this process cleaning off my island. It was much more energetically advanced then talking things out. It was an organic natural cleansing of sorts. He said that a benefactor would initially do this for an apprentice, but that eventually I would need to do this for myself. Another analogy he used was that we wiped our own asses.

I'm getting your priorities turned around. You need to know how to use your own instincts. He felt that one of my ex-boyfriends was demented enough to have wanted to kill me.

Your gut instinct will give you a good read on a situation. White trash is white trash. You can judge a book by the cover. If they look weird, they are. Their good side should be up front. The flip side could also be possible. If it is, it isn't, or if it isn't, it is. It's weird but you really have to look closely to see what is up with people.

I'm grabbing your attention with heightened awareness. You're paying attention. You've never paid attention because your spirit was warped. Not in school and not in music school. Your intelligent edge is unengaged since you don't know how to pay attention or concentrate. Hook it in. Learning is where it is most fun. You have to unplug your learning anxiety. You have to stretch and take walks.

Create a ring of smoke around yourself. Your business is your own. When people are nosy or curious, and you're not interested to discuss your business, say… "Why do you ask?" Get away from personal history. You're always who you were. They type cast you to your past. Be private and amiable. Don't let people assume their way into your life.

You have to clean yourself off from the negative influence of the past. I was fortunate to run into my benefactor. You can't imagine the amount of garbage I have shoveled off your island. You can't imagine what an asshole you were. It took a long time to get you cleaned off to where the old programming didn't matter, this total society influence about what is and what isn't. You were heading towards doomsday.

I'm stretching your attention span. Don Juan had stretched out Carlos's. He grabbed his attention by pulling on his luminous fibers. You never paid attention in school. Sit with the guitar and catch on fire. Catch on fire when you're learning. I could learn all day and be happy. You have to unplug from learning also, or you'll forget your body.

Don't try to become friends with everybody. Don't try to be always expressing yourself. Get away from personal history, because you're not trying to recreate your old bullshit ways. You're trying to put distance away from the old you. You're starting new. You're erasing personal history. Don't let people react to you and treat you like they knew you way back when. Work quietly at your craft.

People assume their way into your life. They ask a lot of personal questions to see if your awake. They're asleep testing to see if your awake.

I walked into a music and bookstore. A strange melancholy feeling pervaded as I perused the rock music section. I was feeling extremely tired. I looked at the young pretty people on the compact disc covers. I had this sadness about I didn't recognize most of the new music. It seemed as though the popular music dream had eluded me while I wasn't looking. Of course my passion for music was as strong as ever. I realized that only a very eccentric teen could ever find me to be their icon. Then I started fantasizing why fantasy is so inspiring. I get to experience their power, heat and direction. As Jonah had said, art is dissected and recreated. Role models are good to have. I took comfort in thinking that although I would probably not be the next target of mass appeal, I liked who I was.

I wandered off to look at the books. I floated around waiting to see if anything stirred my interest. I loved to read inspirational books. It tickled me, but it didn't really produce anything but a good mood and hope. That was worthy. I started honing in on how I lived through others all the time. It was beginning to irritate me about my lack of completion. Were there any books on Rush? I could drink every last drop of them and never get enough. There was a book on Jimi Hendrix's studio sessions. I picked it up and thought this might be something. An almanac mysteriously flew off the shelf. It was by my feet to the right. No one was there. The store clerk walked over and said... "They jump off the shelf sometimes, how are you today?" I took the Hendrix book and left.

I called Jonah to mention the book flying off the shelf. It had been a little startling. He bitched at me for having a propensity for the left side. He said ... who was there? I told him about the store clerk. He said that that was probably the person I would breed with. Then he went into a mockery about what a domestic imbecile I was. Then he made some weird joke about bringing lime to the outhouse.

Jonah said Dan had said that the true meaning of insanity is when people keep doing the same thing over and over again. Later that day Jonah was telling me the story of how to create things in bits. I was really excited because I really laid into other artists to absorb and enjoy their material. I was glutinous with stimulating myself with other people's art, but I was ignorant to producing myself. Finally, in a fit of elation I was able to grasp the bit by bit idea. I saw how easy I could play music bit by bit. I loved improvising. I was negligent in songwriting and recording. I got really elated by how form could be mastered piece by piece. I always had had a problem with form. The abstract always exuded the most masterful attraction. I felt structure intimidating yet also prohibitive. I guess a balance of form and fluidity would be optimal.

We decided to go on another trip. He was driving back to Los Angeles. This would be the fourth time we had done this. The trips always were the best and worst of any type of time that you could have. These are the best times you've had in your whole life, he said. I had to agree with him. The displays of nature that would occur in his presence were absolutely the most fascinating gifts one could ever dream for. Our path along the earth was lined with spectacular visions. One particular moment was around sunset in the Colorado region, where there were five various sunsets in all directions continuously changing. It was a kaleidoscope of vision that could only be the highest source. Time seemingly stopped. We got out of the car. No one was on the highway and the show began.

You shouldn't be afraid to act, he said. Business is acting. Act. Act up. Controllable folly is acting. If you had done the striptease you would have seen the power of women. You would have realized the power that you have. He had given me a "sorcerers task" of doing a striptease in a club. I never even could consider it. He had been very serious about trying to get me to lose my self -consciousness that way. I probably should have, but I failed to be able to do that. That is why I told you to meet young men, to learn about the power that you have. That was another scenario he practically demanded that I had evaded. He said that it was customary of tribal women to educate the younger men in the ways of love. At that time a vivacious overly confident young boy took to chasing my car on his bicycle. He embarrassed me silly. He was far too young even for innocent flirtation as far as I could tell. I had a history of shining up to older men. I did manage a mild encounter with a nineteen - year old. It was very exciting. Even though this was not a real sexual encounter I caught his drift. This man had been much older in spirit anyway. His youthful beauty and intriguing personality were basically just a beauty to behold.

"Your problem is that you judge yourself the way others judge you. Don't do that. To thine own self be true. You judge yourself by your own standards. Be independent of other people's judgments. Don't let their stuff take you down.

The only way any of this stuff is going to come out of a dormant phase, meaning the information he had given me, was through creativity.

Dress masculine to look more feminine, dressing feminine looks more masculine on you. Meditate for health. Get in the lotus position. No fat on this path. The body is the temple of the soul. Extreme good health is the warrior's way.

Jonah said to me that nature liked me. If a natural event was occurring, I could usually not find a reasonable enough connection to feel responsible for it. He would say… Look, that's for us … One time was funny though. He told me to gaze at the sky while he was driving. He told me to cross my eyes, but continue gazing at the sky. I did this for about fifteen minutes.

Suddenly I noticed a cute funny face in the clouds with big crossed eyes. This felt shocking, but positive.

Rousseau moved from Los Angeles. He now lived in the country. He called one night and as we were speaking I sensed a feeling of heightened awareness. He said that he was training my awareness by stretching it. He said that he couldn't believe how dumb I was to not see how my mindset differed from the norm at this point. He said that if I woke up and everything started tripping I should just go about my business. I should learn how to keep my mouth shut, he said.

"We and all the creatures were made from the earth. We are part of the earth's awareness. The earth has its own agenda as well. It has its own favorite toys and things. New York loves me, he said. Manhattan is one of the greatest power spots of all time. New York gave you a boost. The guy who is the big booster gave your business a boost before you even got there. You will continue to do well there. You're looking for magic tricks to appear before you. The magic is in the little things. You should just tune in and shut off the internal dialogue. Turn off the internal dialogue and listen. You don't have time for blabbing and bullshit. You only have time for paying attention. Paying attention to your awareness. Paying attention is listening. Listen to your body. You are a body. Your body is your intellect. Stop letting your mind, rationalize your body, listen and follow your body. Let yourself be free. Stop picking on yourself. Stop worrying about yourself. Let yourself be.

Jonah was coming to N.Y.C. The idea of seeing him always sent me into a quagmire of anxiety. He was generally very pleasant and equally unpleasant. Invariably he would find something completely unseen to me, to find huge offense in. There hadn't been a time I'd seen him that there had been overall peace. However, with the charade of brutal antagonism has always come the mystery and intrigue. His energy and power have been tangibly palpable to me. In the midst of his positive side I feel an ecstasy unparalleled to normal day life. He has put me in heightened awareness on the phone at least one hundred times. I hope he does come by because after the challenges and the intensity of his presence, I have always felt renewed, refreshed and as though my entire life has changed. I am not in the least bit exaggerating that. I never feel the same after one phone call, let alone

a visit.

30 CENTRAL PARK

He said… "This is where the magic begins." We

entered Central Park from about eighty second street. I

could tell instantly what he meant. I shivered with

anticipation having seen several times before. The

landscape had a surreal illuminating glow. There was

nothing so outright as to look unreal. On one hand it

could have looked like just another afternoon in the park.

The sky was cool and had darkish winter hues. The

leaves were changing. Jonah said... There is a connection between Jesus, Don Juan, Carlos and myself. I am definitely a disciple of all of these. They are not arbitrary mentors that I have picked out. Who knows whether Carlos will resurface again? He now knows the unknowable. Who knows whether he was able to gather up the totality of his awareness and got out in a way in which he could resurface.

We walked past a bridge over marshland. There were ducks. The way everything looked was a rare kind of perfect. Nature started to glow. A flock of birds flew overhead. The wind started coming up and going down as though in shaded whispers. I climbed after Jonah as he bounded up and down rocks. He ignored the common trails and wove through the brush. The objective was to get to the Metropolitan Museum of Art. I followed him diligently through the woods. Once he said that it was magic time I tuned into that feeling. Being with him in the woods was often on a different level. I fell into heightened awareness almost immediately. We got up to the highway going through the park. By this point I was in deep heightened awareness. He told me that Dan was a channel for his benefactor. He said that he didn't know if Dan knew exactly what was going on. Maybe Dan knew and didn't care. He said that certain things had happened simultaneously for him. His apprenticeship with Dan, which held extreme power and revelation happened while a multi-million, dollar business was presented to him. He had the high money situation and the great spiritual awakening occurring at the same time. This presented great conflict in his life. He came to New York at that time to ask his brother help about his business. His brother was on a business trip. When he arrived a doorman let him in. He had hitchhiked there from Maine, where he had been fasting. He was very broken up by the events with his benefactor. He was confused. He went to New York to try and relax and put things in order. He had become delirious in Central Park at that time. He was becoming weaker and weaker.

Jonah fell asleep in the park. An Indian man found him. He had on the exact belt buckle that Dan, his benefactor had. A silver Indian head, that was rare. The Indian took him to Greenwich Village and fed him. He gave him some gifts. They took one of the rowboats out on the Central Park Lake. They brought it back to the boathouse. As Jonah and I walked through the tree lined streets we passed a boathouse restaurant. There was a band playing old fifties and sixties songs. He said that by walking through there he was trying to recapitulate what had happened there. He said that it took him twenty years to understand what had happened there. The Indian and him had waded out into the Hudson River and tried to find some island. When they got there it was a cold night. They took rocks from the campfire and buried them under dirt. They slept on top of the rocks for warmth. Then they separated and he went back to Ohio.

He went to another friend's house. He said that he was walking down a dirt road when he realized that he was the omen. I asked him…Omen for what? He said… "For the dawning of the Aquarian age." He became freaked out when he realized this, he said. He began running down the street. When he was running down the street he kept getting revelations. He was running down the street and he was getting lighter and lighter. He was starting to levitate. This freaked him so much, that he made it stop. He feels today, that that was an opportunity missed to achieve enlightenment and lift off to eternity. He realized that he was a messenger of knowledge.

We walked up to "Cleopatra," a statue of an obelisk form 1600 B.C. It was darkening into dusk. I was in intense heightened awareness. His storytelling was laying a thick web of trance around me. It was almost as if I was on another plane of consciousness. Since I have experienced that since this writing I can say that it wasn't that deep of a changed environment but I felt as though I was very intoxicated. He said that he felt as though he had almost died in Central Park in the past events. He had had revelations in Central Park. He said that the New York land loved him. It would give him anything. As we walked down Fifth Avenue he raised his arms, looked at the park and exclaimed…"This is my town. I could have anything here." "This is my town. I own this town." A confirmation came when I had asked N.Y to show me confirmation of this, and at that moment the 1977 Blackout occurred. New York confirmed who my benefactor was. It gave me affirmations. I cooled off after that.

He had arrived at about one a.m. on a Friday night.

He told me that I looked thinner which was a good trait for warriors. This was a sign of success for me. He looked good, perhaps even healthier then in Hollywood. He had that robust glow from living in country air. I felt that strange happy joy at seeing him. We went to the Yaffa Café in the East Village. The healthy food was great. The décor was exotic bohemian and the people were exuberant and attractive. The back-round music was interesting. I felt good in having brought him to the right place. He said that New York was very creative and different from Hollywood. He commended me on my success here. We ate in complete silence with complete relaxation, as we usually did. On the way over he had engaged the cab driver in conversation about his car. He had been eager to know Jonah's knowledge about mechanics. I noticed that Jonah could often engage people by getting them to talk about themselves and their lives. He could never live in a city again, he said. We walked back. I took him past a person I knew who played exceptional Jazz guitar. He played in the subway each evening. I commented on how pure I thought this person was. I mentioned how this person was a

Commanche, and that even though I would not want to live off the land in Manhattan, I thought the guy was rather rugged for having done it. He was super built in body frame, although somewhat mental. Jonah became unglued. He threatened to punch me. This unnerved me because regardless of our unusual association, I didn't see the validity in that type of behavior. I was intimidated by him. He renounced me knowing anyone that was unsuccessful. I had seen him assisting people with problems for years in Hollywood, but I knew what he was getting at. Me being so easily influenced could bring me right down there with whatever malady had occurred for these people. He was also furious that I walked through the streets of Manhattan totally relaxed. He said that I had to watch the street and everything around me when I walked. No talking while you're walking. He again emphasized to be present and not lost in thought as you walk around. He spoke bitterly harshly to me. I hated when he got that way. I couldn't argue or say anything. That had been established years ago. It was my way or the highway, as he put it. Because of the illuminating quality of knowing him and feeling certain ways around him, I wouldn't have jeopardized our situation for anything, especially my self-importance. When he harassed me, which he assuredly did, I assumed there was a purpose behind it. I strived to hear beyond the theatrical folly and know really what he meant. Even when he sounded like an aberrant, what he was saying was usually of sound intelligence. This time it was the cleaning. He ranted for two days about what a hippie artist slob I was. He even wanted my record collection out of the office. I had a home office. I understood his sentiments and actually there was enough space to at least get the records in another room. He was saying throw them out or put them in storage. I didn't feel there was anything about my business that could hold a candle to my record collection. That was a piece by piece part of my lifetime. Unfortunately, although I loved business, I didn't love it nearly as much as my record collection. But I got what he was saying and certainly another room was a good idea. The rest of the cleaning conversation was absolutely true. He had always said that what was in your outside surroundings effected your abilities on an energetic level. So it was more than neatness for neatness sake, which would be valid too, but there was greater benefit and reason to have it that way.

It had been wonderful but intense to see him. We actually survived him leaving the stove and gas on after lighting some incense with it. There was no sound and the gas was running into the room all night. I had gotten a headache and opened the window. The next day we found the stove on. What a miracle that we lived. I guess having the window open helped, but I was shocked to find the stove on. Even with his carrying on, it was an immense honor for him to have shared his intelligence with me. His energy was not common in the least. I just didn't get that feeling around people normally. He was a very attractive man, but that is distinctly not the type of energy or feeling that I am talking about. He carried a subtle feeling of electricity of an unusual sort. Being around him rewired something in me.

Jonah called. He mentioned that Dan and he had taken some time off from working together. He said that Dan's feelings towards him at times weren't good for him. Probably in some ways the way it felt with him toward me. He tried to strong arm me into improvement, and it really was helpful and appreciated, although I had to get the strength inside myself to do it. His emphasis at least pointed out what was what. We commented on Dan's unbelievable brilliance. His benefactor Dan and his wife Kathy were by far the most amazing people I had ever met, by their shine alone. The way I felt in their presence was absolutely the most unusual experience I had had. I often remarked to him how unusual I thought Kathy had appeared. She was super pretty. She looked a little translucent. I don't know if I'm just crazy but she looked illuminated somehow. She had a lovely angelic quality and she was very nice. She was nice in a manner that was self- confident and pleasant. She wasn't gushingly nice, the way I had the problem sometimes of giving over my power to people, in the act of being nice. People in Los Angeles often shine compared to the death warmed over New Yorkers, but she was in a class of her own.

He told me that I had perplexing inability to see dangerous people. It wasn't necessarily the people, but what was acting on some people. He said that I had not learned to defend myself and that I got scared of people because I made them like my mother who had intimidated me. He then said that women have more intuition because they are closer to the earth. Dan could create harmony for everyone, he said. The point that I think he was getting at was to take care of myself. He said that I should pamper my health and treat myself kindly. Relax, clean up, and create good health and harmony. Stop being so uptight.

The tongue is where the inner dialogue lives. When you meditate, the twitching of the tongue is where the inner dialogue is. Different parts of the body are like different brains. The whole body is like a brain. Talk to your tongue. Tell your tongue to relax. This will quiet the inner dialogue. Chant OM to start meditation. Meditation is like a school of discipline. Sit down, meditate and chant OM. It replaces inner dialogue with divine sound. The universe has a frequency. The whole universe is talking. If you can get away from it, the sound of the universe is OM. Duplicate that sound and you are tuning into a channel. The inner dialogue is a channel. Change channels on your radio.

I started keeping a dream journal. Little things

would happen here and there. I dreamed that I woke up in my dream and was doing actual dreaming. Upon reflecting upon this, this morning, I didn't know whether I actually woke up or just dreamed that I had woken up. I remembered that the guard in my building, who was a dreamer, had said to be more aware in the day, to be more aware in the night. In the dream I became more aware of everything around me. I heard Jonah's voice talking to me. I stayed awake a few minutes before going back to my body. I still think that I had only dreamed that I had "woken up."

I called Jonah. When you're ranting in your mind, isolate how tired that makes you feel. Tell yourself to shut up. Tell yourself that everything is going to be alright. Everything is going to be just fine.

In meditation, there are three people involved with inner dialogue. Me, myself and I. One of those is the "flier" talking. The flier talks nonsensical bullshit. Non elevated nonsensical bullshit. It's the idiot on amphetamines. The flier talks about everything. People, are possessed by their flier. This topic was covered well in the Carlos Castaneda book titled.... "The Active Side of Infinity." The flier is the inner voice that is incessant and nonsensical. They say it's like an alien force that feeds on humanities luminosity.

When the assemblage point is in the place of no pity, you do not experience the humbleness of a beggar. The right place is a place of no pity. No pity, for a warrior, is not a place of cruelty, but of ruthlessness, complete indifference. A warrior's ruthlessness is how I am ruthless about being on your case. I am interested in heirs to this knowledge.

When meditating, shut off dialogue. Turn it off or let it go. A lot of indulgence is self -importance. Give yourself a break. Recognize the difference between higher thought and the flier. Higher thought is always striving to be silent by way of command. The flier's voice is always trying to distract you from attention. Incorporate saying the word OM to shut off the inner dialogue during the day. Do Indian Chants. Get creative with it. Get your voice to sing the Indian chants.

You can talk and give commands to your body. The body is the mind. The mind is the body. There are two forms of recapitulation. Formal and Random. They are performed, in order to retrieve energy that was spent in your life. It's like cleaning dirt off your spirit. Formal recapitulation is to list every person and do a head roll exercise to remember and rid oneself of energy expenditure. Random recapitulation is to do the head roll exercises while allowing situations and people to come up randomly in your mind. Recapitulation helps you to replace yourself with new energy. You're helping the assemblage point to move by doing this. "You can fly past the eagle" by regaining the energy by recapitulation. You've given back a facsimile of your awareness to the force that wants our awareness at the point of death.

"Seeing is personal." Jonah said that Kathy had told him that. "There's no such thing as coincidence." His benefactor had proven that beyond a shadow of a doubt to him.

You want to be enlightened. Do not deal with the wrong people. The energy it has taken me to wake you is astronomical. Like Dan, I could have dropped dead from the energy I have put upon you. Dan went beyond the call of duty. Dan would say… what don't you understand except doing it? He exhausted himself. He would say not

to worry about you. I leaked on you. No leaks except
onstage and on paper. Put creativity onstage and on
paper. When you walk, look at the horizon. Ignore
humanity and see how good it feels. Even when they
look at you, see how good it feels to not look at them.
You're always seeking out approval from others. It
righteously sucks. Learn how to disconnect from the
world. This keeps your energy. You have to realize this
on your own. Look to the higher planes. Something calls
us. Man is marching out of the darkness into the light.
The great light. God doesn't describe the eternal. It's not
about words. It's about the absence of words. Get
organized and get busy. Replace inner dialogue with
OM. That is the closest word for God. Accomplishment,
is knowing. Why be led by idiots. This path is about
being an artist. Pick up a pencil, or a paintbrush, or a
guitar. Be a writer, be onstage, be an artist.

Pay attention to the body. There is knowledge in
the body. When you meditate, watch for incandescent
shooting lights, we call tumblers. Hum OM, while you
look for tumblers. Infinity is easier to see at the bridge of
the nose then at the end of the nose. It is where the third

eye is. When you meditate, cross the eyes slightly and focus on the bridge of the nose.

Imaginary is a word to discredit reality. Meditate to cure yourself. The hardest part of doing anything is picking it up. The part of the guitar is sitting down, to do it. Doing something nine times in a row creates a groove. Talk to your body to get healthy. Talk to your brain and talk to your tongue. Heal by relaxing, being quiet and chanting OM. Relax is a command that you give yourself. Imagine a glass wand going to each part of the body and making it well. Gazing is the relaxed concentrated act of staring at something so that you will see it in your dreams.

I asked Jonah some questions. He responded… you can only listen to God. You can't talk to God. You can listen. He's everywhere else outside your head. What's in your head is the alien installation of the flier. When you're thinking shut up and listen. To hear the great spirit turn off the inner dialogue. Shut the mind. You can then have communion with divine force watching over you. Listen for God. Listen in meditation. Listen for divine force that watches over you. You are not alone. You think your thoughts are important. Do not

think. The mantra is … shut up. To achieve self-

realization, you must all day shut the flier up. All day as

much as possible keep your head free and clear. The

point of the messiah was to be like the messiah. Not

worship, but follow. Be a warrior. Shut off the inner

dialogue. Forget the world. Shut off the outer

consciousness and you will perceive and you will leave

the body. You will achieve what Jesus wanted. You must

transcend and become fluid in your dreaming body in

order to leave the world with your consciousness. That is

waking up. Talk to yourself. Give yourself good

thoughts. When you hear thoughts or inner dialogue,

make sure it is you. Who are you? You are the one with

the good thoughts. The bad thoughts are demons messing

with you. Be careful how much attention you pay to your

fellow men. Detach. Fliers are like a virus. Detach your

fibers from the world of your fellow men and walk on

by, he instructed me.

"The world is a stage." Every day when you

meditate, keep talking good thoughts and commands to

yourself. Watch for the tumblers. Listen for the tuner,

(the white noise of quiet that is present. A low hissing sound you can hear of the universe. It can be heard as OM as well.) Take deep breathes. Light incense. Burn candles. Every day meditate for one minute at least. Total perception. "Do what you're doing when you're doing it." That's really critical. Dan had said there should be time for everything. You just need to schedule and organize.

Self-importance and indulging are other forms of excessive inner dialogue. Listen for the tuner and look for the tumblers to achieve perception. Your evaluation of what is important is mental interference. You give your thoughts importance. Your thoughts are a barrier to your evolution of enlightenment.

I'm trying to teach you. You come off like a frustrated artist but you have a good sense of humor.

Off and on over the years I started having fragments of lucid dream experiences. The last one I had about two months ago was the strongest and most definitive. I pretty much forgot what led up to the finale. The last fragment was the few minutes that made this entire path absolutely indisputable to me. I had the sensation that I was either in a car, or my body was flying over the road in the way that a car would just normally drive. I looked around. I observed that it was dawn. It was a country like suburban neighborhood. I looked at the houses and could not read the numbers. I remembered the command to not look too specifically at any given item. I got to a point in the road where there were large gorgeous blooming cherry blossom trees. During this experience I was fully aware that I was dreaming and I was fully aware that I was awake somewhere and somehow. It was as awake as a normal day. It lasted for a few moments and then I was in my bed. The outstanding quality of the experience has fully proven to me the existence of some type of parallel experience that we can achieve. I'm aware that this is commonplace to legions of adept dreamers. I'm aware that this would be impossible to imagine without having the experience. I'm also aware that this was just the merest glimpse of our potentiality. This was the first taste, not the end of what could be experienced. For me, after hanging around with data and roadmaps, the Castaneda books, for ten years, I can say.... This is absolutely real.

I just took a nap and a different but equally distinctive experience occurred. I had a thought about not wanting to be experimented on by aliens. Then I shot through a square opening in a white room. I was in some kind of space. I thought to myself... this is the mind sky. It's the world right inside my mind when I look inside right behind my pupils. With my eyes shut there seemed to be an active world right behind my closed eyes. Then I heard a voice. It said something about how everyone has had teachers that have went before them. It mentioned Gandhi and Bach. Then I heard a voice singing and possibly playing guitar. I was straining to listen not believing this was going on. Then I knew I was back. I opened my eyes and I was in bed.

Jonah called me about ten o'clock the next night. He repeated things to reinforce them. Inner dialogue is thinking to yourself. Sorcerers say that they don't know where that comes from. We claim that those are our thoughts and defend everything that we think. Sorcerers say that it is another mind that incorporates itself into our being. The objective is that when you are thinking, you can instead be listening. You must distract the inner dialogue. You can listen to your environment instead. You have a choice as to what you want. Stuff influences the inner dialogue by what you ingest. The mind is like a garden. Food also will reflect the type of inner dialogue. You listen to yourself think. You listen to what you think is you, thinking. This is not to banish thought. We are frail creatures. We are governed by our inner dialogue. Thought has devastating effects on the physical body. Thought effects the body. External stimulus also effects the body. Danny put the magic back in my life. Man is a magical being that has lost touch with it's magic. We all vaguely still feel the magic. They pump you in the system then they expect you to die. My father thought himself to death. Give your mind and body rest often. They didn't' have all these distractions in the past. The magic has dissipated on the planet. Money as a means to an end is good. The love of money can be negative. Magical things can happen when you shut out the dialogue. Sit up and touch the soles of your feet together. You'll hear dialogue but it won't be your kind of dialogue. Do the meditation consistently. It takes discipline. You're easily distracted by things. I meditate three times a day, morning, noon and night. Reach down and grab your toes. Stay limber, get relaxed. Do it anytime. Stop thinking. When you're thinking you're having a conversation. You're perceiving, in pictures, you're perceiving a place. I've seen my allies. They were incredible people. I was seeing angels. One of my allies is Jimi Hendrix's ally. They came to greet me. They were serene beautiful people. They are my allies. It was a quiet summer day. I was in the tavern that I was renovating. I looked in a mirror. There was an ethereal face in the mirror. It was a peaceful serene face. It went away and another one came. Seven came and the last one was Jimi Hendrix. It was me meeting my allies. Jimi's other. It's the other you. You want to bring that close to you. You can wake up inside your dream. You'll be awake. When you're dreaming, you're attracting your other. It's capable of extraordinary feats. Do it while you are young. You'll lose your awareness if you don't do it in time. You act dumb, but you're smart. You're gullible, but your aggressive. There's a pecking order in society. There is a chain of command to teach the weak. Wise up and stop being a pacifist. Quit being lunchmeat for everyone. Be impeccable. Relate to people. You're not part of the world. Birds of a feather flock together. Do what I tell you. Discipline is what you lack. Learn discipline. An ally is a force in the world. There are different forces in the universe. There's your "other." The "flier's" who have inhabited the planet have vamped the world of it's magic. Now it's every man for himself. It was your good fortune to run into me. I've been trying to fix my own party. Clarity becomes an enemy to a man of knowledge. I don't know how I effect you. It was a disaster how things have effected members of this party. Danny's out of control in some ways. Kathy ran in her own way. She ran away to become Dan's wife. Dan is the most profound person in the face of humanity. It's important to do formal and random recapitulation. It cleans off your island of negative and old energies that weigh down the development of your dream body.

Flip gears from your old self. Start a fire. Be organized. Nothing happens overnight. Keep doing things. Do the guitar right. You're dense, but not stupid. Your problem is discipline. Have faith that you'll get it.

Keep doing your chops on guitar and you will get it or anything else. You have to observe fate. You have to watch how fate works. It's often best to be careful around personal history. You will often be pigeonholed to what you were. That insults who you are now. Having a cloud around you gives you privacy and the ability to not have people hanging the past on you. Your body knows the real you. Be the real you. Be strong. Shed the timid. Let it rip. You're a masculine woman. Be assertive.

When you're meditating, put the palms of your feet together and keep your back up. Relax the roof of your tongue. Listen to outside sounds. You'll hear conversation and possibly music. It's not coming from your thought centers. It's coming from somewhere else. Gazing is important. The fliers have incorporated themselves into the fibers of our being. It isn't us. They feed off us. We are their sustenance. Our magical selves are here. Man possessed magic, before something got mixed in. The fliers feed on a sheath we had as children. It can grow back. Silence turns the flier off. They feed on inner dialogue. Meditation cleans off the fliers, which are akin to mental demons. The silence makes you an undesirable meal. At one time in history we had mythological amounts of magic. We knew from the old testament that people lived to be very old. Something interfered with that. The fliers screwed that up. Indians had their sorcery from ancient Mexico. Imagine two million buffalo. The Europeans devastated everything. They were soulless, mindless, disrespectful puppets with no appreciation for the people that were here. They had lost their magic.

Become a practitioner. One who testifies what I am telling you. I come from an ancient line of seers. My real benefactor is Jesus.

To become a practitioner, you must practice recapitulation. Isolate and be aware of inner dialogue. We talked obsessively about inner dialogue. The outer dialogue is everything outside your head. To form discipline, concentrate on the outer dialogue. There is a bubble. A luminous cocoon. There is a hissing sound which is a vibration of the luminous body. I've called that sound the tuner. Listen to it. Meditate on hearing the white noise hissing sound of the universe. The fliers are masters of deception. Pay attention to the outer dialogue, which is the hissing sound. Sexual energy will quiet the inner dialogue. Jonah said that the tumbler was the easiest to perceive. While meditation focus eyes on brow. There will be subtle light formations in the mind's eye. Look for the tumblers to appear as a greenish blue light that appears to be a bubble going away from you. He also said that I would remember things by writing because I was being stored with creativity. A lot of Danny rubbed off on him, he said. Don Juan also put his personality on him. We inherit personality traits and then take the rest of our lives to sort out stuff. The breathing exercises for recapitulation will restore your life energy that got spent and dissipated along the way. What it is, it isn't, and what it isn't, it is. Things often aren't what they look like. Turn off the self. The real self is the instinctive self.

I talked to Jonah for twelve hours in the last two days. He was very demanding in his treatment of me. He was furious that we had the same conversation for seven years. He told me stress was killing me. I returned his call, planning to speak for five minutes at that particular

time and we continued for seven hours. He talked about
the fliers and how it was like a foreign being that
attached itself to people's minds and that it was similar
to how they used to say that a devil was inside you. You
would think the thoughts were your own but they were
actually the thoughts of this demon type entity. The
internal dialogue was the flier. This was clearly written
about in The Active Side of Infinity, by Carlos
Castaneda. The other quieter voice that was your own,
was the voice of the spirit. It was the intuition and the
real you, that was often buried deep inside a person.
Stopping the internal dialogue was the key to opening
your perception. The constant chattering mind that spoke
in English and in pictures was the internal dialogue. In
meditation the idea was to shut the internal dialogue and
listen to the tuner. The tuner was a name he had devised
to name the hissing you could hear in your ears when
you listened to the outside world. He said that it was the
inside edge of your luminous egg. The light refraction to
look for in meditation he called tumblers. Look for
shooting beams of light on the screen behind your eyes.
Follow them. Try to attach your consciousness to one

and ride away with it. He was referring to the idea that you could astral travel or do dreaming, by holding on to one of these light beams while meditating. The kingdom of heaven is within you. Jesus told about the father and the kingdom of heaven. To prove this, he healed people.

The goal is to enter the kingdom of heaven. To override for yourself, the fliers and the evil that pervades the planet. Do gazing. Then nap and think of what you gazed at. Accumulate light inside the body. The whole point is that there is a whole other cognitive system available to you if you plug into it. The act of recapitulation replaces energy. Following Jesus to the kingdom of heaven is developing the ability to experience the other cognitive worlds available to us. "Be like children." Children can move their assemblage points.

"The hinge of sorcery is the ability to move your own assemblage point." The inorganic beings want your awareness. Do not state that you want to be in their world because it will be forever. Do these things religiously, no pun intended. Recapitulate, read the Castaneda books and highlight them, write, meditate, do cardiovascular exercise, play music......

Sit down and start recapitulation. Inhale left to right, exhale right to left. Let spirit choose what you want to think about for random recapitulation. For formal recapitulation, make a list of everyone you know and go down the list. To recapitulate is to gather back the energy you have put out in the world. You can then give a facsimile of that energy to the eagle that demands your awareness at death. Therefore, you can bypass death by regaining the totality of your awareness. Study the books intensely. Save energy by stopping the internal dialogue.

What I'm about is warning people that in ten years the planet is going to explode. It will not take this kind of abuse, and something completely annihilating is going to happen if there is not a complete reversal of destruction.

Be a warrior. Follow Jesus. Don't worship him. This is about eternal life and not dying like other people. Enlightenment will prevent death. This is about leaving the planet like Don Juan and his party of warriors left the planet.

The other day I dreamed that Jonah was talking to

me. He called and said that he was reading the same stuff that I heard him saying to me in the dream. He said that he knew that Don Juan and Carlos were there also. I remember the environment being of an ethereal like atmosphere in the mountains. It was warm and dark. I was shocked when he called.

Pray for intent. Praying is intending. There are two kinds of people. The black magicians and the seers. Become a practitioner by listening to the tuner. The flier gives us it's mind. By paying attention to the flier, it is eating your luminosity. When you're listening to anything other than your tuner, it's the flier. We love to think. We get addicted to thinking. We get addicted to sex. You remove the flier by doing recapitulations.

Make yourself a prayer closet, or a prayer place. Go inside it. Pray that you can focus all of your attention on the tuner. Pray that you can move the assemblage point. When you walk, recite to yourself… The hinge of sorcery is in moving the assemblage point. When you're praying, you are aligning your emanations with the eagle. Pray to find your hands in your dreams. When you realize you are dreaming, that's the first gate. Find an object. Look at it, then look away, then look back at it. Be relaxed and at ease. Get to a state of indifference.

You have to will something. The will turns into intent. You will something and you will yourself to intend something. You consciously give commands to yourself. Intend instead of random thought. "Shovel the world off your island." You have to learn, to will yourself to intend warrior's commands, so that all of your conscious thoughts are commands. If you are going to pray for something, pray for inner silence. You have to repeat things. That's intent. "Intent, Intent, Intent!" You're willing yourself to see. That was quoting Silvio Manual, one of the most talented of the sorcerers in Don Juan's party. You can only see with inner silence. You're turning off the rhetoric bullshit of the inner dialogue. The inner dialogue is the flier. You can grow back luminosity. You will understand that there is a part of us that always wants to engage us. It's not us, it's the flier. We are willing the flier off the island. We're doing it with commands. It's a celestial virus. The irony is that the most possessed are the religionists. They're full of self- absorption. Jesus said… "Follow me." Self-absorption is being absorbed with the inner dialogue. The camera in front of you will show you how to act. Keep that camera in your mind's eye. It's like having a mirror in front of you to remind you of good acting. Think to yourself.... It's not so important that I have to think about it now. These are the commands of a warrior. Intending yourself to be quiet. Intending distractions off of your island. The best time to do this is when you are out walking. Give all your thoughts warrior commands. Pay attention to your body. Get as much rest as you possibly can.

When you lose the human form you will turn off dialogue and detach yourself from whatever is effecting you. It allows you to then rest your mind. Be relaxed, detached and at ease. Otherwise people burn out their brains. Keep your commands the commands of a warrior. You have to intend yourself to be a warrior. Your commands become the commands of the eagle. You're lighting up different emanations. You're matching the emanations inside with the emanations outside. The other seers got into praying. The new seers saw that they're commands became the commands of the eagle. Why ask for dumb things in this world? The path is to shut off the dialogue. Two times a day set aside to meditate. The sound of silence is the tuner. When you're ranting isolate how tired that makes you feel. Tell yourself to shut up. Tell yourself…. Everything is going to be alright, everything is going to be just fine.

Turn off the dialogue by chanting OM. Do Native American chants. Get creative with it. Get your voice to crackle. You can talk to and instruct the body. Your body is your mind. Your mind is your body. You can tell it to heal. We give objects power. Do recapitulation and the head rolls to regain enough energy to "dart past the eagle." This is the term for giving the force that devours life, a similarity of energetic awareness so that you can retain your consciousness past death. According to the shamans of this party you can evade death, by developing your dream body during life to a state that will transcend the life of the body. You can become enlightened by developing your consciousness to a state that can surpass traditional death. It is said that the exercise of recapitulation will boost and prepare you for this journey. This journey that is within human physical means under strong pursuit of energetic conditioning and balancing. This is the goal of a warrior. This is the journey that Don Juan and his party of warriors made together.

There is a dissolving force in the universe that wants our awareness. By doing recapitulation head rolls you are taking back the energy that you put into those experiences. You're replacing it with new energy. You're helping your assemblage point to move by doing this. You can fly past the eagle by doing this.

Jonah encouraged me to keep a diary of dreams and dreaming. He encouraged me to set up dreaming. Over time bits and pieces began to occur. Be aware as you are falling asleep. Look for your hands in your dreams. One evening I read a chapter in "The Art of Dreaming." By Castaneda before I went to sleep.

The first thing I remembered is lying in a darkened place. Jonah seemed to be around somewhere. I feel a tug on my stomach. I make a complaint about it. Then Jonah says…There's Jesus. I say something to the effect of… "wow." I now get the impression that I am with Jesus, even though I don't see or hear him. I pass behind something that seems to be similar to a large burlap sheet. It's as if I can see into a world behind the sheet, but I get the impression that they don't see me. I come into a room that seems like the inside of a gymnasium. The people are acting out what you would consider a Chanukah play. They are wearing old fashion clothing. What is different about these people is that they seem to be completely free. They are dancing magnificently with no inhibition, yet they are not lewd. They are extremely sexual and free, yet they are not bawdy or lewd. They are like emancipated individuals.

That scene dissolves and I am now in some kind of house. It seems to be a dormitory. I am studying all the people. At one point I am in a girl's dormitory. The place is shimmering with pretty quaint décor. The women are pretty, blonde and vacuous. They wear an expressionless look, but they are very natural. I am aware that I am dreaming and that this is actually another world. Everything is very vivid. Then I woke up in my bed. I am conscious that I just went somewhere. My heart is beating rapidly but I only lightly experience the bodily pain that I am accustomed to feeling after such a vivid dream. I usually get deep muscular aches after dreaming like that.

The purpose of recapitulation is to clean the connective link to the spirit. Reread the "Power of Silence" by Castaneda.

Occasionally he would tell me bits and pieces of what he referred to as his tales of power. He would go from vehemently telling me off, to a mood of great comradeship. I bent to his mood like a willow in the breeze. I would change paces along with him as quickly as he shifted.

He told me how he got his first bible. He walked into a church. A cleaning lady saw him reading it and told him to take it with him. He never heard her exit the room. He told me of another incident where he had walked up to the George Cohan statue in Times Square. A movie was in the process of being shot. As he walked out from behind the statue the director looked at him in shock. The lead actor looked exactly like him and was wearing the same clothes. He also had a heart medallion on. He had a poncho, a straw hat and rolled up jeans. The director said to him… "Who are you?" His eyes had sparkled at him when he said that. He looked up and the marquee in back of him flashed "The Omen" for the movie.

We changed subjects. He told me that at the time of the passing of the Messiah, the sky turned dark, lightening flared, earthquakes occurred and luminous beings were visible. People were really shaken by this. He said that I could have been there. I felt electric as he told me this story. I told him that when he had spoken to me as the other person, I had mentally envisioned a dark rainy hill. He then told me that I should be conscious of how I act. Get out a video camera and record yourself talking, and figure out what you look like acting. Keep the mental mirror in front of you. See yourself, how you act. Stop thinking that acting is phony. People don't dislike you, they dislike your lack of acting.

Keep your mind conscious. Get into a Naguals state of consciousness. Schedule your accomplishments. Get out your checklist. Talk out loud to give your mind and body commands. You're being led around by your flier. Something is holding your talent, your blatant talent, captive. Shut off inner dialogue and cross your eyes, (let

eyes go when you walk down the street.) Figure out who
the tyrants were in your recapitulation. Get the people
that warped your spirit off your island in recapitulation.
Don't evaluate yourself through other people's eyes.

I went to see Jonah in Pennsylvania. I knew he had
been residing in a country environment, but I had not
envisioned the depth of how far out in the country he
actually was. This was a small town in an absolutely
gorgeous area not far from Ohio. I had never been this
far out in the country in North America. It had the same
quality of natural beauty as Colorado or even
Switzerland. I left New York in a state of typical stress. I
made the money for the bus ticket, one hour before
departure. The eight-hour ride was supremely beautiful. I
left at one thirty a.m. By four o'clock I was viewing
things from the bus window that I had never seen. I
couldn't understand how there was any light before
dawn. It was still well before sunrise and yet there was
an errie, incandescence permeating the mountains. We
were going through the Appalachian Mountains. I had
never seen these. There were huge layers of mist and fog
all over the mountains. The sky and land were vivid hues

of bright aqua and purple. I kept trying to wake up more to see this. Every time I opened my eyes a virile explosion of splendor greeted them. The range looked different than any landscapes I'd ever seen. I finally arrived in his town. I walked around a bit, feeling out and comparing his description of the place to what I was seeing. My back hurt and my gear was uncomfortable. I stopped in a tiny café to use the restroom and obtain coffee. There were memorabilia of 1950's music dotting the walls. They immediately gave me one of those stares that questions you through and through. I'm sure I looked exhausted, but I didn't think I deserved that much scrutiny. I went into the restroom. I tried to relax and urinate. My body was extremely frazzled. I felt I was being watched and listened to, which didn't assist bodily functions. All of a sudden I heard a twisting of the door handle. I say… "someone is in here." A moment later there is a loud banging on the door. I imagine that some poor woman or child need to urinate urgently. I call again… "One moment… someone is in here." Another rampage of loud banging ensues. Now I'm angry. I'm thinking… what's with these country assholes. I decided not to pee. I wash my hands and exited. I expected to see a woman or child waiting somewhere. Only men are in the place now. They stare back vacant and wry. Now I'm surprised. Why would a man, start hassling a woman, in the ladies room? This felt spooky. The owner served me the coffee. I'm extra polite to sort of disclose, that even if I look different, if that is what they see, I am not of any bad intent. In retrospect I understand my stance of intending civil relations, since I might have wanted to enjoy the place on another occasion, but by the same token, they sure had a lousy disposition toward assisting weary travelers. I continued on to look for Jonah's dwelling. I walk into the back parking lot that he had described. I climbed the long wooden stairs and noted the big porch. I thought that this had to be the place. A knarled voice growled "Who is it?" I took in the sight of Jonah after not seeing him for two years. His eyes shone more brightly. I saw that comfortable old hippie essence layered on top of what I know to be a more aggressive character. I see the effects of rural mountain life etched serenely on his slightly more withered, but a slightly more fierce, face. He looks to be getting good air. Our greetings are lighthearted and warm. In the range of normal as opposed to the different attitudes that often shift between us. I'm feeling very guarded, because we have operated on so many levels and certain ones do not feel appropriate at this time, because of other people. I would feel guarded anyway because nothing about him could ever be guessed beforehand. No matter what my demeanor he often waxed perfectly congenial to seriously frightening. I walked into his meditation room. The feeling was almost overwhelming. The air was fragrant with incense. There was a distinctive energy in the air. It was one of joyousness, power and peace. He left me alone and I slept for awhile. When I got up we resumed a lighthearted conversation. He showed me around the rather huge apartment. In the room he used for a large gym was a large wheel. It was meant to stretch the back. One would lie over it, and hold onto the handles and roll ones back out. It resembled a huge spool. My back was better almost immediately, not to mention the sheer novelty of this thing. It was massive in size. He then assembled a bicycle for me to ride. Even though I worked out almost every day, I still felt

apprehensive about riding. It had been about seventeen
years since I had been on one. His bicycle resembled a
mini circus ride. It had an awning, lots of colors and a
trailer attached. I adjusted fairly quickly to the riding.
Still, the princess in me was bellowing. I couldn't believe
how far he was going. In the end we went twenty miles.
The trail was gorgeous. It was along the Allegheny
River. The Appalachian Mountains resided in the
backround. We saw woodchucks, chip monks, robins,
rabbits and six deer. We had a picnic at a historic
landmark rock. It had an Indian Petroglyph, that he
estimated at being from around the year twelve hundred
A.D. The rock was covered with people's signatures
from the last thousand years. It was intense to see. We
sat in an area overlooking the river. He told me to stare at
the mountain and to let my eyes lose focus. Then he
directed me to look at the river. By doing that the
mountains appeared to move of their own will. He called
this gazing. It gave the strong sense of an optical illusion.
I really could see them moving. Gazing would help in the
dreaming process. Things you gazed at could be returned
to in dreaming. He thought people had been doing gazing

in that location for perhaps hundreds of years. He then moved off the spot on which he was sitting. Underneath him was a carving of an alien face. It was spooky because it looked so old. He then commanded for us to leave immediately. Miraculously when we got home my respiratory system felt entirely different. I had been having difficulty breathing. I attributed it to my chronic use of Ma Huang, that I used as a workout stimulant. I have since luckily abandoned this practice. My lungs opened after the bike ride in a way that made me more sensitive to what lungs were actually supposed to feel like. I had become extremely congested in N.Y. He attributed it to stress. It felt like the first time I had felt was real breathing was. Doing deep breathing exercises gives a lot of energy. Breathing the country air was a great feeling. The air was delicious. What a change from the city.

Everything was going fine until Jonah decided that I should go into the Army. In retrospect I can almost see his rational. Although frankly, a honest and consistent lifestyle in the gym I thought could also manage what he was after. My health did appear appalling, and his heart was in the right place in wanting to kick my ass into surviving. This was not something I felt was anything less then insane. Being that survival is what I clearly think is the most important thing in life, I felt apprehensive about signing up for something that I perceived as possibly life threatening. The military is no joke, and one can only respect the people that are that committed to effecting change in society as to put themselves at risk in that way. That being said I was legally above the age to be accepted. He was all for bluffing your way in, and again I really like to stay inside the standards that no one is going to take great offense to. There was a discipline problem that I had in my life. The daily challenge was so encompassing, that a lot of his teachings I couldn't get to or even remember existed. It was as if I had amnesia. Only now after such a long time, do I feel ready to settle down into the mechanics of what he showed me. I also felt like I was completely married at the time he mentioned the Army. I couldn't see not being involved where I was involved.

Ten minutes later he had me on the phone talking to a recruiter. I basically became hysterical and handed the phone back to him. There was a day and one half before he had mentioned this. In that interim some very lovely experiences had taken place. For instance, he had transformed the inside of a piano into a huge percussion palette. He had devised several types of brushes and rubber ball mallets, to apply to the wire piano strings. His mastery of playing this instrument was superb. It was an angelic experience to relax in his chair by the window as he wove a dreamy cacophony of orchestral percussion. At one point I even started chanting OM in different tonalities along with it.

After two days he finally went wild about how I was acting like a schoolgirl on vacation. It seemed that when I was not around him I forgot the demeanor with which he liked to be addressed. He basically requested total silence, and only pertinent discussions mentioned. I always forgot that. I always engaged in conversation because I thought that was what people usually do to communicate. I was careful in my questioning of him, so as not to be intrusive. He said that all other chit chat conversation was not allowed. Once he reminded me of this mindset, I was fine with it, it's just at the time I forgot about being serious and silent. I simply forgot. I forgot so many things that it's almost as if I am insane. I don't know why I forget so much. Once I remember, then it comes back to me, but how I forget his entire approach to interaction, I'm surprised at, myself. Part of my forgetfulness is that I operated several different personalities with Jonah. He was Jonah the sorcerer, Jonah the guitar buddy, Jonah the Man, and was most often Jonah the friend. He was Jonah my benefactor and as such teacher. He was Jonah the genius as far as I was concerned. We had a lot of normal conversations so it startled me when all of a sudden I was out of line by not acting like a normal sorcery apprentice. At times I took authority poorly because I thought his apartment was as messy as mine. Initially I didn't understand him being as a superior. At no time would I have questioned his superior intelligence to mine. That I felt was a given. Over time it was obvious how vast his knowledge and experience was.

The day after I returned to NYC I was writing and took a break. Not even fifteen minutes later it all started happening. I closed my eyes and noticed that I was still seeing almost pictures, shapes and light formations. Then

I felt my body relax. I started visiting a variety of scenes.

First I thought I was in my hometown. I saw neighbors.

Then I floated away. Then I saw some kind of wild

island where there were intense large trees surrounded by

muddy banks of water. A group of young men appeared

to be swimming in the mud. Quickly I shifted to another

scene. This time I had the sensation of flying down a

pink corridor as though in some type of hospital. I

became aware that I was doing dreaming. At that

moment for a minute or so, I became awake in my

dream. I flew to a door in a stairwell. I debated how to go

through the door. As I was flying up to the door I

remembered the command to not look at anything too

closely. The edges of the hall looked slightly blurred.

Once I got through the door I willed myself to go back to

my body and wake up. I had an odd sense of being lonely

and a palpable sensation of fear. My heart was not

feeling the accompanying anxiety that I sometimes

experienced when I woke up from these dream travel

experiences. I wanted to tell this to someone. Rousseau

was out. I felt more alone in the world then I normally

would.

The night before I left Pennsylvania became very interesting. We were watching a movie called the Commitments. I made some comment about how it was hard to leave a life so filled with great sex and good music. The way it came out, was that he was stating that during his apprenticeship he had women coming out of the woodwork, and a business, and didn't want to leave. I said.... I know what you mean. I had a very sexy boyfriend and was performing a lot of music. He grabbed me by the hair and pulled extremely hard. I was freaking out. This guy was extremely strong and there was no sympathy between us. It was not like a mock fight or passion where people are kidding and will wind up on the floor making love. Somehow he settled down. This was horrific behavior between us. Never had he been this out of control. Legitimately I could understand his frustration with me, but I felt this was extremely out of order. Miraculously the mood shifted. I became extremely subdued. He decided that now my mind was quiet. This quietness of mind was what he was trying to get me to achieve. He talked quietly for a few minutes.

Then he abruptly decided that we were going to go out and stalk power. That was another chief objective in the sorcerer's world. Countless times that we had driven across America, power had presented itself in extraordinary and magnificent ways. From storms, to rainbows, to allies, to cloud faces, to extreme states of heightened awareness, to birds that didn't really act like birds. "Seeing is personal." Kathy had said, and on our previous trips all sorts of peculiarities had presented themselves to be seen.

He commanded that we leave the house momentarily. I grabbed some food quickly. We had a discussion about his ally earlier. He said that he had been thinking of me during one of the episodes in which his ally had appeared. He had interpreted this as a request on his ally's part, to meet me. This sounded rather intriguing. He then said I was in no condition to meet an ally, and that the shock would unquestionably drive me insane. I told him that I would have been motivated to pursue it, but that I trusted his judgement, concerning my potential reaction. So when he wanted to "go out and stalk power," I thought he was proposing we seek out his ally. Naturally I considered a bit of food in order, first. I used a lot of food to buffer my senses in these somewhat stressful encounters. I would go in and out of heightened awareness talking to him. I felt like my blood sugar was going up and down as well.

He said to walk silently and with the proper hand position for the gait of power. The hand was clasped in a fist with the thumb lying straight across the top. I was still in a state of shock from him most radical outburst. I then felt better that we were going out and that we were going to be doing something. I felt like maybe it was ok now, and that whatever had set him off was behind us now. Miraculously I felt very strong and very good about what was going on as we left the house. In retrospect I see I was going along with the mood changes as quickly as he did.

The night was crisp and beautiful. He told me beforehand to be very quiet. I was jazzed with anticipation and trepidation that he might be taking me to meet his ally. He had said that my meeting the ally could put me in a state from which I might never recover. I thought maybe he had changed his mind and considered me more resilient. The town was relatively quiet for a Saturday night on a Holiday weekend. He told me that the mantra that I should keep repeating in my head was… "The hinge of the mystery of sorcery was in the movement of the assemblage point. He held his hands in the gait of power walk. His fingers were clasped inward with the thumb across the top. He walked in a slightly deliberated fashion with the arms moving slightly back and forth. Off we strode. I matched him step for step. He was relatively quick. Our breathing and steps were almost synchronized. I tried to tone it down when we passed a cop. It was not that we were doing anything wrong. He made me nervous because he said that I was always being noticeable. I had never tried to be invisible. I had thought the point was to be somewhat attractive. Our demeanor was somewhat unusual, so I tried to act "normal." Again I was probably still reacting to my first welcome by the locals which I had considered really odd.

Eventually we got onto the path that runs along the river. There was only the light of the moon. At one point I turned around and the cloud formations had become an incredible linear abstract design. I was surprised. There were stretches of clouds laid out in a very peculiar geometrical design. I hadn't ever seen such a formation. All the while I rambled the mantra in my head. After two or three miles the words faltered at one point. I felt incredibly lucky and proud to be in Jonah's company at this moment. I considered him a real man among men. A man close, to nature and a man blessed by our great creator. It gave me a feeling of spirit to take this walk with him. Earlier in the evening I had witnessed one of the most commanding performances that could ever have occurred.

We had been sitting in his room. He was asking me why couldn't I ever do what he had asked of me. Here he was, one of the greatest teachers of all time, and he was dragging along someone that was like a bratty errant kindergarten student. I had this emotional catharsis about how my memory was dysfunctional. He had me memorize a piece of Shakespeare. I was extremely slow. It seemed to me like there was actually something wrong with my mental ability. We pieced this together for an hour. The idea was to get over the phobia of learning and memorization and to do it slow. I got over the fear part and was able to do it slow.

The dusk was falling in the room. He began to do a play of Shakespeare. He went on and on and on. It became nearly pitch black in the room. I gestured to get light, but he refused it. He did the play of Caesar. It was extremely invigorating, yet frightening. This was not a guy reciting a play. He became the character. His voice rose and fell, and rose and fell. I had the realization that I was witnessing something out of the ordinary. It was completely as if those characters were before me. The magnitude of his presence as he performed this was enough to make me faint. It was as if something was alive in the room outside of us. His memorization was shockingly awesome. I imagined how Dan and Kathy would have appreciated seeing him. They no doubt had similar skill. Jonah had told me how Dan acted.

I remembered this performance as we trotted down the river path. We walked about four miles when we came to our destination. There was a picnic table by the river ledge. There was a very large and old looking tree behind it. Jonah walked up to the tree and began caressing it in what appeared to be a deeply intimate

way. I was a little taken aback by the grace with which
he touched this tree. It wasn't even that it might be
considered odd to so touch a tree, but it was the
eloquence and elegance with which he did. He indicated
that I should also greet the tree. I moved to caress it,
though in a more informal way. I tried to feel what he
was feeling because his gesture had seemed rich with
feeling. I felt a current of energy where my hands
touched the tree. I had a rush of sensual feeling. I didn't
mention it. I still wondered if I understood what he was
trying to convey through these actions. We resumed the
walk home. Over and over I recited the mantra. Once we
were home we remained quiet. He said that the tree was
an old friend. I was fascinated, but he would not
elaborate. It really had been one of those huge, almost
fairytale looking trees. He said that it was quite striking
how entirely quiet the world had been. I would have had
to agree. I kept looking for something, such as an ally or
an evidence of power we were stalking, but there was
almost literally silence for seven and a half miles. He
said that the path was normally awash with the sound of
crickets, frogs, ducks … He said that it was extremely

unusual for it to be silent.

The next day I boarded a bus back to NYC. As we walked across the street two bicycles passed on the roof of a car. He said that this was a good omen. I gave him a strong hug before I left. I still found him very exciting even if I didn't express myself that way because of other associations. I was glad we had wrapped on a high note. His company always elicited terror and tremendous power. This trip certainly had been no exception. His energy boosted me in an incredible way. I felt in an entirely different state of consciousness for weeks after seeing him.

What Jonah had been telling me for years occurred today. He said, that there was going to be a catastrophe where the roads out of town were all closed. I hadn't called Jonah's benefactor Dan for years. In between the collapse of the Twin Towers I called him. I left a message that Jonah was on his way across country on a bicycle. The whole world was in shock.

31. CONCLUSION...FOR NOW

I began this manuscript exactly ten years ago.

While my journal and my life continue, this story must conclude, and the next one begin. Jonah has absolutely lavished me with his personal power and knowledge. To this end my gratitude could never compare. His benefactors as well were inconceivably generous in their seen and unseen support. The journey has just begun. In ten years, I have indelibly proven to myself, that what would have been presented as the rational world, is but the thinnest top layer of our human capacity for perception, and our normal natural ability to experience and participate in other cognitive states of consciousness. The teachings of Jonah, the teachings of Don Juan through Carlos Castaneda, the teachings of Jonah' benefactors Dan and his wife and apprentice Kathy, and the teachings of Jesus all commune in the area of... developing perception and defending the living sentient being, our Mother Earth.

32. 2001-2006 AN OVERVIEW

I continued speaking to Jonah. I had a dream one evening that had again the flying in the beginning and then felt I was in Hollywood. It was nighttime and I felt that I was somewhere out visiting Jonah. I went down broken stone steps leading out into a woodsy type of garden. There were cats following me around. While the dream did not carry total lucidity as some had, I was aware that I was doing dreaming. The next day I spoke to Jonah. He was delighted with my navigations. He said that unquestionably I had been in his backyard in Hollywood because that was an exact description right down to the cats.

At this point, if there's anything I can see about this plan of action, is how to do it, and why. As far as all of his teachings, I can clearly now see how to simply do it. That is where I am at, at this time. That is to be positive about it. Why it took so long to get in order, is almost something I don't know. The constant challenge of daily life has been consuming to the degree that it has steered the focus away from doing this properly. That being said, I feel really great about implementing these structures into my life now. I can still clean up to perfection, eat like a warrior, exercise, live deeply and earnestly. Much has been done. Much has just happened over the maturity of time. The music at long last learned itself. Things are only at the beginning of getting great. This story and outline of how to become a warrior is as vital to me as a guide as I would offer it to anyone else. Getting these things together is about a lifetime. Everything is equal. The world of dreaming and the world of daily life. What do I see in general that I feel I would mention? I see an absolutely gorgeous earth. Every season and every place. The simplest things from the wind to the stars, the moon, the mountains, the oceans and the city streets. I see millions of fantastic people.

This story is really only about a couple of things. It's about my personal journey as an apprentice to a warrior sorcerer. As human beings the physical potential is there for anybody to achieve bodily knowledge and learning in this area. In a nutshell, how to make your life tight enough to have the energy taken back, and cultivated so that your dreaming body is a viable functioning vehicle that you can slip into at the time of physical death to maintain consciousness life to life.

There are serious and grave emergencies going on here. It's not a few trees that are being cut down here.

Heading off environmental destruction and what is likely
to be set off because of ignorance is what is at hand.
Who is the world going to listen to? How is the message
that the scientific community is screaming going to be
heard, and taken on the level of severity it actually is.
Forget about saving the world for your children. Our
own life spans are about to be killed off if action is not
taken to heed these environmental warnings. The leaders
have to get in order about protecting and resurrecting the
faculties of the earth. If there is a chain reaction effecting
the air, water .... we die, we become extinct, as other
species have done in the past. Would Moses, Jesus,
Mohammed, Confucius, Buddha, Krishna, or spiritual
leaders of any nation anywhere ever allow the
destruction of the earth? Who was Jesus talking to when
he performed miracles? When sea or sky was addressed
what were the great seers communicating with? This is a
lot more serious than people are aware of. Money can't
buy air. This is a prayer and a plea that the people that
can address this understand the true seriousness of this.
People as a whole seem interested in having a good
association with whatever they deem to be God. Well,

from what I can see, the planet is God. We have to love
and protect the earth. The bible says…. "Tend this
garden." It doesn't say, kill this garden. I was told not to
be preachy. I was told to express the divine comedy that
we are all a joyous part of. This can be done with
positive energy and spirit. The manpower of humanity is
overwhelmingly able to redirect our systems away from
more toxicity.

Why tamper with magnificence. We have
everything here. The planet is paradise. If it was healed,
it would support everyone ten times over.

Friday, 3pm 2001

33. EPILOGE 2016

Considerable time has passed. I am older,
a little wiser, happier, still feeling hot and
groovy. In a word, fortunate. While my next
writing will reflect a person feeling a far deeper

experience, because that is how I feel life feels in the progression of it, my teachers profound bomb of information has not lost any of its validity or value in the face of huge societal change. His wisdom of pursuing the parallel lives of our natural dreaming abilities and intuitive natures as well as the magic in everyday life is as stellar for the moment of now as it was when I first heard it. The Carlos Castaneda books are the same in that as well. If time is the test of some things, the very fact that my teacher is still steadfast in his convictions some twenty years later, speaks of his devotion to the knowledge he received. On a basic fun level, this is every bit a handbook for positive living and cleaning out all your channels to attract the most abundant, creative and joyous life, tune into other levels of consciousness, and have a healthy appreciation for observing the divine comedy that parades before us. Love the Earth and allow its energy to heal you and love you back. We are never alone. Live your magical life. Much Love,

Jaime Paris

www.ingramcontent.com/pod-product-compliance
Lightning Source LLC
Chambersburg PA
CBHW052027090426
42739CB00010B/1805